THE IDEAS OF
AMERICAN FOREIGN POLICY

MICHAEL DONELAN

The Ideas of
American Foreign Policy

DUFOUR · PHILADELPHIA
1965

First published in USA by
Dufour Editions, Chester Springs, Pennsylvania
© *1963 by Michael Donelan*
Printed in Great Britain
Library of Congress Catalog Card Number
65-17941

Contents

Preface

Like most books on American foreign policy since the Second World War, this book is concerned both with actions and with the underlying ideas, but its focus is the ideas. The great actions of the time are set out roughly in their sequence but the aim is less to tell the story than to illustrate a discussion. This approach sacrifices some of the impact of action, the heat and excitement of the battle. People at the time of events are necessarily far more aware of actions than of ideas. Yet, for that very reason, the approach can contribute to fuller explanations.

The obvious explanation of the character of United States foreign policy since the War is that it has been primarily a defensive response to the actions of the Soviet Union and China and other powers. But, strictly speaking United States policy has responded, not to these actions, but to the American appraisal of these actions. Some of the elements in this appraisal have been common the world over, some have been common to the Western powers, but some have arisen from specifically American habits of thought. It is this situation which this book attempts to illustrate and explore.

If a foreign policy is to win the support of a nation, if an active foreign policy is to be pursued with vigour, it must, it seems, be commanded by an idea, giving a sense of position or of direction. Such ideas are those of independence, of Panchsheel, of containment, of European unity. There is, at the same time, a corresponding dilemma. Policy-makers and, still less, the public cannot constantly reappraise their guide-lines to day-to-day actions and events. Yet, it follows that these determining concepts and slogans may be applied to what are in fact new situations merely through familiarity or imaginative appeal. They may be retained long after they are outdated, inapplicable and misguiding.

In this book, there are many criticisms of American ideas on world affairs and of the policies which these helped to form. But it is clear that while the policy-maker has only limited time for his decisions, the critic has almost unlimited time and the advantage of comfortable hindsight for his criticisms. Though this thought does not diminish the value of criticism, it may make acceptable, here at the outset, a personal expression of respect for the basic purposes of American postwar policy and for the men who carried them out.

In the course of a year in the United States from 1958-9, I was privileged to talk with many politicians and officials of postwar Administrations and with scholars of several universities and organizations. I hope that any of them who chance on this book and recollect the matter, will take this mention of the fact as an expression of gratitude. I am especially grateful to Professor Harold Sprout of Princeton University, in whose Department I worked, and who helped to shape many a fair comment and who expurgated any bad comment which was mentioned to him. I wish also to thank especially Princeton University and the Princeton branch of the English Speaking Union who gave me the Sir John Dill Fellowship for 1958-9 and whose hospitality, in every sense, made the beginning of this book possible.

March 1963

1

One World

No country in history has been so suddenly confronted with international responsibility as was the United States in the Second World War. At the time of the attack on Pearl Harbour, the attitudes of the American people to world affairs were comparable with those of most of Asia today. They were still preoccupied with the problems and opportunities of the New World and with freedom from the Old. The American instinct was still to restrict commitments outside the Western Hemisphere and to maintain isolation from the politics of the great European powers. The energy and attention of the population were largely absorbed by the affairs of the Hemisphere. The expansion of America beyond these boundaries was still slow and reluctant.

At the turn of the century, Secretary of State John Hay, and later more dramatically President Wilson had sought in different ways to arrange a stable system among the powers. From the same time, involvement in Far Eastern politics had become increasingly voluntary and purposive. America's significance in international politics in general had necessarily grown with its economic influence. But this significance lay more in what the United States did not do than in what it did. On the whole in 1941, the idea behind American foreign policy was as it had always been, defensive, the great purpose being the satisfactory arrangement of relations within the Western Hemisphere and the prevention of outside interference in it.

Pearl Harbour and the War and the implications of the War forced the pace of history for Americans as it did in a different

9

way for the European great powers. World-wide responsibilities were thrust on to America not slowly but suddenly, responsibilities far beyond its experience. To this can be attributed many of the mistakes and many of the merits of America's postwar foreign policy. It had shared too little in the past to avoid mistakes and too little in the past to cling to it.

The spirit of American postwar foreign policy is still defensive, and this too accounts for many of its merits and of its defects. Even today only a small minority of Americans welcomes American responsibility in world affairs, a small minority is averse to it, and the great majority are merely reconciled to its necessity. An active foreign policy was less adopted by Americans than imposed on them. It sprang not from positive forces such as economic dependence on the outside world or population pressure or missionary zeal or idealism but from the changed needs of defence.

The basis of Senator Vandenberg's famous repudiation of isolationism in his Senate speech of 10 January 1945 was simply disbelief that 'any nation hereafter can immunize itself by its own exclusive action'. The War was the conclusive demonstration to Americans that if the great powers in the outside world prepared to fight, the United States must inevitably be involved in the catastrophe. The Pacific War drove home the new conception that Americans could no longer look solely eastward to the historic source of danger, Europe; they were surrounded; they were increasingly vulnerable from all sides. Arguing these points in the first of a series of broadcasts in the spring of 1945 in which the Administration explained the proposed United Nations Organization to the people, Assistant Secretary of State Acheson concluded: 'Unless I am entirely mistaken, it is the bedrock explanation of why American foreign policy has got to be directed in one of two ways: either towards organized international co-operation or towards aggressive imperialistic militarism'.[1]

The defensive idea was wider than mere military strategy and wider than the defence of America alone. Strategy was the head but not the heart of the abandonment of isolationism. The great ideas of American postwar foreign policy involved a strong sense of the general good and were not simply a new expedient for safeguarding America. The experiences of the War, its global scope and the revolution in communications had in a hundred ways made the rest of the world nearer to Americans and had strengthened the feeling of community with other peoples. Wendell Wilkie's *One World*, a widely-read account of a world tour in wartime, caught the spirit of the time: 'If I had ever had any doubts that the world had become small and completely interdependent, this trip would have dispelled them altogether... Our thinking in the future must be worldwide.'[2]

The focus of this feeling was determination that there must be no repetition of the tragedy then in progress and a conviction that America must play its part in ensuring this. There was also a sense of obligation to repair a past mistake. 'If our withdrawal from world affairs after the last war', wrote Wilkie, 'was a contributory factor to the present war and to the economic instability of the past twenty years – and it seems plain that it was – a withdrawal from the problems and responsibilities of the world after this war would be sheer disaster.'[3]

The development of United States foreign policy in the postwar years widened to area after area of the world at an unprecedented pace, unequalled even by the development of the Soviet Union's policy. The imperial and mercantile powers of Western Europe had extended their activity in the world gradually, over centuries. The United States in a mere fifteen years moved onwards from peacetime responsibility in Europe, to the Middle East, to South Asia and to Africa.

In considering the guiding ideas of the United States in these ever-growing responsibilities, it is right to begin with the traditional area of United States responsibility, the Western

Hemisphere. The course of American postwar foreign policy relied heavily on the extension of hemispheric conceptions to the world at large. More to the immediate purpose, American policy in the Western Hemisphere and Japan in 1945-6 throws a sidelight on the origins of the quarrel with the Soviet Union.

There was a contrast and a paradox in the realism with which the United States acted in its traditional sphere and the idealism with which it acted outside it, particularly in Europe. In the Western Hemisphere and Japan, the United States sought to further certain ideas ultimately derived from American home traditions, ideas of co-operation, of the rule of law, of democracy; but in doing this, it was nonetheless a great power seeking to impose its own ideas within an exclusive sphere of influence and, so far as such ideas could be imposed by the conventional tactics of a great power, doing so.

At the same time, the United States sought to extend these same ideas to the world outside its sphere and so denied like rights to the Soviet Union. The United States would not accept the imposition of the Soviet Union's ideas in Eastern Europe; it would not accept the conventional tactics of great powers, spheres of influence, balances of power, exclusive alliances, there or anywhere in the world outside its sphere. Whether the United States was right or wrong to act as it did, is not the issue. The point is that the United States acted as a revolutionary power in its relations with two traditionally minded powers, the Soviet Union and Britain, and, unfortunately for its prospects of success, entirely failed to grasp this.

In the Western Hemisphere in the early postwar years, the guide-lines of American policy had long been laid down; they were the search for harmony and security by the increase of inter-American co-operation. The wartime and postwar steps culminating in the establishment of the Organization of American States at the Bogotá Conference in March 1948 pulled together the various aspects of the inter-American system. At the same time, they completed the conversion of the Monroe Doctrine from the policy of the United States alone to the common policy of all the member republics. Not just the United States but all the members were now fully committed to the principle that intervention from outside the Hemisphere in its affairs would not be tolerated.

The growth of political uniformity and of military co-operation was, however, troubled. America's offer in return for the progressive adoption by all of the Monroe Doctrine had for two decades been the principle of non-interference in the affairs of the other republics. This was belied by the quarrel with Colonel Perón and, in particular, by the attempt to influence the February 1946 elections in Argentina against him. The enthusiasm of the United States army in the summer of 1945 for equipping Latin American armies was thwarted for two years by Congressional misgivings at the Administration's Argentina policy. Again, to the north, Canada continued to reject occasional suggestions that it should join the inter-American system. Rumours in 1946 that the United States was proposing American bases on Canadian soil aroused sharp popular reactions. However, a modest agreement for joint facilities in Canada and for consultation was reached in February 1947 and became the basis for extensive co-operation later.

The growth of the inter-American system was one of the main reasons for Article 52 of the United Nations Charter, permitting regional associations. In the American view, there was to be no interference by the Organization or anyone else in Latin America. The point of the new Organization was to extend sane principles to the outside world and not to submerge the already satisfactory arrangements in the Western Hemisphere. At the same time, the other powers found this proviso in the Charter acceptable. Regional associations expressed in miniature the favoured idea of the time, and were later more immune from attempts at interference by outsiders than were national domestic affairs, theoretically much more strongly protected by the Charter.

'I take it as a premise about all discussions of world peace', noted James Forrestal, Secretary of the Navy, in April 1945, 'that the United States is to have the major responsibility for the Pacific Ocean security, and, if this premise is accepted, there flows from it the acceptance of the fact that the United States must have the means with which to implement its responsibilities.'[4] To put the matter in an equally valid way, the war with Japan had given the United States the wish and victory the opportunity to add to its possessions in the Pacific with a view to defence. The means in question were the Pacific islands. After sweeping proposals in 1945 involving Australian, British and French mandated islands had been abandoned for reasons of economy and the resistance of these powers, the United States confined itself in 1946 to taking over Japanese mandated islands and possessions and to reciprocal arrangements with Australia and Britain in the southern Pacific. All these bases were to be strategically subordinate to Hawaii and Guam. The grant of independence to the Philippines on 4 July 1946, the fulfilment of a pledge made in 1934, meant that the base retained there, though important, could not be central to the system.

Beyond the Pacific, the trading and security and missionary interests of the United States had long involved it in the affairs of China and Japan in competition with the European powers. The United States was quite clear in 1945 that it intended to be the dominant power in the area while a postwar settlement was made in accordance with its own ideas.

The overall aim of American policy towards China and the civil war was well stated in one of the policy documents given to General Marshall to guide him in his mission of mediation between the Kuomintang and the Communists which began in December 1945. 'The Government of the United States holds that the peace and prosperity of the world in this new unexplored era ahead depend on the ability of the sovereign nations to combine for collective security in the United Nations Organization. It is the firm belief of this Government that a strong, united and democratic China is of the utmost importance to the success of the United Nations Organization and for world peace.'[5]

These requirements were not as abstract as they might at first sight appear. The United States sought an end to the civil war in China not merely on general policy grounds but so that the weakness of China should not lead to an expansion of Soviet influence and to ensure that China should eventually become a counterbalance to the power both of the Soviet Union and of Japan. The United States had encouraged Soviet participation in the war against Japan and had at Yalta conceded certain historic Russian claims; yet simultaneously it aimed to remove any possibility of permanent Soviet expansion or major extension of influence. In wartime Allied discussions, the United States had supported the great power status of China for much the same reasons as Britain had supported that of France, namely the maintenance of a balance of power in the Far East and Europe respectively.

Unfortunately, the plain upshot of the Marshall mission in 1945-6 was that either the Kuomintang must reform itself, cooperate with the Communists and defeat them in subsequent rivalry for the alleigance of the Chinese people, or it would lose to the Communists; and yet the Kuomintang would not or could not reform itself. Overt American intervention on the side of the Kuomintang, on the other hand, would be likely merely to provoke compensatory intervention by the Soviet Union on the side of the Communists. Both powers had covertly intervened in the closing stages of the war with Japan and continued to assist the two sides to some extent thereafter. In contrast to its refusal to fight a 'political war' in the European theatre, the United States had air-lifted Nationalist troops from western to

15

eastern China to ensure that they and not the Communists should take over control from the defeated Japanese. Correspondingly, the Soviet Union's delay in withdrawing from Manchuria was at least not unfavourable to the Communist cause there. It seemed clear that any large-scale assistance to the Kuomintang would draw the United States into a competition with the Soviet Union, the effects and probably the outcome of which would be disastrous.

The Administration's policy might, it is true, have been different if it had seen a Communist victory in so serious a light as it did after the event. The hostility of Mao Tse-tung's China and its alliance with the Soviet Union were not fully foreseen, partly of course because they were still to some extent in the making. The ideology of Mao Tse-tung's revolutionaries, though a matter for some anxiety, did not weigh very heavily, since Americans generally, in common with most of the world including the Russians, looked on them as 'not proper Communists', as 'agrarian revolutionaries', as, with the Nationalists, 'two dissident factions' of the revolutionary movement, or, in Secretary Byrnes' more homely view, a quarrelling couple.[6] Yet even had the Administration viewed a Communist victory as seriously as according to later critics it ought to have done, even this could not have altered the hard facts of the situation in and about China nor made a policy of intervention or large-scale aid reasonable.

The immediate and overriding problem in the Far East in 1945 was the disarmament and reform of Japan. The United States soon showed that it would not accept the interference of the other powers in the process of refashioning Japan according to its own ideas. No Allied group equivalent to the European Advisory Commission had been set up during the War, but in the summer of 1945, the United States was prepared to accept some such body in deference to the role of its allies in the Far Eastern war and their interests in the peace. But the United States would

16

not accept British and Soviet proposals for an Allied Control Council in Tokyo with powers approaching those of the Control Council for Germany. The arrangement desired by the United States was one similar to that prevailing in the Balkans where the activities of the Allied groups were in practice confined to advice and protest, the initiative being in the hands of the Soviet Union.

In the end, a compromise of form was reached which yielded little of the substance of the American position. In October 1945 the United States accepted a Far Eastern Advisory Commission, to meet in Washington. Britain continued to demand more and the Soviet Union refused to attend the Commission unless more was given. Since, characteristically, the United States was genuinely anxious to secure the co-operation of these powers in getting its own way, in December 1945, an Allied Control Council was established in Tokyo with representatives from Australia, Britain, China, India, the Soviet Union and the United States. On the day that this arrangement was announced, General MacArthur stated that he had not been consulted on it, did not like it, but would nonetheless try to make it work. But remarkably enough, though he was almost the dictator of Japan in the postwar years, General MacArthur did not have much success in this respect. America's allies had some influence on overall considerations, in particular in the late forties when the question of economic recovery and a peace treaty arose. But it was at most a modifying influence. The essentials were throughout decided by the United States.

In the world outside the Western Hemisphere and the Far East, the United States had traditionally fewer interests, fewer responsibilities and less power. Its stake in particular countries of Europe, Asia and Africa and in general was important but on the whole, politically, its traditional role was that of an observer and critic of the European powers which more or less ruled all three continents. When in 1945 the United States found itself saddled with a leading role in these areas, it was thus, so far as its own experience and interests went, writing on a comparatively clean slate. It was disposed, that is, to give the fullest possible play to its highest ideals of national and international order and not disposed to qualify them with less generous principles or to see them so qualified by others.

In practice, of course, as the War drew to an end, the United States was heavily burdened with such pressing detailed problems as the winding-up of military operations, the relief of devastated areas, and the administration and reform of the Axis powers, and these necessarily entailed a large measure of day-to-day improvisation. Equally, however, consciously or unconsciously, the larger issues of policy were governed by certain general ideas of the type of postwar world the United States wishes to see develop. These ideas were most clearly revealed in policy towards the problem which embraced all others, the problem of harmony between the nations and the prevention of war, and in the solution adopted, the United Nations Organization.

The conviction which grew in intensity from Pearl Harbour that America must play its part in ensuring world peace did not necessarily imply that a framework such as the United Nations Organization as established in the Charter of 1945 should be set up. Other frameworks were possible. It was reasonable to wish that the power of the United Nations which had proved so strong in war should be maintained as a unit for the preservation of the peace; but this implied only that the postwar arrangements must aim at maintaining harmony at least among the great powers. It did not imply the form of these arrangements. Yet, in the event, at no time from Pearl Harbour onwards was any alternative to the arrangements eventually made at San Francisco seriously considered. Without explicitly foreclosing discussion, the various grand pronouncements of wartime were all based on the expectation that the core of these arrangements was to be an organization similar to, if an improvement on, the old League of Nations.

The basic reason for this assumption was the very memory of the League, buttressed by the almost universally accepted belief that with America's participation, it might have been successful. The Covenant of the League had expressed the highest Western ideals of the international order; the United States had not so much rejected these as been persuaded to reject the outside world altogether in favour of isolationism; this time, the United States was willing to play its part in the outside world and to devote its power and influence to the success of the ideals.

Indeed, having made up its mind to accept a leading role in world affairs, the United States would do so on no other terms. The United Nations Organization was a renewed attempt to revolutionize the principles of the international order in a direction which was, generally speaking, natural to all the Western nations; but it was also an attempt in which the United States led and on which it insisted. The United States, Administration and people, was not willing to enter actively into the affairs of the outside world on the traditional terms and conditions of that world. The abolition of the old order and the building of a new order were a condition of the abandonment of isolationism.

This attitude on the part of the United States, essentially revolutionary but for the most part unconsciously so, governed its approach to the whole of postwar international relations including in particular the European settlement; the United Nations Organization was only the summit of the matter. President Roosevelt's summary of America's attitude in his address to Congress on the Yalta Conference may be taken as the text for the discussion which follows: 'I think the Crimean Conference was a successful effort by the three leading nations to find a common ground for peace. It spells – and it ought to spell – the end of the system of unilateral action, exclusive alliances and spheres of influence, and balances of power and all the other expedients which have been tried for centuries and have always failed. We propose to substitute for all these a universal organization in which all peace-loving nations will finally have a chance to join.'[7]

Of the various expedients of the old order which the United States sought to abolish, the widest was the concept of the balance of power. This concept was later to become the basis of Western policy towards the Soviet Union, though the name itself was avoided; in 1945, it was neglected under any name with the most far-reaching consequences.

The history of Russia gave the strongest grounds for believing that as the War came to a close, it would take advantage of its victorious position to extend its power in Europe; and indeed there were American commentators who pointed this out. More direct indications were also available during the War, sufficient at least to arouse suspicion. William T. Fox of the Yale Institute of International Affairs based an analysis of the likely course of European events on the Declaration of Principle adopted in June 1943 by the Union of Polish Patriots in Moscow. 'Whilst the declaration serves notice to the Western World', he wrote, 'that the Soviet Union strives for hegemony in the Eastern European tier of states along its borders, it also gives assurance that formal incorporation of great new areas into the Soviet Union is not contemplated' . . . 'Beyond the belt of friendly régimes is Germany. Here Allied pressure from the West and Soviet pressures from the East will reach some type of equilibrium' . . . 'In the next belt are the states whose political orientation will be more towards the British and American power nucleus. Here one may expect Soviet diplomacy to limit itself to inhibiting as far as practicable the complete consolidation of these areas into an aggressive anti-Soviet coalition.'[8]

If American policy-makers had appraised the future in these terms, it is possible that the Western military campaigns in Europe would have been directed differently and more fortunately. It seems unlikely that any degree of political calculation in these campaigns could have greatly affected the fate of Eastern Europe; but it is likely that the crucial case of Germany could have been decided for the better. As it was 'some type of equilibrium' was indeed struck down the centre of Germany, leaving a radical instability at the heart of Europe.

More than this, throughout the crucial period of fluidity in Europe in 1945-6, there was a standing prospect of a power vacuum in enfeebled Western Europe arising from American attitudes. These were exemplified in Roosevelt's 'momentous announcement' at Yalta, in Churchill's phrase, that he anticipated the withdrawal of American forces within two years. President Roosevelt, that is to say, preferred to rely not on the old concept of the balance of power, but on the new concept of co-operation: co-operation with the Soviet Union in Eastern Europe, four-power control of Germany, and, for longer-term stability and security in Europe, on the guarantees to be given in the United Nations Charter.

Events took a parallel course with regard to the old expedient of spheres of influence. The United States declared their abolition, and, apparently oblivious of the revolutionary nature of its demand, expected the other great powers to comply; and they did not. As the War drew to an end and in its aftermath, the Soviet Union and Britain were engaged in a traditional manœuvring and bargaining to safeguard their interests, the Soviet Union in Eastern Europe, Britain in the Mediterranean. The United States was an uneasy spectator of this process and in particular of the arrangement made by Churchill and Eden in Moscow in October 1944 whereby in return for primary responsibility by the Soviet Union in Rumania and Bulgaria, Britain should have primary responsibilty in Greece, both parties having equal responsibility in Yugoslavia. This arrangement, said Churchill, was confined to the immediate problems of restoring order in those countries; it was a practical arrangement, not amounting to spheres of influence.[9] This, however, was a distinction without much difference, and the setting-up of Soviet puppets in Rumania and Bulgaria, the British intervention against the Communists in Greece and the silence of each on the actions of the other roused the deepest suspicions in the United States. Britain's intervention in the Greek civil war in the winter of 1944-5 was greeted with as loud an American popular outcry as were any of the current actions of the Soviet Union.

There was similar unease at Britain's policy in Italy. Britain had little difficulty with the Soviet Union in arranging in 1943 that the Allied Control Commission should consist of British and American representatives only, leaving the Soviet Union with no more than an observer and with membership of an Advisory Council which had negligible influence. The Soviet Union's occasional protests later at the neglect of its representatives seem to have been made mainly as a parry to American protests at Soviet disregard of the Allied Control Commissions in the Balkans. The United States on the other hand was in a state of constant agitation at Britain's manœuvrings in the internal politics of Italy in 1944. Here as in Greece, it seemed clear that Britain's policy was based on support for reactionary monarchy with a view to ensuring continued British influence.

In the course of 1945-6, the results if not the methods of British policy were gradually seen to be in line with the ideas of the United States. The actions of the Soviet Union on the other hand took on an ever darker complexion. As the weary round of protests, negotiations and conferences continued, American appreciation of the Soviet security interest in Eastern Europe deepened. American publicists went far in expressing sympathy and in excusing Soviet actions on these grounds. In the last resort, however, the United States would not accept a Soviet security sphere, involving the ruthless imposition of puppet dictatorships, as the answer to the problem. The United States was disposed to have faith in the feeble democratic tradition in Eastern Europe and to believe that it could be so fostered that never again would these countries abet the near destruction of the Soviet Union. 'Our objective', Byrnes told Molotov in a discussion on Rumania, 'is a government both friendly to the Soviet Union and representative of all the democratic elements of the country.' The United States believed, he said, that the Soviet Union would be safer with friendly populations than by imposing 'friendly' governments.[10]

In the end it became clear that the Soviet Union would believe none of this. It pursued its own ideas in the countries of Eastern Europe as unswervingly as did America in another country towards which America had similar feelings. Once, in October 1945, Secretary Byrnes 'asked Ambassador Harriman to request an interview with Generalissimo Stalin . . . I wanted him to present to Stalin directly an amended proposal for a peace conference . . . and to discuss the situation in Rumania and Bulgaria. The result was a revelation. When the ambassador started to present our views on these European questions, Stalin interrupted to say that what he wanted to hear about was our view on the control of Japan. Mr Harriman was as surprised as he was unprepared, and my surprise was even greater.'[11]

The third expedient of the old order rejected by the United States was that of exclusive alliances. American attitudes to the Soviet Union and Britain, as we shall notice more fully in the next chapter, were such that the United States considered itself if anything a mediator between these two old-world powers. But in any case, special relationships were undesirable in themselves. As late as 16 March 1946, Secretary Byrnes said in reaction to Churchill's Fulton speech, 'We do not propose to seek security in an alliance with the Soviet Union against Britain or in an alliance with Britain against the Soviet Union. We propose to stand with the United Nations . . .'

The ideas which underlay the United Nations Charter and which the United States sought to substitute in all aspects of world affairs for the ideas of the old order, were a compound of many elements, all interconnected, and were not summarized at the time in neat phrases such as later became common in American foreign policy. They were fused in an all-embracing vision of One World at peace. As an approximation, however, the three main ideas which the United States hoped to establish were the ideas of co-operation, of the rule of law, and of the conduct of affairs by reasonable discussion. These, roughly, were the ideas which Americans most admired in the conduct of home affairs; which the United States now sought to further in the Organization of American States and to impose in Japan; which it now relied on in its dealings with the Soviet Union and the other powers; which underlay its belief in four-power control in Germany, its attitude to the re-establishment of governments in Eastern Europe, its policy on Europe as a whole; and which reached their peak in the United Nations Organization.

International co-operation nowadays bulks so large on the world scene that it seems less an idea than a commonplace. There is nowadays an international grouping about almost every public question; names like UNO, NATO, EEC and a hundred more are the common coin of discussions of world affairs; the approach to almost any question is to handle it collectively or to show cause to the rest of the world why it cannot be so handled. All this is in marked contrast to the spirit of the inter-war years at least in the higher ranges of world affairs. The degree of growth of co-operation is in fact so great as to amount to a revolution, one of the most significant and certainly the most hopeful that has ever taken place in world politics.

The growth of co-operation is rooted in a general international reaction to the interwar disunity and its outcome and to the ever-decreasing practical size of the world; but it also owes much to the enthusiasm and leadership of the United States. American enthusiasm for this ideal springs from the whole American tradition, the myth of the building of America; but, so far as the American approach to world affairs is concerned, one aspect of

American attitudes is of particular significance: the attitude to power. When in the autumn of 1944 James Forrestal sponsored a seminar at Princeton on the Foundations of National Power, one of his notes for his address was: 'Our problem – to achieve accommodation between the power we now possess, our reluctance to use it positively, the realistic necessity for such use, and our national ideals.'[12] Whatever the brute facts of practice in American history may sometimes have been, power as an idea was troublesome to the American conscience, connected as it was with the wars and tyrannies of the unregenerate outside world. The solution to the problem was the exercise of power in cooperation with others. In the old ideal of Wilson: 'There must be not a balance of power but a community of power, not organized rivalries but organized peace'.

These attitudes were expressed in 1945 not simply in the foundation of the United Nations Organization but in the association of smaller powers in the Security Council; in 1946, not simply in America's whole approach to the peace treaties but in the pressure on the Soviet Union at the Paris Peace Conference to give due weight to the views of the smaller Allies. In these cases, the United States was not simply seeking the widest participation with a view to maximum stability of the decisions reached; there was also an element of genuine reluctance to overrule others by the pressures of power. The most momentous example of all was the American attitude to atomic power. It is an easily-accepted and yet historically astounding fact that for four years of frustration and trial from 1945 to 1949, the United States was the sole possessor of a source of power sufficient to coerce the entire world and was utterly unwilling to do so. On the contrary, in the American view, the problem of the atomic bomb, of modern weapons in general, of the absolute necessity of preserving peace, was the greatest of all reasons for the pooling of power, for co-operation in disarmament and a world security system.

If the United States showed optimism as to the prospects for its ideal, if it habitually disregarded difficulties and avoided precautions, this sprang in part from a conviction that there was simply no alternative to success if the world was to have peace. 'From my close association with Franklin D. Roosevelt', wrote Secretary of State Stettinius in his memoirs, 'I know that he was primarily motivated by this great ideal of friendly co-operation among nations. At the same time, he had no illusions about the dangers and difficulties of dealing with the Soviet Union. He emphasized many times that we must keep trying with patience and determination to get the Russians to realize that it was in their own selfish interest to win the confidence of the other countries of the world. We must help them see, he said, that co-operation with other nations was the only way they or we could have a peaceful world.'[13]

By the time of Roosevelt's death the first open cracks in four-power unity had already appeared, over Poland, and the idea of co-operation took on a special aspect. Speeches and articles by Acheson and Dulles in 1945 admitted the sceptic's maxim that allies always fall out so soon as the common danger is passed; but all the more reason then to try to channel the united effort of wartime straight through on to the common tasks of peace in the United Nations Organization and its agencies. Co-operation, that is, had a way of breeding its own unity.

At the same time, however much the great powers might accept the idea of co-operation and however great its self-strengthening effect, co-operation would not in fact be possible unless there were common views on certain fundamentals. Of these the most important was whether national security was to continue to be sought by primitive methods; or whether, as in the American view, it was henceforth to be sought by acceptance of the rule of law.

The basic meaning of the United Nations Charter to Americans was that it was an attempt to write down a law for the nations. The consistency with which American statesmen, particularly Republicans, have reverted this ideal in their widest reflections on international relations has in the first place two detailed explanations: the fact that so many of them have been trained in the law; and the fact that the remainder have at least acquired a little history. The Anglo-Saxon part of the world is, on the whole, comparatively very proud of its history. The feature of which is perhaps most proud, following the emphasis of nineteenth-century historical writing, is the growth of the rule of law.

The underlying explanation is, however, that the rule of law is one of the most deeply admired ideals of the American people as a whole. 'Despite a certain superficial indifference to the niceties of law observance', wrote John Foster Dulles in 1957, 'Americans have developed a profound respect of law as the basis of social and civic life. We conceive of man-made law as an effort to apply the moral law to the conditions of time and place. Our constitution is the oldest basic written law in the world today. The concept of law permeates our entire political system and gives it a stability and moderation rarely matched among contemporary governments. We yearn to see the behaviour of nations in their relations with one another rest upon the foundation of agreed legal principles derived from moral concepts.'[14]

In the interwar years, the best efforts of American statesmen were devoted to the pursuit of this ideal. As a contribution to the prevention of war, the United States relied heavily on the incantatory effect of words, moral or legal. Among many moral admonitions, that once given by Secretary of State Hull to the Italian Ambassador is outstanding in its paradox. The United States 'while taking every precaution to keep aloof from political and military involvements abroad, strongly feels that each civilized country right now has the unshirkable responsibility of making a real contribution to promote peace'.[15] From the beginning of the century to the nineteen thirties, the United States negotiated no less than ninety-seven international agreements laying down procedures for conciliation and arbitration in the event of a dispute.[16] This whole laborious network had no apparent restraining effect on the subsequent world catastrophe, yet the strength of the ideal was such that it survived the War intact. The preoccupation of Americans early in 1945 with the mechanics of the world organization and the exaggerated hopes which many placed in the signatures to the United Nations Charter reflected this old belief in legal undertakings and agreed procedures as a guarantee of peace.

At the end of the Second World War, Americans tended to the belief not that the rule of law should be the goal and hope of nations but that it should forthwith be adopted by them in entirety: laws, disarmament and police force. And, in the event, the Charter did contain much optimism of this sort in that it laid down an almost complete substitution of security by justice for security by power. When the Charter failed in this respect, a common American belief was not that its attempt to substitute justice had been too great but that it had been too little.

This was a frequent view in the discussions of the early fifties of a review of the Charter. In a speech of August 1953 dealing with the inadequacies of the United Nations Organization, Secretary Dulles said: 'A third inadequacy came out of disregard for the fact that world order, in the long run, depends not on men, but upon law, law which embodies eternal principles of justice and morality . . .' Dulles went on to quote from Robert Taft's book *A Foreign Policy for Americans* the view which Taft had urged consistently from 1945: 'The fundamental difficulty is that it (the United Nations Organization) is not based primarily on an underlying law and an administration of justice under that law. I believe that in the long run, the only way to establish peace is to write a law, agreed to by each of the nations to govern the relations of such nations with each other and to obtain the covenant of all such nations that they will abide by that law and by decisions made thereunder.'[17] The enduring attraction of this ideal to Americans was exemplified in its adoption by Mr Nixon in his nomination campaign in 1959 as part of his attempt to strengthen his popular image as a statesman rather than as a politician. It was also exemplified at that time in President Eisenhower's revival of proposals to reduce the right of veto, the main respect in which the Charter had limited the substitution of justice for power.

These statements by Americans looked, in effect, to the replacement of international politics by international law. American Administrations were not in practice as optimistic as this and neither was the Charter of 1945. The Charter required the renunciation of armaments and the use of force, and the settlement of disputes by peaceful means; but the system was to be operated, not by the judgements of an impartial tribunal, but by the discussions and decisions of the nations themselves. At the same time, though the Charter avoided the extremes of legalistic optimism, it adopted democratic optimism on a scale which it is scarcely possible to exaggerate. The notion was that the discussions and decisions of the nations were to be conducted by a semicircle of reasonable men, debating and voting in public.

Certainly the Charter provided that conventional diplomatic means should be tried before a dispute was brought to the Security Council; but this would necessarily mean in practice that the disputes which reached the Council would be precisely the most momentous and intractable. Moreover, in the American view, the principles of reasonable discussion and consent to the majority view were to be followed even in the normal diplomatic processes. Though the comments which follow are cast in terms of the United Nations Organization, they apply almost equally to the American view of the making of the peace settlement, four-power control of Germany, and the whole approach of the United States to its postwar dealings with the Soviet Union and the other powers.

The belief that public debate and majority decisions should be the method of the United Nations Organization was common to all the Western countries. All hoped that the United Nations might be sufficiently united on fundamentals to make parliamentary democracy workable. Americans, however, felt an exceptionable degree of confidence that the method would work and hence, more important, an exceptional degree of surprise and anger when it did not. The explanation of this lies in the character and traditions of Americans, the instinctive friendliness and optimism about human nature, the political myths of democracy, enlightenment and reason. From another point of view it was the nemesis of isolationism; conviction of the necessity for One World was not equalled by appreciation of the world's diversity. These and many other American characteristics combined to produce an exceptionally strong tendency to believe that if only the statesmen of all nations could be brought together in reasonable discussion, then it must be possible for them to reach agreed solutions. If they could not, then this must mean that one or other of the nations was at heart an outlaw from humanity.

Reasonable discussion did not mean dry intellectualism but friendliness and frankness in a style jokingly described by President Roosevelt to the Dumbarton Oaks Conference when opening its work on the drafts of the Charter: 'A conference of this kind always reminds me of an old saying of a gentleman called Alfred E. Smith, who used to be Governor of New York ... He said that if you can get the parties into one room with a big table and make them take their coats off and put their feet on the table and give each of them a good cigar, you can always make them agree. Well, there was something in that idea.' Roosevelt frequently expressed the idea that acquaintance and understanding must surely lead to agreement. On the same occasion, he said: 'I got to know him (Churchill) and he got to know me. In other words, we met and you cannot hate a man that you know well . . . Later on, Molotov came here and we had a grand time together. Then during the following year, at Teheran, the Marshal (Stalin) and I got to know each other. We got on beautifully . . .'[18]

On an earlier occasion, in March 1944, Roosevelt told a gathering: 'And I think the Russians are perfectly friendly; they aren't trying to gobble up all the rest of Europe or the world. They don't know us, that's the really fundamental difference.'[19] Roosevelt was later criticized by Americans for gullibility towards the Russians; yet the truth seems to be that the instincts underlying his appraisal were and are shared by the majority of Americans, and probably in a simpler form than in the case of the President himself. Those who doubted the possibility of friendship with the Russians at the time were mainly men with special reasons for repressing optimism such as isolationists and uncompromising anti-Communists.

The extreme result of the idea of a world run by reasonable discussion was the inclusion in the United Nations Charter of voting. The system adopted contained, it is true, one important limitation, a source of resentment to some of the smaller Western nations. The United States proposed at Dumbarton Oaks that a majority in the Security Council must include the votes of all five permanent members, the Big Three, France and China, provision, that is, for the veto. This was suggested because neither the Administration, nor Congress nor the people could be expected to accept a complete sharing of control of American foreign policy with a new, untried international body, particularly as regards the use of American forces for security action. With only the very widest limits, however, it was expected that the great powers like anyone else would accept the decisions of the majority. 'It is not to be assumed,' said the explanatory statement of the five powers of 8 June at San Fransisco, 'that the permanent members . . . would use their "veto" power wilfully to obstruct the work of the Council'.

This idea of the decision of disputes by majority vote was the climax of the revolution which the Charter was intended to work in world affairs. The influence of acquaintance and frank discussion would not necessarily lead to unanimity among the powers but it should dispose the unconvinced minority to accept the opinion of the others. Above all, fundamental agreement on the absolute necessity for unity and harmony would produce overriding compulsion to submit. Such was the common interest of the powers in peace, so few were the apparent grounds for dissension that no doubt only superficial disputes would arise for the Council's decision, and those in the minority on such issues would be able to give way without great loss to their interests. It was on this astonishingly optimistic basis that the great revolution was attempted, an attempt which was to lead in 1946-7 to the pathetic spectacle of the enormous issues of world affairs being submitted for a solution to the counting of heads.

On traditional standards, so long as the nation-state has the final responsibility for the security of its citizens, nations require to be convinced and not outvoted. If they should not be coerced by power, they cannot be coerced by votes. If a consensus among the powers emerged, then no voting was necessary; if it did not emerge, then no amount of voting could produce action. In traditional terms, the Security Council would have been at most a forum for continuous contact between the powers as an additional means of maintaining sufficient understanding among them for united action to be negotiated or unilateral action to be accepted in moments of crisis. It would have been, in a later phrase, a permanent summit conference. According to the new dispensation, however, the majority in the Security Council was to exercise the functions of sovereignty, not indeed because anyone had found evidence of a disposition among the powers to surrender their sovereignty, but because of a faith, that, with the defeat of the Axis, all mankind would henceforth be united by a common conception of peace and of the means to achieve security, or, at least, by a common conception of what was reasonable.

Not only was it extremely unlikely that this faith could be justified in the postwar world or for many years; but in addition the Soviet Union gave certain direct evidence in advance that it was not. The most general assessment of the Soviet Union might well have been expected to expose the utter improbability that it too would suddenly abolish the methods of the old order and commit its security to international co-operation under the rule of law and democratic decisions. To the radical doubts which might thus have been awakened, the Soviet Union added indications of an attitude quite at odds with that of the United States during the planning of the United Nations Organization, even if these were perhaps to some degree obscured by differences of approach between Stalin and Molotov, even if it was by then perhaps too late.

Both at Dumbarton Oaks and at San Fransisco, deadlocks developed between the Soviet Union and the other four sponsoring powers on the extent of the right of veto; in particular, at San Fransisco, the Soviet Union argued that the right should apply even to the inscription of items on the Security Council's agenda. The stubbornness with which the Soviet delegates argued their case for limiting the competence of the Security Council may well have had the paradoxical effect of reinforcing the American assumption that the Soviet Union, like itself, attached great significance to the future role of the Security Council in world affairs. On the other hand, Stalin at any rate gave clear indications that he did not.

The Dumbarton Oaks deadlock was quickly solved at Yalta by Stalin's ready acceptance of the American formula. However, to quote Secretary Byrnes, 'I was deeply disturbed by the clear evidence that Stalin had not considered or even read our proposal on voting in the Security Council even though it had been sent to him by diplomatic air pouch on December 5. This was February 6, and it occurred to me that if in those sixty-three days he had not familarized himself with the subject, he could not be greatly interested in the United Nations organization. It was all the more impressive since this certainly was the only proposal on the agenda with which he was not entirely familiar.'[20]

Similarly, the further deadlock at San Fransisco was an important point in Harry Hopkins's special visit to Stalin at the time; but when Hopkins raised the matter, it was at once clear that 'the Russian leader was not informed on what was the crucial issue of the San Fransisco conference'. Hopkins explained the point and Molotov intervened to defend the Soviet delegation's stand; but Stalin 'told Molotov he thought it was an insignificant matter and that the American position should be accepted'.[21]

These exchanges on the veto suggest not only that the United States and the Soviet Union attached a very different scale of importance to the United Nations Organization in the postwar world, but in particular that the Soviet Union had no expectation of subjecting its policies to public discussion, judgement and vote. Stalin's attitude of indifference suggests that he believed either in unilateral action or that the precedent of the Big Three wartime meetings would be followed after the War, and that, like the drafting of the peace treaties, all matters crucial to the great powers would be settled by bargaining among them. Molotov's attitude to the veto as expressed by the Soviet representatives at Dumbarton Oaks and by himself at San Fransisco gave a clear warning of the vigour with which the Soviet Union would use this right if need arose.

However, it seems probable that in agreeing to the five power statement on the use of the veto at San Fransisco, Molotov, like Stalin did not seriously consider that such need would in fact arise. Though seeking stubbornly to take precautions, he perhaps scarcely believed that the United States truly intended to allow its policies, and correspondingly to require the Soviet Union to allow its policies, to be discussed and decided by the votes of such powers as Australia, Brazil, Egypt, Mexico, the Netherlands and Poland, the original non-permanent members of the Security Council. It no doubt seemed incredible to the Soviet leaders that the most momentous and intractable disputes in world affairs were to be settled in a public forum in front of a battery of microphones and television cameras. If the United States insisted on a complicated ritual in a remote Pacific city as indispensable to its role in world affairs, then it must be held and must be repeated annually in another suitable city; but without doubt, the realities of international relations were to lie elsewhere as they had lain for centuries. The Soviet Union probably never appreciated the extent of the change which the United States hoped to see in the conduct of the outer world. The Soviet Union was probably still less able to appreciate that the United States was revolutionary in its intentions than the United States was to appreciate that the Soviet Union was traditional.

In the first months of peace in 1945, the main 'idea' of Americans in their outlook on world affairs gradually became one of dismay at the actions of the Soviet Union, and, in 1946, of resentment and growing anger. Incident after incident revealed to the Administration and to those of the population not fully preoccupied with home affairs, a sudden aloofness and coldness on the part of the Soviet Union, ruthlessness and deception in Germany and Eastern Europe, audacity and stubbornness in the settlement of Europe and the Middle East. It was these crude rebuffs to American friendliness, these blatant affronts to Western opinion as a whole, which began the spiral of hostility which grew eventually into the East-West conflict.

At the same time, with its revolutionary approach to the problems of postwar world affairs, the United States had expected more of the Soviet Union than on any reasonable calculation it was likely to get. The United States became as a result too angry with the Soviet Union or angry in the wrong way. The failure of the United States to appreciate how novel were its expectations, how conventional were Soviet aims and how historically typical were its methods, contributed, that is to say, to the growth of the extremist ideas about the Soviet Union and the nature of the Soviet threat which deeply influenced American policy from 1947 onwards.

The same considerations arise from the fate of the United Nations Organization and, in particular, from the debates in the Security Council and General Assembly in 1946. Elated with victory over Germany, the Soviet Union was in a mood to take the rewards of victory. It would have been difficult, probably impossible, to dissuade the Soviet Union from this course by any means; least of all could this be done by debate and voting in any open assembly. The airing of issues in the Organization when private diplomacy had failed had only two results. One was the enrolment of opinion in the West and to some extent elsewhere behind the Western Governments, balanced perhaps by the further exacerbation of the Soviet mood. The other was an additional and misguided element in the anger of the United States towards the Soviet Union.

The United Nations Organization was the highest embodiment of the new principles which the United States hoped to see established in the conduct of world affairs. The frustration of its working by the 'everlasting No' of the Soviet Union was perhaps the most cruel disappointment which American opinion had to suffer. It was the focus of American popular amazement at Soviet conduct and thus a powerful contributant to the gradual American belief that the Soviet Union was motivated by some unique and extraordinary wickedness. The Russians had agreed to the United Nations Charter, they had accepted the Organization along with all other nations as the centre of the new world order, and yet now they deliberately sabotaged its operation. With the example of the Fascist demagogues as witness, it was overwhelmingly clear that the world's affairs must be settled by sincere and reasonable discussion among the nations if there was to be peace. And yet for week after week Americans heard the perverse propaganda, the abusive tirades which were the Soviet Union's reaction to the public pillorying of its policies. The Soviet Union, as Americans saw it, totally refused to co-operate with men of goodwill, to accept the rule of law, or to follow the dictates of honest discussion and reason. It was an enemy; more than an enemy, it was an outlaw, an outcast from humanity; it was, in a word, Communist.

As to the further results of American expectations in 1945 about the postwar world, the most general and the most obvious was two years of disillusionment, hectic improvisation and painful readjustment of the broad lines of policy. The fault of the United States was not that it sought to change the methods of international relations but that it failed to see how great was the change it sought and how small were the chances of acceptance by the Soviet Union, and to prepare itself accordingly. It would be unreasonable to criticize the United States for pursuing the idea of co-operation, and, more cautiously it is true, the subjection of ever-increasing areas of affairs to the rule of law and of all other areas to reasonable discussion and agreement. It was impossible for the United States and the other Western nations to accept a Soviet sphere of influence in Eastern Europe in the form in which it was imposed.

But the United States might well have appreciated from its knowledge of the Soviet Union and from its own attitudes to the Western Hemisphere and Japan how unlikely it was that the Soviet Union would share these ideas and how likely that it would act as it did in Eastern Europe. If this had been done, the fate of East Germany might have been different and, to that extent, the situation of Europe, more stable; there would have been reserves of policy-planning behind the laborious, benevolent and, in the event, almost entirely irrelevant memoranda which, as we shall see, were America's main wartime preparation for the European settlement; the United States would not have been harassed and dismayed, and Western Europe governments with it, by setback after setback in the two chaotic postwar years, with little to rely on but improvisation and courage.

In the longer term, the American ideas of 1945 progressed and prospered. The Soviet Union, in clinging to its traditional ideas of the exploitation of victory and the attainment of security, certainly confirmed the unlikelihood that it would ever again have to endure the sufferings which had struck it four times or more in five generations. But it seems probable that this threat was already past, that the modern dangers were significantly different, that its methods were accordingly as outmoded as they were brutal. Above all, by pursuing this course, it sacrificed the prestige and power and the great body of enthusiastic or friendly opinion throughout Europe and beyond which its victory and progress had brought it.

As to the United States, the idea of international co-operation in which it most trusted for peace and security continued to strengthen throughout the world, not merely in the alliances against the Soviet Union but in every direction. The United Nations Organization fell for a time into the background of world affairs; the idea of the rule of law, now admittedly confined to one half of the world, needed little invocation when the accent of policy was on building the Western Alliance; but both re-emerged strongly in the mid-fifties.

The crisis which dispelled the wartime vision of One World modified the American attitude to power. American power overshadowed the Western Alliance in the late nineteen-forties and fifties, causing an undercurrent and sometimes outbursts of resentment among Western populations and influencing Western policies by reaction. Earl Attlee once said of Britain's decision to make atomic weapons: 'We couldn't get co-operation with the Americans. That stupid MacMahon Act prevented our acting fully with them. And they were inclined to think they were the big boys and we were the small boys; we just had to show them they didn't know everything.'[22] The essentials of this remark applied to all the Western European countries and to Western Europe as a whole and were fundamental to developments there in the nineteen fifties. Nonetheless, the common tone of the Western Alliance was unprecedented in its reliance on agreement rather than on power. No country has ever made so little use as the United States of overwhelming power as a substitute for reasonable persuasion nor gained so steadily from it.

In this as in most other discussions of America's approach to the postwar world, a recurrent theme has been the optimism of its ideas: optimism in the idea of the rule of law, optimism as to the influence of friendliness and frank discussion, optimism about co-operation with the Soviet Union. Why was this so? Hard-headed, even cynical forecasts of postwar circumstances were not lacking among the leaders of American opinion and among publicists. Americans as a whole, as we have seen, were prone to exaggerated faith in legal undertakings, in charters, in the unifying effect of constitutions on peoples of widely differing origin. But in an influential book in 1943, Walter Lippmann wrote: 'We should not have learned the lessons of our failure in the past especially the lesson of the failure of the League of Nations, if in our projects for organizing world peace we did not fix our attention first of all on the powers capable of organizing it. Blueprints, covenants, contracts, charters and declarations do not create living associations . . . The will of the most powerful states to remain allied is the only possible creator of a general international order.'[23]

Similarly, Secretary of State Stettinius voiced the general official view when at the Senate Foreign Relations Committee hearings on the Charter he emphasized that 'the provisions for the Security Council recognize the special responsibilities of the great powers for maintaining the peace and the fact that the maintenance of their unity is the crucial political problem of our time'.[24] Certain publicists adopted a cynical approach to the Charter. The journalist John T. Flynn reasoned at these Hearings that an analysis of past wars showed the great powers to be the aggressors and concluded: 'Practically everybody is restrained from making war by this Charter except the war makers; and if you try to stop them, they will veto your effort . . .'[25] Again, William H. Chamberlin argued in his book, *America, Partner in World Rule* that as an organization to prevent war, the United Nations Organization was of little value because it had no means of dealing with the only powers capable of large-scale war. At best, he believed, it might permit the great powers to impose peace on the smaller powers, if by exception, they were unanimous.

Such pessimism was generally dismissed because the spokesmen were isolationists like Flynn or, like Chamberlin, were noted for their hostility to Communism and hence to the Soviet Union. They were simply asserting dogmatically that the unity of the great powers would not continue and had special reasons for doing so. Nonetheless, leading politicians, Democratic or Republican, had their own brand of foreboding, at least in private. In a diary note of a discussion in April 1945, Forrestal wrote: 'Dulles indicated great misgivings as to whether the hopes of the nation for an international peace organization flowing out of Dumbarton Oaks and San Fransisco might not be raised to too great heights.' Men had striven to solve the problem of organizing peace for centuries; a final solution overnight seemed unlikely. 'He said that his own preference was to start for the ideal but to have a foundation of hard reality; in other words, that the holding of meetings between the three nations that now exercise power – Russia, Britain, America – was highly desirable; that these three could, so to speak, provide the umbrella under which the other nations of the world could come in and between all hands try to work out a lasting peace.'[26]

These views of leaders of American opinion necessarily raise the question why, in the event, optimism and not shrewdness and caution was the keynote of the American approach to the postwar world. One explanation is no doubt that, in other moments, these men were inspired by the same vision of the extension of American ideals as were Americans at large. Another explanation lay in the conviction that in the modern age there was no alternative to co-operation and the rule of law and of reason if the world was to have peace, and in refusal to endanger the chances of gaining acceptance for this ideal by suspicions, reservations and precautions.

There is also a further explanation. President Roosevelt, like the American people in a different sense, was overshadowed by the memory of America's rejection of Wilson. Roosevelt's optimism, if not calculated, was at least an instinct of profound statesmanship. It was a necessary optimism. The American people in 1945 was unpredictable in its enthusiasm for world affairs. Even in the nineteen fifties it was felt necessary by the Administration in proposing a new policy departure to promise 'light around the corner', the dawn of a just and lasting peace. In 1945, no other mood than optimism, no other basis than the abolition of the old order, no other framework than the establishment of American ideals in the United Nations Organization could have been sure to win the American people's abandonment of isolationism and acceptance of a leading role in world affairs.

2

The Tough Line

Whether from the viewpoint of the time or in retrospect the main characteristics of American foreign policy in 1945-6 were uncertainty and improvisation. In the eyes of many domestic critics and friends overseas, the United States and the new President in particular were floundering. The main reason for this situation was that there was no generally agreed idea of the nature of world events and of America's response to them. The conduct of the powers in 1945 rapidly belied the idea of One World, but to establish this, to abandon hope, to develop new ideas, took time. American policy in those years, in Secretary Marshall's mild phrase, was developed 'to meet a series of crises and was therefore of a somewhat disjointed nature'.[1]

By the end of 1946, however, a tough, realistic pattern of policy was being hammered out in practice. Only the further pressure of events and open confirmation in a major Presidential statement were needed to give strong impetus and direction to American policy. This confirmation was given in the Truman Doctrine of March 1947 in response to the crisis in Greece and Turkey, and the 'tough line' of Secretary Byrnes widened into the great new policy departures of that year. At the same time, other currents of opinion were strengthening in the United States in 1946 and these too eventually entered powerfully into the Truman Doctrine, giving a special temper to the policy which followed. In this sense, the 'tough line' of 1946 was only an interlude. The idea of 1945 of One World was abandoned;

in 1947, the idea of a struggle of two worlds, Freedom against Communism, was substituted.

The world in which these developments began in 1945 was a world overshadowed by the Big Three; China and France were great powers mainly by courtesy. Though Britain did not have the resources of the other two, its traditional status was buttressed by its role in the War, by the prestige of victory and by the armed strength at that time at its disposal. This last point became important to the American Administration in 1946, worried by the speed of America's demobilization and unable to make headway in Congress with peacetime military service. Though it was realized that Britain was faced with a great task of postwar reconstruction, the extent to which wartime developments had undermined its economic position in the world was not appreciated. This mis-estimate was not lessened by the discussions of the American loan of 1946 and was even aided by the conspicuous part which Britain simultaneously played in the United Nations Relief and Rehabilitation Agency. Despite a common impression in 1946 that Britain was probably going to the dogs under a Labour Government, the basic difficulties were not clear, even to the Administration, until the crisis of early 1947 and the Marshall Plan studies later that year.

The natural Anglo-Saxon partnership, significant in a hundred day-to-day respects even before common cause was joined against the Soviet Union, was to some extent offset by suspicions. There was the American mistrust of Britain as an old world power, apparently justified by events in Italy and Greece, and of the British as cunning masters of the old diplomacy. 'Some people are already saying, you know, that we are being taken for a ride by the wily British', was one question by the interviewer in a Treasury-State Department broadcast on the loan to Britain. 'Then there's the matter of the lend-lease settlement, Mr Acheson, what about that? Isn't it a pretty generous settlement?'[2] To the British, on the other hand, the abrupt ending of lend-lease was a harsh, disturbing blow.

Britain still retained the imperial foundations of its power, even though the end was being sought quickly in India and elsewhere. American suspicions on this account were strong, if largely submerged, during the War and continued, very vocally, during the process of independence. In the vast area of the world from Morocco to Malaya, and Cape Town to Canberra, the United States had few peacetime responsibilities but it had a pronounced attitude. 'Is that Churchill's idea on all that territory out there, he wants them all back just the way they were?' was a question put to Roosevelt at one wartime Press conference. 'Yes, he is mid-Victorian on all things like that.'[3] The lines of division of command in the Far East and other understandings implied American acceptance of the legal argument that the colonial territories of the victorious powers should be restored to their prewar status at least as a starting-point for a change. Still, the attitude of Americans on the ground to the difficulties of the colonial powers in restoring their control was unenthusiastic and sometimes unhelpful. The independence of the Philippines was cited as an example of how these matters ought to be handled.

In 1945, the question of Communism did not dominate American attitudes to the Soviet Union any more than it did in the case of the civil war in China. Most Americans deeply disliked the Soviet system, but a major point was that the Comintern had been dissolved. The Soviet Union was an unpredictable dictatorship; interwar events in Russia and the German-Soviet agreement of 1939 were not forgotten; but it could be hoped that the Soviet Union had learned its lesson and that it recognized from the assistance of wartime, the peaceful intentions of the United States towards it.

In business circles there was much talk of a vast new postwar market for American goods in the Soviet Union. Suppose, on the other hand, there was trouble with the Russians, what did this mean? Uneasiness in the Administration in 1946 at the relative decline in America's military power still rested on confidence in a basic, overwhelming superiority over the Soviet Union. It was this high estimate together with the comparatively low returns produced by the Administration in the later conflict with the Soviet Union which largely accounted for the explosion of popular frustration in the early fifties. Certainly the Soviet Union had great natural resources but, unlike the United States, it lacked techniques. The skilful Germans, the clever Japanese were one thing, but the Russian Bear, for all his heroism, was a clumsy creature and quite another. It was reckoned in 1946 to be unlikely that the Soviet Union would make an atomic bomb until 1952 and then only with the help of spies, traitors and captured Germans. The picture of Soviet backwardness and hence inferiority was maintained by a constant stream of popular books and articles by diplomatists and journalists in 1945-7. It was not seriously shaken, even in the official mind, by the explosion of a Soviet atomic bomb in 1949 and persisted until the earth satellites of 1957.

In the spring of 1945, there was a vocal section of American opinion which derided the possibility of co-operation with Communists, but probably the majority of Americans had a fair measure of confidence. Roosevelt wrote to Churchill on 12 April, the day of his death, 'I would minimize the general Soviet problem as much as possible because these problems, in one form or another, seem to arise every day and most of them straighten out ... We must be firm, however, and so far our course is correct.'[4] By the summer, the difficulty and stubborness of the Russians was becoming increasingly apparent, but still, as Archibald MacLeish, then an Assistant Secretary of State, said in a broadcast report on the San Fransisco Conference: 'The vital interests of the United States and the Soviet Union conflict at no point on the earth's surface'. Both were independently rich in resources, needing little from the world outside; both were 'young, strong, self-confident countries with their own business to attend to'. Without minimizing existing differences, there was still 'no reason in logic and no reason in substance why the Russians and ourselves, given the will – given the will on both sides – to solve the problems which now face us cannot make and preserve a strong and lasting peace'.[5]

Because of its differences with Britain, the apparent absence of any fundamental cleavage with the Soviet Union, and, above all, because of its desire for the unity of the great powers, the United States did not envisage a special partnership with either of the others. In his 'Iron Curtain' speech at Fulton, Missouri on 5 March 1946, Churchill roundly declared that 'neither the sure prevention of war nor the continuous rise of world organiz-ation will be gained without . . . a special relationship between the British Commonwealth and Empire and the United States'. In the controversy which followed most Americans seem to have agreed with the official comment of Secretary Byrnes ten days later on 16 March: 'We do not propose to seek security in an alliance with the Soviet Union against Britain or in an alliance with Britain against the Soviet Union. We propose to stand with the United Nations.'

The missing element in these American attitudes to the other major powers was an idea of the manner in which the postwar settlement would be arrived at and of the form which it ought to take. Britain and the Soviet Union had more or less clear ideas of their interests in the Mediterranean and Eastern Europe and settled down to establishing them. The United States had few particular interests in Europe and, by way of principles for the settlement, was equipped only with those same equitable notions embodied in the United Nations Charter. It appeared to expect that the substance of the European settlement would be made in the conference chamber rather than in the field and to expect that the matter would be transacted by impartial debate.

The State Department, it is true, appears to have been a hotbed of realism but its influence on large-scale policy in the last years of the War was small. So, for that matter, was that of Secretaries Hull and Stettinius. The State Department was not entrusted with the work on the United Nations Charter; to a great degree, the Charter is a monument to Leo Pasvolsky, ironically enough a Russian refugee, and to the group of experts he headed. On other aspects of large-scale policy, Roosevelt's dislike of professional diplomatists caused him to use a 'little State Department' of his own in which the most influential figure was Harry Hopkins. Not a fixed organization but a varying group of advisers, the 'little State Department', while displacing the State Department proper, was not itself fitted for organized analysis of the likely course of postwar events.

The neglect of the State department and the liking for *ad hoc* advisers could be illustrated from almost any of the great power conferences of the War years. No policy official of the State Department accompanied Roosevelt to the second Quebec Conference in September 1944; this, on the other hand, was the occasion when Secretary of the Treasury Morgenthau caught the fancy of Roosevelt and Churchill with his plan for the reduction of Germany after the War to a 'pastoral state'. As regards the Yalta Conference, Byrnes records: 'Not until the day before we landed at Malta did I learn that we had on board a very complete file of studies and recommendations prepared by the State Department . . . Later, when I saw some of these splendid studies, I greatly regretted that they had not been used on board ship. I am sure that the failure to study them while *en route* was due to the President's illness.'[6]

It seems likely that these studies were exclusively technical. At all events, if the State Department was directed to produce broad appraisals of the likely conduct of the other powers, they were ineffective. One document prepared by the State Department made some impact, the Declaration on Liberated Europe.

It was inserted by Byrnes into the Yalta discussions, it pleased the Big Three and was adopted by them. Its crucial provision was that the three governments would jointly assist the setting-up of interim authorities in liberated countries 'pledged to the earliest possible establishment through free elections of governments responsive to the will of the people'. Though not without its loopholes, this, as Byrnes commented in his memoirs, made a useful basis for subsequent protests to the Soviet Union about Eastern Europe; but more to the point would have been a direct appraisal of whether there was the least likelihood that the Soviet Union would hold free elections there. Quantities of detailed studies were prepared during the War but as to general principles, the notion was, in the words of the Postwar Programs Committee, a high-level group of advisers to the Secretary of State on long-range postwar policy: 'The Government should examine each territorial dispute on its merits and should seek a solution which would contribute to peace and orderly development in Europe'.[7]

The confusion caused in American policy in 1945-6 by the unexpectedness of almost everything that happened was made worse by personal and organizational factors. The deaths of Roosevelt and Hopkins meant that responsibility was suddenly thrust on to a President who was inexperienced in international affairs and on to a State Department unaccustomed to the very highest role. The Department and the Foreign Service were small in comparison with the number of postwar problems to be tackled. Throughout 1945-6, both were in process of piecemeal expansion and re-organization. The State Department was assimilating part of the work and many of the personnel of organizations which had rivalled or displaced it in many spheres of overseas work during the War.

To the unsettlement and friction thus caused must be added the fact that Truman and Byrnes did not work easily together. This led in April 1946 to the decision that Byrnes would resign once the minor peace treaties were concluded but the work dragged on until the end of the year and General Marshall did not take office until January 1947. This situation was in itself unsettling for the work of the Department but in addition, Secretary Byrnes's frequent absences abroad meant that it was difficult for him to lead in policy-planning, while, at the same time, he apparently did not wish to delegate the initiative to Under Secretary Acheson. Since Departmental machinery was also weak in certain respects, day-to-day decisions were often hesitant and unco-ordinated as well as lacking in strong overall direction.

The Cabinet had necessarily to divide its attention between foreign policy and the great problems of the return of the nation to a peacetime footing. Truman did not, however, lack advice on foreign policy questions; he had too much. The Secretary of War and the Secretary of the Navy had equal access to the President with the Secretary of State and had equally strong views on foreign policy. Furthermore, the two service Secretaries and to a great extent, the whole Administration were deeply involved in the continuous wrangle on military strategy and the shape of the armed forces in postwar conditions. 'It is hardly too much to say', wrote Walter Millis in a note to Forrestal's diaries, 'that the battle over unification (of the armed forces) – for which "all hands", to use one of Forrestal's favourite naval phrases, were about equally responsible – delayed the nation for a year or two in grappling with the already dire state of world affairs.'[8]

These various difficulties, the confusion of ideas and the confusion of organization, meant that when in October 1945, President Truman made in his Navy Day speech his first full-dress statement of American foreign policy, its basis was still no more than twelve 'fundamental principles of righteousness and justice'.[9] These, restless critics commented, were certainly fine principles but they did not amount to a policy.

In fact, however American policy was already beginning to fall into a pattern and this pattern became increasingly clear as 1946 progressed. Two developments foreshadowing the great decisions of 1947 were outstanding. The United States fell into a more and more conscious partnership wtih Britain and the other countries of Western Europe in resistance to the Soviet Union. Correspondingly, its general interest of 1945 in the European settlement hardened into a refusal to accept the situation in Eastern Europe and into more or less formal declarations of involvement in the security of the various areas of Western Europe.

These developments were first noticeable in Italy, the first liberated nation. By the end of 1944, American and British views had already grown together in support of the coalescence of centre groups into a Christian Democrat Party in opposition to the Communists. Then followed in May 1945 the United States warning that it would if necessary expel Yugoslav troops from Venezia Giulia. The discussions on the Trieste and reparations issues at the London Conference of foreign ministers that September showed that Italy was now definitely under American patronage against the claims of Yugoslavia and the Soviet Union. In Greece, American protests at British actions subsided in 1946 as awareness of Communist strength and intentions grew and as a quarrel broke out between Britain and the Soviet Union on events there.

This quarrel was a by-product of the Iran crisis of spring 1946. Of Soviet thrusts in the Middle East, the proposal at the London Conference that Tripoli should be made a Soviet mandate was the most optimistic; the pressure on Iran and Turkey, the most serious. In the 1907 agreement, Britain and Russia had laid down spheres of influence in northern and southern Iran respectively, but while Britain had subsequently developed its position in the oil areas of the south, Russia after the Revolution had done little to further its interest. In 1944, however, during the negotiations between Britain, the United States and Iran, the Soviet Union also pressed Iran for certain oil concessions. In the autumn of the following year, the Soviet Union adopted the tactic of sponsoring a revolt in Azerbaijan, its old sphere of influence, subsequently demanding a large measure of autonomy for it and the establishment of a joint Soviet-Iranian company to exploit its oil.

The United States and Britain sought to dissuade Iran from raising the issue at the first meeting of the Security Council in January 1946. They apparently feared that a public exhibition would straightway be made of the disunity of the powers on whose unity the functioning of the Council depended; and this was what in the event happened. In retaliation for the raising of the Iran issue, on which the two Western powers backed Iran, the Soviet Union raised Britain's actions in Greece, a matter on which in accordance with the Anglo-Soviet understanding it had hitherto remained silent, and for good measure inspired the raising of the question of Indonesia. In the further debates in March, the quarrel grew fiercer, and Mr. Gromyko, the Soviet delegate, walked out of the Council. The benefit gained from the debates was resolutions noting that the parties were to continue negotiations and requiring that the Council be kept informed.

Another outcome of the debates and of the crisis in general was to further strengthen the association of the United States and Britain. The similarity of views on most issues was clear in the January session; next came the episode of Churchill's Fulton speech; then the March debates demonstrated the growth of a working partnership in practice, even if this was still not acknowledged in theory. The partnership was still further strengthened by the trouble over Turkey.

Soviet pressure on Turkey from the spring of 1945 for a revision of the Montreux Convention and for a base on the Dardanelles was another case of Soviet probing on historic lines. Turkey relied initially on the support of Britain but in November 1945, the United States intervened even though it was not a signatory to the Convention and traditionally had little political concern in the area. In July of the following year, the Soviet Union followed the tactic of stirring up a separatist agitation in north-eastern Turkey and proposed to Turkey the joint defence of the Straits. It also declared that the whole issue was a matter for the Black Sea powers alone. In this crisis, Turkey appealed not to the United Nations but to the United States. The United States informed the Soviet Union of its support for Turkey's view and implicitly reasserted its right to intervene. In this state the issue remained, alive but quiescent.

The most momentous advance in American involvement in Europe in 1946 was made in Germany. At the close of the War the Big Three had an administrative programme for Germany, announced at Yalta and Potsdam and based on four-power control, but, beyond that, no common idea of the kind of Germany and hence the kind of Europe which should emerge from the War. In America's and Britain's case at any rate, they had only the vaguest individual ideas. It was felt that a postwar 'cooling-off' period would make for better joint decisions in the end.

In the event, disagreement developed simultaneously on both levels. The most dismal aspect of the German question in 1945 was the refusal of the Soviet Union to treat the country as an economic whole despite the agreement to this effect. Straightway for economic purposes and increasingly for all purposes, the eastern zone was closed off from the three western zones and from the West. Since the parts of Germany were economically interdependent, the United States and Britain faced the alternatives of prolonged destitution in their zones or prolonged support by their taxpayers. By the summer of 1946, the United States was beginning to lose patience and turned from protest to action. It invited the administrative merger of any other zone with its own, and in July, the American and British zones were merged for these purposes. The Bi-zone, formally established in January

1947, was directly speaking the outcome of economic circumstances, but it foreshadowed the general decision of that year to
abandon the search for co-operation with the Soviet Union. In
retrospect, the Bi-zone was the first step towards a republic of
West Germany.

On the higher level, a variety of ideas circulated within the
Administration in the war and immediate postwar periods for the
settlement of Germany, including dismemberment and the Morgenthau Plan for pastoralization. The one idea which was apparently absent was that the Soviet Union would simply hold on
to whatever it was allowed to conquer. A proposal was also
tentatively discussed from 1943 for a security guarantee by the
great powers, and in the autumn and winter of 1945, Byrnes
sounded Molotov and Stalin. Finding an apparently favourable
response, at the Paris Peace Conference the following April,
Byrnes proposed a treaty to be valid for twenty-five years, whereby the four occupying powers should guarantee the continued
disarmament of Germany, appoint inspection teams to ensure
compliance, and promise joint action by majority vote, including
the use of force, in the event of violation by Germany.

This was an unprecedented offer on the part of the United States
even though it was in effect only a special application of the
principle of co-operation for security. More was to follow. The
disingenuous objections of the Soviet Union amounted to a
rejection of the treaty though the United States continued to
press the idea throughout 1946-7. Beyond this, beyond the
general refusal to co-operate in Germany, in July, Molotov made
a speech which included dire references to the Morgenthau
Plan, obviously designed to sway the German population towards
the Soviet Union, with a particular eye to the forthcoming
elections.

Two months later, on 6 September 1946, Secretary Byrnes
delivered a carefully mediated speech at Stuttgart. The Stuttgart speech, in effect, buried Roosevelt's 'momentous announce-

ment' at Yalta and promised that even though agreement could not be reached on four-power co-operation, the United States would maintain its own commitment to European security. While reassuring the German population on the dismantling and reparations policy of the Western allies, Secretary Byrnes declared: 'It is not in the interests of the German people or of world peace that Germany should become a pawn or a partner in a military struggle for power between East and West . . . Security forces will probably have to remain in Germany for a long period. I want no misunderstanding. We will not shirk our duty. We are not withdrawing. We are staying here. As long as there is an occupation army in Germany, American forces will be part of that army.'

This speech, looking as much to the future as to the past, a warning as much to the Soviet Union as to Germany, had dramatic repercussions in the United States. During 1945-6, the United States had taken steps in Europe and the Middle East which were unprecedented in peacetime: the pressure on the Soviet Union in Eastern Europe, the more and more overt partnership with Britain in European affairs, the commitments to Italy, Iran, Turkey and now in Germany. Why was all this happening? The United States and the Soviet Union had no common border; both seemed self-sufficient; whatever the future of armaments development, an attack by the Soviet Union on the United States was still not easily imaginable by most people. It was this kind of doubt which inspired ex-Vice President Henry Wallace, a politically powerful member of Truman's Cabinet, to deliver suddenly an outright denunciation of what he called 'the get tough with Russia policy.' In a speech in New York on 12 September he declared: 'We should recognize that we have no more business in the political affairs of Eastern Europe than Russia has in the political affairs of Latin America'.

The national and international sensation caused by this challenge were considerable, even though the domestic political

factors involved were more or less taken into account. The issue
admittedly subsided with the enforced resignation of Wallace a
week later. The 'tough line' continued as before. At the end of
the year, America announced the discontinuance of its aid to
the United Nations Relief and Rehabilitation Agency, which
had necessarily meant aiding governments which it disliked, in
favour of bi-lateral aid. The loans to Britain and France of 1946
had already been overtly directed at strengthening the anti-
Communist front in Europe, foreshadowing the Marshall Plan.

Still, the question raised by Wallace needed answering. Clarifi-
cation of America's stand was necessary whether to buttress
Western European governments, to consolidate American policy,
or to scotch the domestic campaign which Wallace was seeking
to get under way. So far as they attended to world affairs, the
American people seemed satisfied that the United States should
not accept Soviet actions in Eastern Europe, that it should continue to protest. They also seemed satisfied that the United
States should take a firm line against Soviet pressure on other
independent countries. In more specialized circles, broad conceptions were strengthening, no longer cast in terms of One
World, but of older ideas, now extended. 'What is the Western
Hemisphere? Where are its frontiers?' wrote one commentator.
'The idea to which we are adjusting ourselves is that the frontiers
of our national security zone lie wherever American interests are
at stake and that they reach anywhere that peace is endangered.'[10] Still, such ideas would need to be brought home
forcefully to the American people if any very public and
dramatic advance in American intervention in Europe were to
be decided on and the nation's support for it secured.

What conception of the Soviet Union would such an appeal
to the American people contain? The historic nature of the
Soviet Union's thrust in Eastern Europe, in the eastern Mediterranean, and in Iran were noted by commentators at the time.
Hamilton Fish Armstrong wrote in *The Calculated Risk* that

Soviet policy in Eastern Europe was considered by 'many experts and fair minded editorial writers . . . as unfortunate and un-called-for but not unnatural carryovers of the ingrained sus-picion towards the West which had developed in Russia, not without some reason, from 1918 on'.[11] 'I do not doubt', wrote Byrnes, 'that their ultimate aim is to dominate, in one way or another, all of Europe'; the right policy, he thought, was that contained in Marx's dictum of 1853: 'If the other powers hold firm, Russia is sure to retire in a very decent manner'.[12]

There were, however, more ominous trends of thought. It was already becoming common ground that the confrontation in Europe was solidifying in the two groupings, 'East' and 'West'. But more than this, the division was already being exaggerated to cover the whole world; it was a 'bi-polar' world. More still, excited and dramatic currents of opinion were gathering strength in America which saw the issues as a conflict of ideologies. The Russians were refusing to co-operate, were engulfing Eastern Europe, were probing elsewhere, were wrecking the United Nations Organization not because they were Russians but be-cause they were Communists. The alarming strength of the Communist parties in Western Europe was not to be seen as the result of the Soviet Union's prestige, as the outcome of the social and political circumstances of those countries, as a menace to be combated in those terms; it was to be seen as another arm of a massive, global campaign against freedom directed by the Communists of the Kremlin.

In the winter of 1946-7, American foreign policy was thus approaching a cross-roads. The question before America's leaders was not only whether they were prepared to continue the ever-growing commitment to the security of Europe; but in what terms they should present this commitment to the American people.

3

Communism

As early as the autumn of 1945, Britain asked for American assistance in Greece. A year later, in October 1946, Secretary Byrnes told the British Minister of Defence that the United States would do everything possible to aid Turkey economically but hoped that Britain would continue its responsibility on the military side. On 20 January 1947, the British government published a White Paper admitting that the economic position of Britain was 'extremely serious', and on the following 7 February, a blizzard accompanied by a critical coal shortage was sufficient to bring half British industry to a halt. Against this background, on 21 February, Britain sent notes to the United States in which it stated that it could not continue financial assistance to Greece and Turkey.

The United States Administration accepted the responsibility without hesitation. The Communist rebellion in Greece, the pressure of the Soviet Union on Turkey must be resisted. More than this, the collapse of either country would have serious repercussions in Western Europe; and, more still, if the Soviet Union should successfully intimidate Turkey, its path to further pressures in the Middle East would be greatly eased. In particular, the proposal for a Soviet oil concession was before the Iranian Assembly and a Soviet success in Turkey would be bound to influence the verdict. By 12 March, the necessary consultations with Britain, Greece and Turkey had been held and on that date President Truman presented to Congress a Bill for Assistance to Greece and Turkey. The financial aid asked for was $100 million for Turkey for security purposes and $300 million for Greece, half for security purposes and half for economic recovery. In addition Congress was asked to authorize the sending of civilian and military advisers and instructors to the two countries.

The Bill and the President's address in which he presented it had a far stronger impact on American opinion than any foreign policy measure since the San Francisco Conference. The immediate impression among policy-makers was that an historic transfer of responsibility in the Middle East from Britain to the United States was taking place. It was not fully appreciated that the recovery of Britain from the exhaustion of the war would need the work of a decade or more. An air of finality attached to Britain's weakness and the transfer of responsibility seemed more far-reaching than it later proved to be.

Nonetheless, Britain's call for assistance was symbolic of an overall relative decline in its power, and awareness of this general decline soon began to grow. 'The power of England', wrote one commentator in April 1948, 'was so long regarded as a great and fixed quantity that the spectacle of its undeniable decline is as confusing as it is disturbing . . . In referring to the world power constellation we still speak of the "Big Three" but also of the "Big Two".'[1] The 'bi-polar' image of the world was and has remained for Americans primarily an 'East-West' image and not an United States-Soviet Union image as it has tended to be, for instance, for many in the European left-wing. Nonetheless, the image of the 'West' contained the element of leadership. Until spring 1947, there were two leaders. Now, gradually and disturbingly, there was one.

The momentous nature of the President's proposals aroused sharp misgivings among the American population. President Truman had anticipated the dislike of military intervention, the strongest traditional taboo of peacetime America, and his address dwelt on the economic aspects of the Greek and Turkish needs and gave but two sentences to the military needs. It was also a comparatively simple matter for spokesmen of the Administration to deal with the objection that the United States was 'bailing out' Britain and financing its imperialist policies and that Greece and Turkey were 'feudal' states.

On the other hand, the President had overestimated the extent to which the ineffectiveness of the United Nations Organization had prepared the public for action independent of it. His address simply stated: 'We have considered how the United Nations might assist in this crisis. But the situation is an urgent one, requiring immediate action, and the United Nations and its related organizations are not in a position to extend help of the kind that is required.' While the facts were on the President's side, the feelings of a large section of the population were not. The storm raised was strong. The United States was by-passing the United Nations; it was not only intervening but doing so unilaterally; the spectre of power politics had been raised.

In the end, the detailed objection was met by an amendment to the Bill, based on a suggestion by Walter Lippmann, which directed the President to withdraw the aid if Greece or Turkey so requested or if he found that some inter-governmental organization could accomplish the task or if the United Nations Organization declared itself able to accomplish it; and in this form the Bill passed through Congress and was signed by the President on 22 May and put into immediate operation.

Wider issues were, however, raised in the President's address than the immediate needs of Greece and Turkey. President Truman took the occasion to make a general declaration of United States policy. This declaration, soon named 'the Truman Doctrine', raised great public debate at the time. The idea of the world situation which it stated was to play a powerful guiding role in American foreign policy in the following years.

'The peoples of a number of countries of the world have recently had totalitarian régimes forced upon them against their will. The Government of the United States has made frequent protests against coercion and intimidation, in violation of the Yalta agreement, in Poland, Rumania and Bulgaria. I must also state that in a number of other countries, there have been similar developments.

'At the present moment in world history nearly every nation must choose between alternative ways of life. The choice is too often not a free one.

'One way of life is based upon the will of the majority, and is distinguished by free institutions, representative government, free elections, guarantees of individual liberty, freedom of speech and religion, and freedom from political oppression.

'The second way of life is based upon the will of a minority forcibly imposed upon the majority. It relies upon terror and oppression, a controlled Press and radio, fixed elections, and the suppression of personal freedoms.

'I believe that it must be the policy of the United States to support free peoples who are resisting attempted subjugation by armed minorities or by outside pressures . . .'

This declaration was far more important than the particular decision to support Greece and Turkey. It was, in the first place, an open and authoritative statement of the policy of resistance to Soviet expansion. But it was more than this. It was a statement of the policy in ideological terms. The East-West quarrel was not a clash of nations but of ways of life; the policy of the United States was not to protect independent countries but free peoples. The impact of the declaration in this respect on American and world opinion was profound. It was not the cause of the ideological view which Americans henceforth took of world affairs, but it did much to precipitate a state of opinion already forming.

Soviet spokesmen took up the challenge. Ideological controversy between Soviet and Western spokesmen had lapsed since the early years of the War. Such unfriendly Soviet doctrines as that the War had originated in the conflicts of Capitalism were still preached to the Soviet population but hardly clouded international relations. Now, in September 1947, Comintern was revived in the shape of Cominform and the idea of two irreconcilable camps, Capitalist and Socialist, was blazoned forth. The corresponding Western idea of a world divided into two, the 'free world' and the Communist world, became a commonplace of thought and speech. International affairs were now commonly shaped in the crudest of categories. The propaganda surrounding the issues between the Western powers and the Soviet Union became still more vague and emotive through a profusion of abstractions. Words like Democracy, Capitalism, Imperialism, Totalitarianism, Communism were elevated from convenient pieces of shorthand to powerful arguments in policy making and public debate.

Ideological language is so marked a feature of the American approach to world affairs that there is some danger of exaggerating its significance. However much Americans may like to speak of the role of the United States in world affairs in ideological terms, the basis of United States policy has been the pursuit of security and other conventional interests. The United States has been a revolutionary power in its attempts to introduce democracy into international relations, in its support of the United Nations Organization and of the ideal of co-operation and the like; but the spread of democracy or of any other creed within nations has not been a standing objective of policy.

American opinion has always favoured the growth of democracy round the world. Where the United States has been responsible for constitutions, as in Philippines and Japan, it has automatically assumed that democratic institutions on the American model should be established. But the United States has if anything been backward in seeking to promote democracy in the independent nations over which it has influence. This has resulted partly from the practical desire to buttress rather than weaken friendly dictatorships, for instance in Asia, against Sino-Soviet and Communist pressure, and partly from a traditional pessimism about the outside world and the value of attempting to reform it.

'Is it not time', Chester Bowles once wrote, 'to revise our pessimistic, and somewhat arrogant, assumption that democracy is practical only for a highly developed, educated people?'[2] The Truman Doctrine raised some suspicion that the Administration's intention was to launch an 'ideological crusade' on behalf of democracy against Communism, but this was denied by official spokesmen and the issue swiftly died down. The suggestion has been made from time to time in the United States, as elsewhere in the West, that the Soviet Union gains through having a fervent creed to offer to other nations. But the evidence for this has not been impressive and Americans have remained happily deaf to the idea that the United States should turn missionary and should preach a dogma round the world.

If not the spread of democracy, at least the support of 'freedom' has been a major aim of American policy since the War. However, even, here the ideological element has been restrained in practice if not in oratory. While Americans have commonly been sceptical of the suitability of democratic institutions in outlandish countries, they have been somewhat more enthusiastic for free institutions of one sort or another and more deeply outraged by the denial of them, for instance by the Soviet Union in Eastern Europe. Even so, there has been little desire for a crusade for freedom in this sense.

The freedom which United States foreign policy has actively supported is independence, whether as regards colonialism or the ambitions of the Soviet Union. In a manner comparable with traditional British policy, the United States since the Second

World War has conceived its national interest as lying in supporting the independence of states against rival great powers, its motives ranging from economic considerations to considerations of the balance of power. The phrase 'free peoples' in the Truman Doctrine, President Eisenhower's emphasis on 'freedom' as the true world revolution, Mr. Dulles' concepts of 'roll-back' and 'liberation' in Eastern Europe, all had, it is true, a powerful idealistic content beyond the requirement of independence. However, the significance of this was mainly that it contributed to the American assessment of the enemy, the Soviet Union. Americans, that is to say, for all the rhetoric of their leaders, did not picture themselves as a nation crusading for certain ideals, but they did picture the Soviet Union as a power whose purpose was to crush those ideals.

While the United States pictured the Soviet Union as intent on spreading Communism throughout the world and was determined to resist it, this is not the same as to say that the aim of the United States was to prevent the spread of Communism. Just as Americans did not wish to impose their own way of life on other nations, so they did not in principle greatly care what way of life those nations adopted instead. They of course deplored certain kinds of régime and, above all, Communism; but whether through conviction or, more usually perhaps, through traditional aversion to unnecessary intervention in the outside world, they commonly maintained the distinction between private attitudes and national policy. The fact that a régime was Communist was not in itself grounds for interference; on the contrary, the United States was even prepared to give informal support to some Communist powers, as the case of Yugoslavia showed. The crucial point for American policy-makers and for most Americans was whether or not a régime was friendly. In the case of Communist régimes, this meant whether or not it was under the control of the Soviet Union or China.

Certain members of the Republican Administration can be

said to have carried their personal hatred of Communism over into the conduct of national policy, particularly in relation to Far Eastern affairs, and in general the ideological tone of that Administration was higher. When President Eisenhower said of the Geneva agreements on Indo-China: 'I will not be a party to a settlement which makes anyone a slave', he was probably thinking as much of the character of Ho Chi Minh's régime as of the supposed satellite status of North Viet-Nam.[3] There was moreover an important obscurity in American concepts in that the United States tended to assume that the adoption of Communism by a state was equivalent to incorporation in the Soviet Union or China until the contrary was proved up to the hilt. In consequence, Americans rarely made a distinction between resistance to the Soviet Union and China and resistance to Communism.

Yet, with these qualifications, it remains true that the aim of American policy has not been resistance to an ideology as such but resistance to the expansion of hostile powers. Despite some confusion of concepts and for all the fog of popular oratory and propaganda, American statesmen seem on the whole to have been fully conscious of this even though they have often hesitated to make the point clearly.

The main significance of ideology in the international actions of the United States thus lies in the fact that it considers the Communist ideology to be the motive of Soviet foreign policy. Both the United States and the Soviet Union greatly exaggerate the extent to which the other is concerned to spread its ideals or cares about the political faith of other countries provided they are friendly or subject. Each, except in rhetoric, appears to be well aware of the truth about itself; but not about the other. Until 1947, as we saw in the previous chapter, Americans did not usually appraise Soviet foreign policy in ideological terms; from 1947, they almost invariably did. Henceforth, they no longer pictured the Soviet Union as a state pursuing its view of its interests; they pictured it as a state, motivated by a Communist creed, seeking to establish world Communism. The Administration's main contribution to this new climate of opinion was the Truman Doctrine; the contribution of independent experts was made in many books and articles, of which the most influential was the anonymous article by 'X' (George Kennan) on *The Sources of Soviet Conduct*, published first in *Foreign Affairs* in July 1947 and subsequently, for a wider public, in *Life* magazine.

According to Mr Kennan, the two main explanations of Soviet antagonism were the Communist ideology of antagonism between the Socialist and Capitalist camps arising from the Communist theory of history, and the necessity for the Soviet rulers to maintain the fiction of the danger from the Capitalists as a justification for their dictatorial powers. Therefore, whatever the tactical manœuvres of the Soviet Union, 'basically the antagonism remains. It is postulated'. The 'secretiveness, the lack of frankness, the duplicity, the wary suspiciousness and the basic unfriendliness of purpose . . . these characteristics of Soviet policy, like the postulate from which they flow are basic to the internal nature of Soviet power and will be with us, whether in the foreground or the background, until the internal nature of Soviet power is changed'.

This view of Soviet conduct was widely accepted thanks to a favourable climate of opinion. 'For reasons which I do not understand', wrote Walter Lippmann in his book *The Cold War*, an attack on Kennan's thesis, 'Mr X decided not to consider the men in the Kremlin as the rulers of the Russian State and Empire'; he omitted 'from his analysis the fact that we are dealing with a victorious Russia' and had 'become exclusively preoccupied with the Marxian ideology and with the Communist revolution'. These and other criticisms were, however, powerless to restrain the trend of opinion which seized on and, it is fair to say, exaggerated Kennan's thesis. Henceforth, for most

Americans, the main point about the Russians was that they were Communists. Henceforth, books, articles and speeches on foreign affairs were considered incomplete without capsule accounts of Communist ideology and the World Communist Conspiracy. The only limit to this enthusiasm was that the tediousness of Communist theories inhibited the majority from any close examination of them.

Ideological excitement about the Soviet Union was, on the whole, much stronger among popular groups than among policy-makers. President Truman tended strongly towards down-to-earth and even homely explanations. He had little sympathy with the 'great wave of hysteria' which began to develop in the United States in 1949-50, and as to the Soviet Union, 'You can understand the Russian situation if you understand Jackson County. But you have to recognize that the people of Jackson County came out of the Dark Ages in A.D. 900 while Moscow emerged from the Dark Ages only in 1917'.[4] Nonetheless, as instanced in his memoirs, Truman habitually thought of America's enemy as 'Russian totalitarianism', and his feeling for the ideological aspect of affairs was clear enough in the tone of the Truman Doctrine.

Secretary Marshall's instinct was practical rather than ideological, for men and measures rather than for ideas, or at any rate, vague ideas. The presentation of the Marshall offer of economic aid to Europe in which Marshall had more share than in the Truman Doctrine three months earlier, studiously avoided ideology. In his broadcast report on returning from the London Conference of November 1947 Marshall explained the European situation in terms of a political vacuum which the Soviet Union was seeking to exploit.[5] Walter Lippmann had written that autumn that 'the contest between the Truman Doctrine on the one hand, the Marshall line and the support of the U.N. on the other is the central drama within the State Department, within the Administration, within the government as

66

a whole'.[6] Lippmann may perhaps have exaggerated in speaking of a 'contest' but a ferment there undoubtedly was, and the prominence to be given to ideological explanations was a factor in it. There was a marked attempt in the official speeches in support of the Marshall Plan, an unsuccessful attempt however, to draw back from the ideological view of world affairs.

An example of Secretary Acheson's attitude was his exposition of the world scene to Senator Vandenberg and other Senators on an afternoon in February 1947, an occasion which was decisive in enrolling their support for the projected assistance to Greece and Turkey. He touched both on the unbridgeable ideological chasm between East and West and on the character of the Soviet Union as an aggressive and expanding power. As an historical analogy, he pictured a world divided between two powers as it once had been between Rome and Carthage.[7]

In a speech in January 1950, Acheson said: 'I hear almost every day someone say that the real interest of the United States is to stop the spread of Communism. Nothing seems to me to put the cart before the horse more completely than that. Of course we are interested in stopping the spread of Communism. But we are interested for a far deeper reason than any conflict between the Soviet Union and the United States. We are interested in stopping the spread of Communism because it is a doctrine that we don't happen to like. Communism is the most subtle instrument of Soviet foreign policy that has ever been devised and it is really the spearhead of Soviet imperialism which would, if it could, take away from these people what they have won . . . their own individual independence, their own development of their own resources . . .'[8]

Exact generalization about the attitudes of State Department and other advisory officials is clearly not possible. However, it can be said that most probably shared in some degree the views put forward in the following two typical quotations from expert sources. In a study guide on Major Problems of United States

Foreign Policy, the international studies group of the Brookings Institution wrote in 1947 of the Soviet Union's 'resumption in the past two years of its prewar role as the spearhead of a world Communist revolution'.[9] The second quotation, from 'Historicus', writing in *Foreign Affairs* in January 1949, includes the notion of 'tactics' and 'strategy', adopted readily and uncritically from Communist apologists and very influential in appraisals of Soviet policy. 'Tactics of the moment may swing this way and that, but the Marxist doctrine to which he (Stalin) is committed is uncompromisingly revolutionary. In that doctrine, world Communism is the supreme aim, Soviet power, the major instrument by which it will be achieved.'[10]

Power and responsibility no doubt helped to dispose Truman, Marshall and Acheson against exaggeration of the extent to which the Soviet leaders were the servants of a doctrine rather than *vice versa*. In his time, Secretary Dulles was also guarded on this point while nonetheless obscuring the Soviet Union behind Communist ideology and emphasizing the latter. Perhaps the most considered public expression of his views was an article in *Foreign Affairs* in October 1957: 'United States foreign policy since 1945 has been forced to concern itself primarily with one major threat to the peaceful and orderly development of the kind of international community the American people desire. This is the threat posed by those who direct the totalitarian system of international Communism. Because orthodox Communism represents a materialistic and aetheistic creed it is inevitably repugnant to those who believe in the supremacy of the spirit. Because it seeks world rule through the domination of all governments by the international Communist party, it is repugnant to all who understand its purposes and, as patriots, cherish national independence . . .'

On another occasion, Mr Dulles gave an equally confused definition. At the Caracas Conference in March 1954, Guillermo Toriello, the Guatemalan Foreign Secretary, at one stage in his remarks, exclaimed: 'What is international Communism?' Mr Dulles's magisterial reproof was as follows: 'It is disturbing if the foreign affairs of one of our American republics are conducted by one so innocent that he has to ask that question. But since the question has been asked, it shall be answered. International Communism is that far-flung clandestine political organization which is operated by the leaders of the Communist party of the Soviet Union. Since 1939, it has brought fifteen once-independent nations into a state of abject servitude. It has a hard core of agents in practically every country of the world. The total constitutes not a theory, not a doctrine, but an aggressive, tough political force, backed by great resources, and serving the most ruthless empire of modern times . . .'[11]

These quotations show that while even American policymakers viewed the Soviet Union to a very marked extent in terms of Communism, a certain ambiguity nonetheless remained. Sometimes Communism was an organization controlled by the Kremlin; sometimes it was a doctrine controlling the Kremlin. Sometimes Communism was the spearhead or instrument of Soviet imperialism; sometimes the Soviet Union was the spearhead or instrument of world Communism. In academic circles, there was for many years a controversy on whether the Soviet Union was motivated by national interests, by ideology or by a compound of both. These conceptual difficulties did not greatly trouble Americans as a whole. They were firm in picturing the Soviet Union not so much as a state pursuing its view of its interests but as a state seeking to establish world Communism. It was symbolic of the attitude of Mr Dulles, for instance, that there were said to be three books which he was never without: the Bible, the Federalist Papers, and Stalin's Problems of Leninism. Still the conceptual difficulties are worth noting because they reinforce the fact that there was, in truth, no absolute validity in the American choice of picture of the Soviet Union.

Distinctions between the Soviet Union's view of its interests and Soviet Communism as 'motives' of its conduct owed too much to the mechanistic concepts of psychology to be entirely convincing. On the one hand, it could be said that the Communist doctrine of a world struggle for Communism against Capitalism induced attitudes of fear and hostility towards people and countries which were not Communist. On the other hand, a national mystique and suspicion of the outside world were traditional in Russia, particularly in the classes from which the post-Revolution leaders were drawn. These attitudes had been reinforced in the present generation by the reaction of the West to the events of 1917, by the Russian view of the politics of the thirties and by the sufferings of the War which were their outcome.

Equally, the guidance which Communist doctrine could in fact give to Soviet foreign policy did not lend itself to clear distinctions. When Mr Kennan explained Soviet conduct in terms of Communism, it seems that he was not intending to offer a complete picture of the nature of Soviet foreign policy, even if he was read as so doing. In private discussions in the winter of 1946-7, Kennan had put forward the view that Communist doctrine acted as a prism through which the Soviet Union saw the world but was not the mainspring of Soviet action.

The latter might well be said. Communist enthusiasts had expected the millenium at the time of the Russian Revolution. When it became apparent that the event was still distant, the new rulers of the Soviet Union were left to make up the intervening steps for themselves without much help from the classic or contemporary ideologues. Communist ideology necessarily became whatever the Russian leaders said it was. As Mr Gomulka is reputed to have once remarked, 'the dialectic of history proves that some things which were revolutionary yesterday are counter-revolutionary today.' To ask whether the Soviet rulers were inspired by Soviet national interests or by Communism was a little like asking whether the Vatican is inspired by the interests of the Church or of Christianity; in each case, the one might be said to be the only meaning which they can give to the other.

Despite these considerations, Communist ideology could nonetheless be seen as the motive for the limitless ambitions of the Soviet Union. Next to its baffling unfriendliness, Americans in 1946-7 most sought an explanation of the ruthless probing by the Soviet Union; the explanation of Communism fitted admirably. Even granted that Communist ideology could give the Soviet rulers little guidance on day-to-day policy, on 'tactics', Communism gave the spirit, the 'strategy', the final aim of policy. The Soviet Union, unlike Imperial Russia, aimed at world conquest; the explanation must be that it was following the Communist doctrine of world revolution. Indeed, the Soviet Union's leaders took every opportunity to proclaim the fact; what could be more certain than that it was so?

On further consideration of Communist ideology, however, or of the circumstances of the world, doubts could be raised even on this aspect of the matter. America's leaders also proclaimed in their rhetoric a stirring, millenial vision, a vision of the expansion of Freedom and of a just and lasting peace; but how these ultimate visions stood in relation to their doubtless no less noble day-to-day inspiration was by no means so simple a matter as it might appear to be. As to the Russians, though the comparison has probably been influential, the Communist claim to predict what History will bring may well be in a different category from Hitler's statement in *Mein Kampf* of what he intended to do. Communists in Capitalist countries, anxious to achieve the local revolution which will bring them to power, are naturally zealous to help History along its revolutionary path; but it was frequently pointed out by Western theorists that the Soviet leaders appeared to be under no such compulsion to strive to accelerate the inevitable. Neither, it seems likely, has the influence of Communist enthusiasm or of Communist zealots overcome the habit, traditionally especially marked in Russia among the European peoples, of separating theory from practice. However fervent the Russian vision of the millenium, whatever their ideology might tell them about 'strategy', there might be nothing to prevent a period of 'tactical' co-operation with the 'Capitalists' of indefinite length should they choose.

Admittedly, the Russian vision of the millenium was objectionable; but this was not because it was menacing but because it was unintelligble. And this was a feature not in the least confined to Russian ideas of the ultimate course of history. Mr Krushchev, in particular, was greatly addicted to such warnings to Americans as: 'We will bury you' and 'Your grandchildren will live under Socialism'. But Stalin had buried Lenin and Mr Krushchev had buried Stalin; and what 'Socialism' would mean by the time of Russia's and America's grandchildren and whether it would be unsatisfactory was anybody's guess.

As to why the Soviet Union did not choose 'tactical' co-operation with the Western powers in the years after the Second World War, the condition of the world and the interests of the powers had to be taken into account. The circumstances of victory and traditional Russian aims and methods would serve to explain immediate postwar Russian policy, as many American commentators recognized. The ambitions of the Soviet Union under Stalin could scarcely be described as limitless; the areas in which he sought to advance were traditional and the areas and events in which he was not interested were apparently legion.

As to the Soviet Union under Mr Krushchev or China under Mao Tse-tung, the ambitions of any great power today are bound to be increasingly unlimited because of the changes which are taking place in the world. If one contrast with the days of Imperial Russia is Communism, another is communications. Because there is now One World of a very shrunken size, no great power, whether it be the United States or China or India, need be or dare be parochial and isolated. The United States in 1945 was not alone in reading the lessons of the times; it was to be expected that the Soviet Union should take the same course, if more slowly. The restless, natural urge, to advance beyond the predecessor, to take the next step, to intervene in further fields, one of the most simple and most potent driving-forces in world politics, now has almost unlimited scope. The interests of a great power may be affected by events anywhere in the world. It thus tends to seek influence in events everywhere.

In this situation, rivalry between the great powers is inherent. Certainly, it was crucial in the postwar years that the mood of these powers and their method of intervention differed greatly. The United States sought co-operation and friendly régimes overseas, whereas the Soviet Union under Stalin and China, at least so far, have preferred varying degrees of subjection. But to picture this difference in terms of the influence of Communism was not entirely convincing.

If distinctions as to the motives of the Soviet Union between Soviet national interests and Communist ideology were dubious, what did it matter that Americans habitually adopted the latter picture? Americans tended to see the Soviet Union as an incarnate ideology; the British, the French and others in the West tended to a much greater extent to see it as a state; but what difference did this make? In any view, the policies of the Soviet Union were intolerable and must be resisted. This surely was the long and the short of the matter? In fact, however, America's choice, America's idea of the Soviet Union, product of the American temperament and outlook on world affairs, had the most potent influence on American foreign policy from 1947 onwards. Resistance to the Soviet Union was magnificently achieved; but at a cost. The chapters which follow contain a detailed commentary on this theme. The broad outline of the matter is suggested here.

One of the most striking characteristics of American foreign policy during the Truman and Eisenhower Administrations was its tenseness, the excitability of the atmosphere in which it was created, the ever-present threat of an explosion of popular opinion. There were many reasons for this, ranging from the unprecedented scale of the East-West conflict and America's unique burden of responsibility to the fierce limelight, created by the Press and other media, in which policy was made. One reason, however, was basic. The United States did not consider itself to be entangled in the endless toils and vicissitudes of a peacetime rivalry between the powers; it was at war. Like all wars, the 'cold war' would be an episode of limited duration, a high tension event to be eventually followed by a return to the normality of peace. The idea of a 'just and lasting peace' lay deep in the American tradition and was a commonplace of rhetoric under the Eisenhower Administration in particular. An optimistic attitude, the promise of 'light around the corner' seemed necessary to maintain the support of the population for America's foreign policy.

To the permanent crisis atmosphere, the state of suspense and expectation thus created, the conception of the Soviet Union as less a state than the incarnation of a creed made its own powerful contribution. The fear and hatred of the Soviet Union and China went far beyond a steadfast repugnance for human wickedness. The added element sprang in great part from the inordinate significance attributed to Communist mythology, from fear and anger at the Comumnist creed. Because Americans are in some degree a visionary people, they can be shaken by a vision. The oppressive sense of a world conspiracy of ideas was also partly responsible for the hysterical hunt for domestic 'traitors' with its dire effects on the personnel and to some extent the course of policy-making. Fear of Communism was not the only reason for McCarthy-ism but it was the element which gave the whole movement of discontent its weapon and its effect.

Once they were at war, Americans believed in total victory, in unconditional surrender by the enemy, and this attitude was strengthened in the case of the 'cold war' by the belief that the Soviet Union was, above all, Communist. The United States was not dealing with a state but with a state whose purposes were aetheism, materialism and totalitarianism; there could thus be no legitimate aim but victory. Just as the individual could not compromise with Communism, neither could the state seek to establish a *modus vivendi* with the Soviet Union. The American approach to the quarrel with the Soviet Union was not to end it but to win it.

This approach necessarily had the deepest influence on the methods adopted by the United States to deal with the Soviet Union. Though the Communist *bloc* could not be obliterated, it could and must be sealed off and the rest of the world immunized from its influence until by internal processes it collapsed. Granted that this might seem an impossible and potentially explosive approach to another great power, it was nonetheless morally unthinkable ever to admit the alternative, ever to tolerate an intrusion of Sino-Soviet influence, to give an inch for the sake of a mile. This attitude did little harm and perhaps even did good in the first few years of the East-West quarrel when, on any view, the need was to stabilize the situation in Europe by restoring Western strength; thereafter, in changed conditions, it acted as a straitjacket.

Because of the hatred of Communism the Soviet Union and China were considered to be not merely wicked but totally wicked in every facet of their characters and actions. Conversely, the self-righteousness of the United States in dealing with the two powers was greatly increased to the detriment of its policy. To take some examples, the United Nations Organization had not fallen below expectations because it was in some respects misconceived but because of the deliberate malevolence of the Soviet Union. The Chinese were not hostile to the United States because of the whole history of Western treatment of China but because the Chinese leaders were Communists. It was perfectly proper for the United States to seek oil concessions in Iran but it was not merely undesirable but outrageous that Soviet Communism should seek the same. Chinese intervention in the Korean War did not show that the United States had been imprudent in seeking to conquer North Korea but confirmed that China was an outlaw, an enemy of humanity.

Unlike ordinary states, Communist states, in the American view, had not legitimate political interests. In fighting the Soviet Union and China, the United States did not simply pay prime regard to its own interests and those of the West but neglected to pay even secondary regard to the justifiable interests of its opponents. One outstanding case was the decision to attempt a security system in the Middle East under Western patronage; this was not seen as a challenge to the Soviet Union but simply as a timely precaution against a Soviet offensive which must be impending. Another was the American refusal to accept the neutralization of the Indo-China states bordering on China, implicit in the 1954 agreements. Because it took so seriously the Communist theory of world revolution as a denial of the international political order, the United States habitually underestimated the extent to which it must continue to observe this order in its dealings with the Communist states if worse chaos was not to follow.

The Soviet Union and China were, in the American view, two states almost totally different from anything that had been seen before. They had at their disposal an agreed and unalterable framework for policy laid down by their ideology. They were almost immune from uncertainties, blunders and confusion in pursuing their interests. Statements of fears or requests for an understanding on this or that aspect of affairs were a trick, were scarcely worth exploring, were a mere tactic in the great offensive. With iron unity and organization, the Soviet empire rolled forward like a juggernaut. Inspired by a uniform creed which overcame all the normal tensions between states, this great horde of variegated peoples was monolithic and unbreakable. Nothing could be done by subtlety to weaken it and confuse its advance. There was no course but absolute frontal resistance at every point, inflexible, ironclad 'containment'. It was thanks largely to the uncritical obsession with Communist ideology and the alarming picture of the opponent thus conjured up that one of the most marked characteristic of American policy was a tense and hampering rigidity. In its handling of the Soviet Union and China, the United States, to use a cliché which happens to fit exactly, scared itself stiff.

Emphasis on the ideological nature of the threat from the Soviet Union and China had a final consequence. It led Americans into an exaggerated belief that all nations must enrol on one side or the other of the East-West quarrel and see world affairs in Western terms or be suspect as Communist fellow-travellers. In the words of the Truman Doctrine, 'at the present moment in world history, nearly every nation must choose between alternative ways of life'. The East-West quarrel turned not just partly but almost entirely on issues which were fundamental to all humanity; there were 'two worlds' and only two.

This interpretation necessarily had the deepest consequences for American policy in areas outside Europe which did not share the American preoccupation. It meant, moreover, that almost all world problems were one problem. The problems of the Soviet Union, the satellites, China, overseas Communism, Asian nationalism, economic development, the growth of international co-operation were all seen in one overpowering light. The diversity of the world, of its issues and movements, was underestimated or lost.

So great was the concern of the United States with the menace to the world of the Soviet Union and China that its best energies were directed towards opposition rather than to creation. The

two greatest American activities under the Truman and Eisenhower Administrations, the Atlantic Alliance and economic
aid programmes, were not developed in pursuit of American or
Western aims but in defence against Communist aims, and hence
their weaknesses. The main impulse behind United States foreign
policy was traditionally the impulse of defence. The terrifying
vision of world Communism ensured that this somewhat barren
approach continued even after America's rejection of isolationism and acceptance of leadership in the outside world.

If these were the broad effects of the American emphasis on
Communism in world affairs, what was the origin of this
attitude? To revert to the Truman Doctrine in the spring of
1947, why did the President clothe assistance to Greece and
Turkey in a general declaration and why was this declaration
given a markedly ideological character?

One reason for making a general policy declaration was simply
that such a statement was greatly needed both by policy-makers
at home and by America's friends abroad. In the world at large,
it had become depressingly clear that the Soviet Union held the
initiative; no end to the series of crises provoked by it at will
seemed in sight. It was essential that the Soviet Union should be
given a general warning of intended resistance by the other leading world power, the United States. However, so far as these
grounds went, the Truman Doctrine need only have been a
declaration that the United States had an interest in the continued independence of lesser powers which it intended to
pursue. There were other still more important reasons why a
general declaration was made and it was these which injected
the ideological element.

During the period of preparation of the President's Message,
Senator Vandenberg made it a condition of his support that the
proposals on Greece and Turkey should be clothed in a general
statement, and Truman agreed. Both appreciated that there
would be opposition among the public and in Congress to this

new departure in the exercise of American power. Apathy and opposition could only be overcome and support evoked if the wider issues were presented. Truman records that the first draft of his Message sent to him by the State Department was over-loaded with facts and figures, making it sound like 'an investment prospectus', and that he returned it, asking for 'more emphasis on a declaration of general policy'.[12]

It is clear from the account of the affair given by a member of the State Department that public relations were considered all-important by the State Department and other interested de-partments from the very earliest stage of drafting. 'There is no question that the information officers, with their sensibilities attuned to the public, made a powerful contribution to the Truman Doctrine'. A group of policy and information officers from the State, War and Navy Departments which produced 'the most significant document used in the drafting of the Truman Doctrine' believed from the first that: 'We should couch it in terms of a new policy of this government to go to the assistance of free governments everywhere. We should say we are prepared to back any country that is a democracy. We should relate military aid to the principle of supporting democracy. We should say that the United States will support free governments to the point where they can defend themselves. The only way we can sell the public on our new policy is by emphasizing the necessity of holding the line: Communism versus Democracy should be the major theme. We should emphasize the idea of a common purpose with all democracies.'[13]

This, the need to 'sell the public on our new policy', was the main reason for the general policy statement called the Truman Doctrine and the reason for its ideological tone. The idea of freedom versus tyranny or, as was understood, Communism versus Democracy, was the idea most likely to stir the imagin-ation of the American people and most likely to persuade them to support a powerful foreign policy. Mere realism about the nature of world politics, a mere appeal to America's interest in the independence of small powers would make little impression on the population; the note of ideological danger must be struck.

The American people was predisposed to an ideological approach to world affairs for a variety of reasons. One obvious reason was that in the immediate postwar period the United States, compared for instance with many of the European powers, had few tangible interests outside the Western Hemisphere. Had Americans been more accustomed to the affairs of colonies, concessions, overseas investments, business concerns and practical interests of all sorts, they would have been less inclined to see the world in an ideological light. In general, the decades of isolation had necessarily not been a good preparation for realism about the politics of the great powers.

A related and equally simple cause was American nationalism, that is, pride in the American way of life. America was the best and most prominent feature of the world scene and the best and most prominent feature of America was the American way of life. Americans were very aware of the achievement of their country, the unique experiment in human liberty, the historic flight to freedom and opportunity from a hostile world, the immense prosperity gained, and they knew and were ready to exaggerate the envy of the world towards them. What, therefore, was more likely than that the world, having schemed to draw America out of isolation into its dark affairs, should now be organized as a vast conspiracy to ruin it? The form of the threat to America might of course have been taken as military rather than ideological, and it is true that the immediate reaction to the Truman Doctrine was a war scare and talk of World War III. Even today the belief persists that the Soviet Union might perpetrate a new Pearl Harbour, might suddenly decide to deluge America with nuclear bombs. However, until the Soviet Union possessed these weapons itself from 1949-50, the general belief was that it would not dare to attack America overtly, and thereafter the nuclear stalemate was held to make an overt attack the least likely. The likely method was the slow erosion of the 'free world' around America whether by arms or by subversion until, in the words of Mr Dulles, 'Soviet Communism' takes over 'country after country and completes the encirclement it has planned in order to isolate us, to weaken us and eventually to strangle us.'[14]

A characteristic of American popular thought is extremism, a liking for clear-cut distinctions, preferably couched in a sharp formula or phrase. So the American imagination was struck by 'one world' or 'two worlds' but not by the idea of manifold diversity of beliefs and problems. When in 1946-7 popular interest in the quarrel with the Soviet Union was seriously roused, the impression was not simply that there was a quarrel with the Soviet Union; there was 'a growing tendency to think that the world is irrevocably divided into two parts that must inevitably clash with cataclysmic consequences and that therefore each part must now organize itself for its own defense'.[15] This dramatic belief in opposites, dividing the entire world, was summed up in the phrase 'a bi-polar world', current in 1947. As one commentator noted, 'We like the term "bi-polar" because it is arresting'.[16] The same was true of the phrase 'East-West'. This liking for extremes was also exemplified in the total distinction of wickedness and righteousness between East and West, the free world and the Communist powers.

From the winter of 1946-7, commentators began to expound the idea that there would be neither peace nor war between East and West but rather an indefinite period of enmity. This half-and-half situation was repugnant to the American temperament, even more so than the idea of 'limited war' when it was debated by theorists ten years later. The American tradition with regard to the rivalries of the powers was either peace in isolation or intervention in war. American opinion in the postwar period was still unattuned to indefinite involvement in these rivalries. To

Americans, it was unacceptable that a world in which America was involved 'might continue to live in the present nightmare that is neither war nor peace nor even an armed truce, with the two sides attempting to contain and counter-contain each other; with none of the world's critical problems solved; with economic and social distress increasing in scope and intensity; and with mutual suspicion and psychological warfare intensified'.[17] The events of 1947 produced widespread talk of ending the whole quarrel at once with a 'preventive war'. Good sense in the event ensured that troubled peace was accepted; but characteristically it was called not peace but 'cold war' and was faced to a great extent like war.

It was to these popular attitudes that the Truman Doctrine appealed in order to gain support for the Administration's foreign policy, and the appeal was successful. In doing so, however, the Truman Doctrine confirmed or at very least did not combat an existing and potentially dangerous trend of popular opinion. In 1947 and in the years that followed popular enmity towards Soviet Communism certainly gave the Administration the support it needed; but at a cost. Emphasis on the ideological factor in world affairs went far beyond what the leaders of the Truman Administration would have desired. It led ultimately to an obsession with Communism which boomeranged on the Administration and on its policies. The characteristics of American policy towards the Soviet Union and China were partly the result of policy-makers' own preoccupation with Communism but partly they were the nemesis of their public relations efforts, their attempt to stir the imagination of the American people.

The United States is no exception to the rule that the majority of a nation's population is most of the time little interested in foreign affairs. A high level of interest is attained only at moments of crisis or of dramatic events. A poll of American opinion in October 1945 found that 7 per cent regarded foreign policy issues as the most important problems facing the American people whereas in March 1947, the month of the Truman Doctrine, 54 per cent thought them the most important. This was the peak level of interest from the beginning of 1945 to the end of 1949. Yet though the interest of the population as a whole is as intermittent in the United States as elsewhere, it is probably true to say that in no other country is foreign policy so sensitive to popular opinion or what passes as such.

On the institutional level, the President, the Senate and the House of Representatives have each some power in the making of foreign policy and each is of course subject to popular influence by elections and by the constant need to maintain general popularity. Equally the influence of American popular opinion on policy-making is not confined to constitutional channels. It is a safe judgement from the character and actions of the Secretaries of State since the War that they have been guided by their own conception of the national interest rather than by considerations of popular acclaim. Nonetheless their views cannot have been uninfluenced by the climate of opinion and by the need for political compromise and acceptable presentation to the public. Because of the intensity of action of social organizations, interest groups, journalists, broadcasters and pollsters, public opinion beats more fiercely on American policy-makers than on those of any other country.

There is an exceptionally excited and dramatic note about public expressions of opinion in the United States. 'Thus', Professor Almond writes, 'the Press conference of Secretary of State Marshall in the spring of 1947 in which he urged the American people to "keep calm" produced what amounted to a war scare. The volatility and potential explosiveness of American opinion must be constantly borne in mind if panic reactions to threat are to be avoided'.[18] The political climate of Washington, an almost exclusively governmental and therefore somewhat inbred city, is particularly heated. James Reston once remarked that 'if you tell Congress nothing, they go fishing; if you promise nothing, they go fishing; if you tell them all, they go wild'.[19] As President Eisenhower said at a news conference during the Berlin crisis of spring 1959: 'I personally think that the American people is more soberly aware of the true situation than a lot of people around this town. We are so close to ourselves around here that we have a great possibility of stirring ourselves up'.[20] The excitability and influence of popular opinion is increased by the fact that large sections of the American population are still only just reconciled, at least emotionally, to the need for any foreign policy at all. The policy-maker is always to some degree on the defensive, and aware of tepidity or suspicion, is forced to give his proposals popular appeal if they are to succeed.

Through these various channels of influence, popular opinion began from the spring of 1947 to exert a particular form of pressure on the thinking and planning of foreign policy-makers. Ten days after the Truman Doctrine, the President announced a security test on all previously untested federal civil servants. This, together with several later measures, resulted in the conviction in the summer of one federal employee for breaches of security and, in the autumn, in the unexplained dismissal of ten from the State Department. By the spring of 1948 a subdued nervousness about internal Communism was widespread, the Un-American Activities Committee was given a new lease of life and a large appropriation, and controversy over the allegations of disloyalty brought before it became common. In August, the journalist Whittaker Chambers accused various former government officials, including Alger Hiss, until recently an Assistant Secretary in the State Department, of pre-war membership of the Communist Party. At first the case caused more sensation than anxiety since Chambers produced no evidence, but in the autumn charges and evidence worth considering were brought forward and Hiss was indicted by a New York Grand Jury in December.

From January to October 1949 the leaders of the Communist

Party of the United States were on trial. In May 1949, the first Hiss trial opened; in November the second. In an atmosphere of mounting anti-Communist frenzy, of reckless allegations and declarations from Press and pulpit, of loyalty checks and committee inquiries, a peak sensation was caused by the accusation against the Chairman of the Atomic Energy Commission of mismanagement to a degree potentially dangerous to national security. Lilienthal had little difficulty in disposing of the charge and was acquitted in October. In December, he resigned his post. In January 1950 Hiss was found guilty. Finally, in March 1950, with the charge that eighty members of the State Department were guilty of disloyalty, the egregious Senator McCarthy stepped into the limelight.

The career and success of Senator McCarthy were one of the most complex episodes in American history. It was an explosion of popular demagogy in the old religious and political style in which the open cause was only one among many other causes more or less concealed. Notably, on the domestic side, there was revulsion from the New Deal and Republican frustration at two decades of exclusion from office. On the international front, the great cause was impatience and anxiety at the course of world events and anger at the inability of the Administration, with all America's power, to find decisive solutions.

There was first the interminable 'cold war' in Europe. Then in August 1949, the fall of Peking and the subsequent rapid conquest of China by Mao Tse-tung's armies suddenly awakened the American people from three years of comparative inattention to Chinese affairs, and they awoke with alarm mounting commonly to anger. The most populous country in the world had fallen to the arch-enemy, Communism. It was incredible that this could not have been prevented. Someone must be responsible.

In June 1950, the Korean War broke out and by the autumn, the situation was once again critical under the impact of the Chinese intervention and by the following year had settled into a frustrating stalemate. The vague feeling that something was badly wrong somewhere was intensified. In such an atmosphere the Administration's opponents found ready support in making the Administration the scapegoat. More than this, the 'socialist' domestic policies of the Administration and the prevailing concern with domestic Communism gave plausibility to the most damning explanation of the Administration's errors: infiltration by Communists.

'As the United States position in Korea became more and more acute,' to take one typical outburst, 'evidence mounted of our betrayal by reds and pinks in high offices in Washington . . . Replacement of Dean Acheson and his pink cohorts would be a welcome relief to the American people. It should be demanded at once! . . . Our diplomacy has been party to the betrayals and intrigues with Communist infiltrators. And hisses can still be heard in the weeds that have overgrown other high government offices. Had we not been betrayed at Potsdam, at Teheran, at Yalta . . . there would have been no Korean crisis'.[21] In a somewhat more temperate tone, Senator Styles Bridges produced his twenty-point 'blueprint for victory', the general theme of which was recognition of a global conflict with Communism and of which the whole mood was a foretaste of the 'positive foreign policy' promised on the Republican victory of 1952. Point eight demanded that 'this administration rid the State Department of the architects of disaster, the termites and muddled incompetents whose thinking has led us from victory to disaster, to war, in five short years.'[22]

The campaign against the Administration, focusing in attacks on the State Department and the United Nations Organization, had a serious if not precisely measurable effect on both the personnel and the course of American foreign policy making. Men were purged as a result of the most trivial suspicions. Some were hounded out as being responsible for Far Eastern policies in which they were little or not at all involved. The prestige of the

State Department, growing slowly since the War and decisive for the recruitment of high calibre men, was seriously undermined, and its *morale* was badly shaken. As to policy, the climate of opinion deeply influenced Far Eastern policy in particular and it was of course the decisive factor in the Republican victory of 1952 and an important factor in the whole temper of Republican foreign policy thereafter.

As to the underlying causes of this campaign, fear of domestic Communism was, as we have noted, only one element. Senator McCarthy was the chosen prophet of a host of national discontents. For all that, among all the other elements, this fear had a decisive importance in that it brought the whole movement to explosion, and gave it, in the anti-Communist inquisitions, its cutting edge. It was this element, moreover, which gave a specific direction to foreign policy thereafter. As to the origins of this fear of Communism at home, it was no doubt ultimately attributable to the same ideological temperament of the American people which produced the emphasis on Communism in world affairs. Nonetheless, something further can be said. There was an interaction of domestic and world ideas; fear of Communism at home and in the world each heightened the other. The 'great wave of hysteria' about domestic Communists can only be explained by the vision of a world Communist conspiracy led by the Soviet Union. McCarthy-ism was in the last resort only a grotesque caricature of the ideological content of the Truman Doctrine.

4

Containment

'What course the free world should take in face of the threat of
Russian totalitarianism was a subject I had discussed with my
foreign policy advisers on many occasions in the year just passed.
To foster our thinking in long range terms, I had approved the
establishment in the State Department of a Policy Planning
Staff. George F. Kennan, one of our foremost experts on Russia,
was to head this group.'[1] President Truman's account of the
setting-up of the Policy Planning Staff in May 1947 can be sup-
plemented by the blunter terms of Forrestal's diary note: 'There
has been a notable lack of any central planning on American
policy. Marshall has undertaken to correct this by the creation
of a planning group which will work directly under him and
outside the departmental framework.'[2]

It was in the event in an entirely personal capacity that George
Kennan provided what was to become the dominant strategic
concept of America's foreign policy in the late forties and fifties,
the idea of 'containment'. The argument of Mr Kennan's anonymous article *The Sources of Soviet Conduct*, first published in
July 1947, fell into two parts. First, as we saw in the last chapter,
Mr Kennan argued that the Soviet Union's basic unfriendliness
of purpose 'will be with us, whether in the foreground or the
background, until the internal nature of Soviet power is
changed.' Mr Kennan then suggested the general character of
America's response. 'In these circumstances, it is clear that the
main element of any United States policy towards the Soviet
Union must be that of a long term, patient but firm and vigilant

88

containment of Russian expansive tendencies.' Beyond this there lay hope in eventual internal changes in the Soviet Union, a mellowing of its hostility. The United States could do something to further this process by offering the spectacle of high *morale* and high ideals to the Communists and to the world as a whole.

We saw in the last chapter that it is doubtful whether Mr Kennan meant to offer a complete analysis of the Soviet problem. It is equally doubtful whether his aim was to propose an American policy in response. His purpose seems to have been the more modest one of warning Americans of two unwelcome and as yet unaccepted facts: first, that the quarrel with the Soviet Union, arising as it did from ingrained hostility, was likely to be of long duration; and next, that America's policies would in consequence have to be characterized by a quality for which Americans were not famous, namely, patience. But if this is what Mr Kennan meant, it is not quite how his article was read. His analysis was looked upon, as we saw, as expert confirmation of a tendency to consider the Soviet problem entirely in terms of Communism; and similarly his word for resistance, 'containment', was seized on far more readily than his message of patience. So striking and so welcome was this metaphor to the American imagination that it became the controlling concept in the development of the policies pursued by the United States from 1947 to the late nineteen fifties. It remained, that is to say, the controlling concept long after the Republican Administration had rejected 'containment' as a word.

The Sources of Soviet Conduct offered little more on the substance of United States foreign policy than that it would have to be exercised at 'a series of constantly shifting geographical and political points, corresponding to the shifts and manoeuvers of Soviet policy'. This statement was at least not incompatible with a policy of the greatest subtelty and flexibility, and one moreover which used to the full all the methods of modern statecraft, military, diplomatic and economic. The policy which in the event developed and for which the name containment was adopted was characterized on the other hand by a high degree of rigidity and of emphasis on armed strength. The main features of United States foreign policy in the late forties and fifties can be summarized as the building of a military line around the perimeter of the Soviet Union and China, and the subordination of diplomatic and economic activities to this end.

The policy was global in scope with a marked lack of discrimination in methods between the various areas of the world. The main instruments were the North Atlantic Treaty Organization and, subsequently, the 'northern tier' in the Middle East, the South East Asia Treaty Organization and the various security treaties in the Pacific region. The line thus drawn was clear-cut or this at least was the aim; there was no room for a no man's land between the areas of American influence and the borders of the Soviet Union and China, for neutrals or neutral belts or the like. The role of diplomacy in the policy of containment was for the most part confined to the negotiation and maintenance of the defensive alliances. Diplomacy was little used for contact with the Soviet Union and China, save for propaganda purposes, and neither was it used as a weapon against the Soviet Union's alliances. Economic assistance ranging from the Marshall Plan to the Mutual Security Programme, when not a response to humane considerations, was similarly directed to defensive ends and to buttressing the military line. The whole purpose of American policy was defence against the Soviet Union and China. The use of diplomacy and economic power to promote co-operation for other ends was comparatively restricted.

The policy called containment, thus briefly summarized was not simply the inevitable response to inescapable facts, namely the actions of the Soviet Union and China; it was a mixture of empiricism and presupposition. The emphasis and omissions of containment, its element of rigidity and indiscrimination be-

tween areas of the world owed much to the ideological conception of the enemy and to the idea of 'two worlds' and total
victory. Even the mere word 'containment' had a certain influence
of its own on the character of policy. Perhaps the best way of
illustrating the element of preconception in the policy of containment is to consider the manner in which it was extended
from Europe into Asia from about 1950 onwards.

Containment developed first in the context of Europe. Between
1947 and 1950, Europe was the focus of American attention and
effort in world affairs and containment with all its characteristics was well enough suited to conditions there at that time. It
became increasingly clear from 1946-7 onwards and remained
so at least until the death of Stalin that diplomatic initiatives
towards the Soviet Union could have little but propaganda value.
Particularly if it was granted that the Western powers could not
agree to ratify the Soviet conquest of Eastern Europe and East
Germany, a negotiated settlement or even an understanding was
impossible. The clear necessity was to revive and consolidate the
countries of Western Europe, first economically and then, when
the *coup d'état* in Czechoslovakia in February 1948 had overshadowed these countries with fear for their security, militarily.
In gradually shifting from economic to military assistance and in
devoting its diplomatic and economic effort to supporting the
conception of 'Western Europe', the United States was basically
in harmony with the countries of the region. In response to the
views of some of these countries, the United States accepted
neutralism or limitations of military commitment; it drew the
sharp line in Germany with common consent. Though there
were important differences of approach to world affairs, they
were for the most part latent; they were overridden by a
common estimate of the immediate dangers and the immediate
needs.

The case of Asia was very different, as indeed was the case
of Europe from the death of Stalin in 1953 onwards. When at

the fall of China and the outbreak of the Korean War in 1949-50 the United States began to pursue a vigorous policy throughout Asia, it at once became clear that the majority of the countries of the region did not share the preoccupations of the United States. The outlook of these countries on world affairs, like their social conditions and aspirations, was radically different from that of the Western countries. Whether this outlook was right or wrong, it meant that the methods for dealing with the dangers to the region could not be the same as in Europe. The co-operation and community of viewpoint on which containment in the European style depended would not be forthcoming.

Since the majority of Asians opposed the diplomatic isolation of China, the attempt to achieve this did little to restrict China's influence; at the same time, it damaged the standing of the United States and sacrificed any possibility of weakening the Sino-Soviet alliance and of reducing the hostility and suspicion of China towards the surrounding world. The mounting of economic assistance programmes in terms of resistance to the Soviet Union and China and Communism was in some respects a hindrance to America's pursuit of the independence, stability and friendship of the countries concerned. Political and territorial conditions in Europe made the concept of a no man's land between the areas of influence of the great powers irrelevant but the conditions in Asia made a rigid rejection of this concept perilous to the ultimate objectives. The attempt to defend the region by miniature NATOs and European-style arms assistance was unacceptable to the major Asian powers and incurred political odium out of all proportion to the military gains. Containment in Asia went far towards deserving Walter Lippmann's caricature criticism of Kennan's original thesis: 'The policy can be implemented only by recruiting, subsidizing and supporting a heterogeneous array of satellites, clients, dependents and puppets. The instrument of the policy of containment is therefore a coalition of disorganized, disunited, feeble or disorderly nations, tribes and factions around the perimeter of the Soviet Union.'[3]

The application of containment to Asia thus requires some explanation beyond that provided by the situation in Asia. This explanation lies in the interpretation of China as, above all, a Communist power, a part of one vast Communist *bloc* with the Soviet Union. Faced with a Communist power, as we saw in the last chapter, no other policy was conceivable than rigid, righteous, uncompromising military resistance in which all countries which believed in good against evil would join, until total victory was achieved and the enemy collapsed. This, the policy of containment, was the right policy against Communist Russia; it was equally the right policy against Communist China.

Until the early 1950s American policy in Asia had no grand guiding idea in the sense that it had in Europe. While the Truman Doctrine and the original containment thesis were cast in world terms, they were generally considered in relation to Europe only. World events to the majority of Americans meant European events and to a lesser extent Japanese events. This emphasis also prevailed in the efforts and attention of policy-makers. Communism was not taken very seriously as a global phenomenon. There was occasional anxiety among some as to the activities of the Communist parties in Latin America. Some attention was paid to the growth of rebel activities in Asia from 1947 onwards. But Asian events were on the whole seen in the light of the struggle for independence against the European powers and only in the case of the Philippines, already independent, were the rebels in serious danger of being considered genuine Communists by most Americans. The majority of those who watched Chinese events saw the forces of Mao Tse-tung as 'agrarian revolutionaries' and shared Stalin's view that they were not proper Communists. Communism meant for the most part Soviet Communism; the Communist danger in the world was the Soviet danger and this was not great in Asia. Correspondingly, the phrases 'containing the Soviet Union' and 'containing Communism' were interchangeable; containment in Asia was thus not yet needed. The criticism that containment would require ramshackle alliances around the whole perimeter of the Soviet Union was not originally very telling. No one at that time was considering such alliances, was thinking, that is, of Asia in the context of containment.

The fall of China, the ensuing world crisis and the outbreak of the Korean War worked a swift transformation in this picture of Asia. A vigorous Asia policy was built at emergency pace. The background was popular shock at the course of events and angry demands for an explanation of China's hostility, of the ingratitude of the Chinese to their onetime benefactors, of China's treaty with the Soviet Union and partnership with it in the quarrel over Chinese entry to the United Nations Organization, and finally of China's intervention in the Korean War. The explanation lay to hand: China was a satellite of the Soviet Union; in the same way as the Soviet Union, its policy was attributable to its Communism.

In the American view, the ideology of China overshadowed all others factors in its conduct; the common ideology of the Soviet Union and China overshadowed all the differences between them. China was above all part of the 'Sino-Soviet bloc', of the Communist camp, was an identical enemy to the Soviet Union and required an identical attitude on the part of the West and of all other free nations. The conquest of China by Communism had brought the struggle of 'two worlds' to Asia; it was now truly a global struggle; what was more essential than the application of the policies for resistance so well tried in Europe? The simplicity of this extension of ideas to Asia was well illustrated by Chester Bowles in his book reporting on his time as ambassador in New Delhi from 1951 to 1954. 'With our firsthand experience in Eastern Europe, it has been natural for most Americans to think of China as another satellite of Soviet

Russia.' 'As more and more Americans begin to turn their attention to Asia, their first reaction is frequently, "Well if NATO has worked so well in Europe, why can't we do the same thing in Asia? Why not a military alliance of the free nations of Asia under the leadership of the United States?"' 'The sixty-four dollar question for most Americans is, "What about Nehru and Communism?".'[4]

Though the American ideological picture is the main explanation of the preconceptions in containment and of its indiscriminate application throughout the world, some place must be given to another explanation of a more traditional kind. When the United States proposed the formation of SEATO in 1954, Pandit Nehru commented that it came close to 'declaring a kind of Monroe Doctrine unilaterally over the countries of South East Asia.'[5] The comment was a shrewd one in that it related SEATO to an American tradition of immense influence in most of the major steps of postwar American foreign policy. It was more than mere phrase-coining that the Truman Doctrine was so called; the Truman Doctrine was indeed a Monroe Doctrine for the entire free world.

The Truman Doctrine made the necessary adjustment of the old Doctrine to new conditions, the necessary extension of the borders of the Western Hemisphere to the borders of the free world. With the extension of the traditional borders went the extension of the traditional border mentality. The widening of America's role in the world did not mean the supercession of the old attitudes but the widening of them to embrace new fields. The American approach to world problems is not finally explicable without an appeal to this border or frontier tradition. Every instinct suggested to Americans that there must still be as there had always been a clear-cut line between the world of freedom and the world of tyranny. If this line could no longer be formed by the Atlantic and Pacific coasts, then it must be constructed. Free men must organize themselves to resist any encroachment across the borders of the free world by the enemy. This world must be isolated from contact with the other and the influence of the other must be sealed off or contained.

From the beginning of the Cold War, the language of American foreign policy was permeated with linear imagery, with lines, dykes, moats and barricades, all tending to the picture of the 'fortress free world' as a modern version of 'fortress America.' A commonplace image was that of the Soviet Union 'pushing, receding when rebuffed but like a great tide seeping in elsewhere if there is an opening'.[6] It was essential to 'erect a sure dam against the Red flood'.[7] Republican rhetoric was particularly prone to the imagery of 'moats' and 'citadels'. An influential source of particular phases was General MacArthur who combined the military habit of thinking in terms of lines of defence with a power to publicize it. Pronouncements by him in 1949 were the origin of Secretary Acheson's famous delineation in January 1950 of a Pacific 'defense perimeter'. As an example of MacArthur's own style, in his speech of 19 April 1951 to Congress, he said: 'Our strategic position then (in 1945) shifted to embrace the entire Pacific Ocean which became a vast moat to protect us as long as we held it . . . We control it to the shores of Asia by a chain of islands extending in an arc from the Aleutians to the Marianas . . . From this island chain we can dominate with sea and air power every Asiatic port from Vladivostok to Singapore . . .' This chain, MacArthur went on, must include Formosa; if it fell, the integrity of the 'littoral defense line' would be gone, the Philippines and Japan would be threatened and it 'might well force our western frontier back to the coast of California, Oregon and Washington.'

When also in April 1951 the Senate passed the momentous resolution endorsing the commitment of American troops to Europe under NATO, a *New York Times* editorial commented that 'we now also recognize that the security of these Powers so directly involves our own security that we are prepared to draw the first line of our defense across Europe and to station along that line six divisions, or all that can be provided at the present time.'[8] The same line was to be continued round the Sino-Soviet world under the Republican Administration. Speaking the following autumn, Governor Dewey for instance declared: 'We must draw a line in the Pacific and put it in a treaty for all to see – just as we have done in the Americas and just as we have done in Europe.'[9]

A similar combination of linear imagery with the European example occurred in the phrase 'the Bamboo Curtain'. The fascination exercised by this imagery can be best seen in the shock which ensued when the 'barricades', supposedly formed by America's alliances, were 'leapt over' by the Soviet Union. General Willoughby, MacArthur's one time Chief of Intelligence, testifying before the Senate Foreign Relations Committee in 1958, described a series of Pacific defence lines, and went on: 'This southern barrier (Thailand, Indo-China, Malaya) however has already been vaulted by the Russians. Like the Middle East where they have vaulted the Baghdad Pact and are now in the rear of it in Syria-Egypt, they appear to have done so in the south-east in vaulting our line, Thailand, Indo-China, Malaya, and now have reached Indonesia . . .'[10] The idea that the line of an alliance was as much a physical obstacle as the seas around the Western Hemisphere coastline is still more clearly illustrated in the following extract from a *New York Times* editorial of 5 March 1959: 'The idea of the Baghdad Pact was to create a defensive belt against Russian Communist subversion. Many critics felt that it failed in this purpose when the Soviet Union reached over and made economic and military deals with Egypt, Syria and Yemen.'

Linear imagery was not of course confined to Americans. One of the British classics of the containment period, Barbara Ward's *Policy for the West* which appeared in 1951 drew on the metaphors of 'sea' and 'dyke' for its most powerful passages. The celebrated *Times* leader at the time of the eruption of Soviet influence into Syria in 1957 entitled 'Parachute Drop' derived the force of its title from the barrier image. However, American writing and rhetoric was exceptionally replete with this kind of metaphor reflecting an exceptionally pronounced tendency to think of defence against the Soviet Union in linear terms.

The central metaphor, the word 'containment' itself raises a further aspect of containment mentality in which the United States was certainly unparalleled among Western nations. 'Containment' was a military metaphor. Its appearance in the article *The Sources of Soviet Conduct* was perhaps due to the mere chance that Kennan was at that time teaching at the War College in Washington. Its adoption as the description of American foreign policy was perhaps in some degree symbolic of what was certainly a fact: the wartime mood in which the United States approached the problem of the Soviet Union.

The policy of containment was so strikingly military in character that it is tempting to lay stress on the influence of military personnel in the conduct of American foreign policy. Containment gave priority to the building of a line of military alliances and to the maintenance of the armed strength of the free world; diplomatic and economic effort were subordinate to this task. There was at the same time a marked influx of military personnel into the government. Surely there was here an element of cause and effect? Let us notice some examples of the role of the military. In the critical years of the outbreak of the Cold War, the direct responsibilty for Japan lay with General Mac-Arthur and in Germany, with General Clay. Behind them stood not the State Department but the Joint Chiefs of Staff and the War Department with their own powerful influence on policy. Other soldiers, for instance, Admiral Leahy, had in addition to their official status a personal status as advisers to the President. Secretary of State Marshall was a soldier. The influence of successive NATO Supreme Commanders is to be taken into account beginning with General Eisenhower, subsequently President.

Military men became involved in foreign policy in great numbers at lower levels. Until the late forties, the State Department was still too small for its responsibilities and in need of reorganization to meet new conditions. From 1949, when these defects had been to a great extent remedied, the State Department was under a heavy cloud of suspicion. The armed services on the other hand, though equally in a turmoil of reorganization, had large supplies of officers, often with experience in political administration, becoming redundant from purely military functions as a result of demobilization. As the Cold War crisis grew, as the State Department lost favour, the armed services were on the initiative, irreproachable in public eyes.

From about 1950, the training of military officers in international politics with a view to staff positions with NATO and with overseas missions was intensified. Military missions in the capitals of the world were often larger than the regular diplomatic staff. 'The five national war colleges (and even their subordinate staff schools) more and more shaped themselves to produce men who would be, it was hoped, capable of filling this rather new type of command and staff position . . . One had to go to places like New London or Pensacola to see the intricate combat trainers in which men are now taught how to fight ships or airplanes in combact action. The war colleges had advanced to higher issues.'[11] In the late forties, and to a lesser extent later, it was difficult to entice sufficient prominent and capable Americans into ambassadorial posts; soldiers frequently supplied the deficiency. As an instance, the ambassador in Moscow between 1946 and 1949 was General Bedell-Smith, subsequently Under Secretary of State to Mr Dulles.

These soldiers in many key positions cannot have failed to have the deepest influence on the formation of American foreign policy. Is it then too much to ascribe the character of the policy of containment at least in part to the influence of the 'military mind'? In fact, to interpret the matter in this way would be to reverse the true order of cause and effect. The influx of military personnel into government was not the cause but rather the outcome of the American 'wartime' approach to foreign policy in the contest with the Soviet Union. The ebullience of the military and the character of the policy of containment were two hand-in-hand results of the fact that America pictured itself as being at war with the Soviet Union.

Two generations of isolationism alternating with war suggested to Americans that war and peace were two sharply defined periods with sharply differentiated methods. There was peace which was the time for diplomacy and for negotiation; and there was war, the time of intervention, the time for the military. In war, the military must be untrammelled by political considerations in the pursuit of unconditional surrender of the enemy, of total victory. In war, the role of diplomatic and economic effort must be to support the military effort. In the 'cold war', it was thus natural that the military should be on the initiative compared with the civilians and should find general favour with the public and should in a hundred ways find their entry into government and their influence there facilitated.

On occasions, there were waves of unease in Congress and among the public at the increasing 'power' of the military, in the conduct of affairs, but in the last resort this 'power' was only the reflection of the wartime mood of the American people, a mood which, to take the highest example, in the crisis of the early fifties played some part in their election of a soldier to the Presidency. The intense interest of Americans in military affairs, military controversy and military news of all sorts was for the most part commonplace enough, but in some degree it expressed a specifically American mood in the postwar years. As Mr Dulles once said, 'If I make a speech, if I say anything about the military in the speech, this is immediately reported in the Press and oftentimes it will make a headline. What I say about the non-military seldom, I'm afraid, gets reported in the Press, and that is typical of the way things go. The military seems to catch the public imagination and it is played up by the Press much more than the non-military, and that is unfortunate.'[12]

Though military power became in the end the heart of the containment strategy, this was not so at the outset in 1947. Marshall Aid to Europe was widely looked upon by Americans as the first application of containment and in 1947 it seemed the ideal application. Military aid to Greece and Turkey had weighed on the conscience of Americans and if Marshall Aid was likely to lighten their pockets, at least it coincided with their generous instincts and their desire for peace. There was no doubtful element in relieving economic distress; it could only be good. The *coup d'état* in Czechoslovakia in February 1948 was taken more as a crushing argument for Marshall Aid than as a signal for military preparedness. The main threat to Western Europe still seemed to be the possibility of victory by Communist parties; economic recovery would remove the conditions in which these parties flourished.

The Czechoslovakia crisis and the Berlin crisis of 1948-9 paved the way in Congress for the NATO Treaty, ratified in August 1949; the announcement of the Soviet atomic test eased the passage of the Mutual Defense Assistance Act of October 1949 whose purpose was to put military teeth into the new alliance. But even at this stage, Congress insisted on writing into the preamble of the Act that: 'Economic recovery is essential to international peace and security and must be given clear priority'. The shift of emphasis was only finally worked by the outbreak of the Korean War in June 1950. A certain pull between military and economic aid to Europe continued until the winding-up of the European Recovery Programme a year later, but broadly speaking Korea swung the Administration and Congress and the public over to a military focus.

At about the same time, the winter of 1949-50, the 'Atomic Bomb' began to move more into the limelight of world affairs and to become an intense idea in public discussion. To look first at the earlier years, the Administration had long been in advance of public opinion in recognizing the need for greater military power and as early as the autumn of 1945 had proposed Universal Military Training; but this was unpopular however much the United States might be at Cold War because of its implications: expenditure and conscription.

In his State of the Union Message in January 1947, Truman declared with reference to the United Nations: 'We live in a world in which strength on the part of the peace-loving nations is still the greatest deterrent to aggression'. But this deterrent meant not so much the atomic bomb as conventional forces. For such need for a deterrent as there was centred on Europe and the use of the atomic bomb in defence of Europe was unthinkable. 'The Kremlin realizes that we will never use it unless we are directly menaced or attacked', wrote Hamilton Fish Armstrong, reflecting the common opinion in 1947. Truman's deterrent was first and foremost sufficient armed manpower to give confidence to American diplomacy and to check any thoughts by the Soviet Union of aggression in Europe. To this end, Truman pressed with increasing determination from 1947 onwards against an unwilling Congress and public for the revolutionary objective of peacetime conscription; and in June 1948, thanks in some measure to the shock administered by the *coup d'état* in Czechoslovakia, a first grudging and limited measure of conscription was wrung from Congress.

The atomic bomb at that date was still kept in the background. It was of course being further developed. 'In all my dealings with the Atomic Energy Commission', wrote Truman, 'I made it a practice to conclude each discussion with the admonition that we must keep ahead (i.e. of the Russians) . . .'[13] More than this, in the absence of powerful conventional forces and of willingness to provide them, the United States was dependent on the atomic bomb whether it liked the strategic implications or not. When the first modest proposals for rearmament were put to Congress in the spring of 1948, the advocates of reliance on air power within the Administration began to gain the upper hand. It seems that for Truman himself the heart of these proposals was Universal Military Training, but against a background of hot inter-service rivalry, Secretary of the Air Force Stuart Symington decided to adopt a different emphasis in his testimony, advocating the enlargement of the air force to seventy groups. The Finletter Committee Report on Air Policy declared that 'our military security must be based on air power'; Congress and the public favoured this approach; Symington's programme was adopted. That summer agreement was reached for the stationing of B-29 bombers in Britain and the numbers on the continent, as yet only a token force, were strengthened.

For all that, reliance on airpower was still more a haphazard state of affairs than a deliberate choice, with the implications publicly accepted. In 1949, America's atomic bombs were still lodged with the AEC and were not apparently in military hands. They were, in other words, locked away in a Presidential cupboard, a potential *deus ex machina* as they had been in the closing stages of the War. Even the air power which might carry them developed only slowly. At the time of the Korean outbreak, there were not seventy but only forty-eight air groups.

The contradictions in these attitudes were manifest. Notably, there was repugnance for the use of the atomic bomb and at the same time, reliance on it. The fact was that until 1948, the United States did not begin to think out a coherent defence policy and until about the autumn of 1949, the public was not very concerned about what exactly it was. One reason for this was perhaps preoccupation with the inter-service quarrel on the organization of the armed services, though this seems to have been more an expression than a cause of the uncertainty on policy. The basic reason was simply that until 1948-9, the military danger and the need for a firm policy did not seem serious.

To the public, the atomic bomb was an unthinkable weapon for European defence partly because it was not much thought about. It was generally assumed that knowledge of America's atomic power would deter the Soviet Union even if it wanted to attack which was, in itself, unlikely. A powerful air force as a deterrent symbol was adequate. For the strategists, there were certain obvious snags in reliance on air power. What would happen when the Soviet Union broke America's monopoly of atomic weapons? What would happen if a minor conflict broke out which atomic power could not solve? However, the Finletter Report reckoned that the Russians would not develop atomic weapons until sometime after 1952, and Truman, as we saw, was determined to 'keep ahead'. As to minor outbreaks, the United States would be likely to have the help of one or more friendly powers. Any deficiency simply had to be made up by optimism. The Administration imposed a ceiling on defence expenditure and the planners had to cover commitments as best they could within it.

Against the general background of mounting East-West crisis, the first shock given to this attitude on defence was the announcement in September 1949 that the Soviet Union had held an atomic test. The public received the news without great alarm; tests did not mean that the Russians had an operational bomb; it had anyway all been done by spies and captured German scientists; the United States was still way ahead.

Military advisers seem, however, to have been put into some commotion. The outcome was twofold. First, Truman decided that the United States should develop the so-called Super Bomb or, as it eventually turned out, the thermonuclear bomb. This was a continuation of the policy of 'keeping ahead', though it soon began to be recognized that the footing had changed profoundly. It was one thing to deter the enemy with atomic bombs; it was quite another to deter him with bigger bombs than he had. As early as January 1948, Hanson Baldwin, military correspondent of the *New York Times* was writing that: 'The best and only defense against atomic bombs, long-range globe girdling planes, inter-continental missiles and induced plagues would appear to be strong offense—the threat of worse blows against the enemy homeland than the enemy can deliver against us'.[14] The trouble with this kind of race was that there might come a 'saturation' point, a point at which bigger was no better than big. Then what?

Apparently in recognition that sufficient equality in atomic weapons between East and West was now a definite prospect, the Administration also began to lay plans for further raising the level of America's conventional forces. At the same time, the autumn of 1949, the debates on the Mutual Security Act were giving rise to the first widespread public discussion of defence policy. The most stirring of the revelations made at the Committee hearings was General Bradley's statement that: 'We have repeatedly recognized in this country that the first priority of the joint defense is our ability to deliver the atomic bomb'.[15] In reality, whatever may have been the thinking of the Chiefs of Staff, the public had not recognized this fact or at any rate not with the sharp awareness of its implications which the closeness of war now enforced; and on the whole, they did not like it.

Then in June of the following year came the great upheaval, Korea. The ceiling was lifted from defence expenditure. In September, Truman promised to increase the American troops in Europe, and the following April after the prolonged 'great debate', the Senate endorsed the promise. Assistance to Europe for armaments under the Mutual Security Act was now flowing at high pressure. The armies were now to be raised, part American but mainly Western European, which would make reliance on atomic weapons unnecessary, save perhaps in the very last resort.

Summarizing the common view of NATO strategy in the winter of 1949-50, one observer wrote that while the West could never hope to equal Soviet conventional forces, it was thought essential 'to build up a Western European force that would be capable of holding the Russians in check while the large armies needed to meet them on equal terms were being raised and transported. Until such a force was in existence, the defense of Western Europe would have to continue relying largely on the "deterrent effect" of Western defense preparations—including the atomic bomb—on the ambitions of any would-be aggressor. Knowledge of the Atlantic powers' determination and growing strength would, it was hoped, keep the Russians in a state of passivity through the period of maximum danger.'[16] Early in 1950, there were twelve Allied divisions in continental Europe facing some eighty Soviet divisions. The original NATO target was twenty divisions by 1951, and 35 by 1954, but when the Korean War still further increased the feeling of danger, the aim became thirty-six divisions by 1952 with some thirty to forty more to follow as soon as possible thereafter.

Two years later, in February 1952, the NATO Council, meeting in Lisbon, received a comprehensive report on NATO's defence position, including the economic base, prepared by the Temporary Council Committee, known as the 'Three Wise Men', Averell Harriman, Jean Monnet and Sir Edwin Plowden. The report re-affirmed the continued need and the economic capacity of the allies to achieve a high level of conventional forces, and it was endorsed by the Council. The communiqué of the Lisbon meeting stated: 'NATO nations agreed to provide approximately fifty divisions in appropriate conditions of combat readiness and 4,000 operational aircraft in Western Europe as well as strong naval forces.' Early in 1952, in other words, the NATO powers still aimed to be able eventually to hold the military line in Europe with conventional forces without the need for immediate recourse to atomic weapons. Though ominous signs were appearing of a re-imposition of a defence expenditure ceiling, this re-mained the policy of the Truman Administration until it handed over at the end of the year.

'I have said and will say again and again that there is only one issue in this campaign. That issue is—"The mess in Wash-ington".'[17] The Republican attitude on taking office at the be-ginning of 1953 summarized in this campaign remark by General Eisenhower, was to have done with the Democratic Party and all its works; with its 'Socialism', its corruption, its toleration of Reds and Pinks, its Korean War, and, not least, its whole policy of containment. During the campaign there was much talk of abandoning a static policy, of substituting a 'posi-tive foreign policy', of America seizing the initiative, and, still more extreme, of 'liberation' of Eastern Europe and of 'roll-back' of the Iron Curtain, of Soviet power.

In the event, after the new Administration had taken office, it became clear that all these were slogans expressing only the impatience and frustration of the American people at the course of world events and the lack of progress towards final solutions. 'Liberation' and 'roll-back' in Eastern Europe, were only a dramatic re-affirmation of America's refusal to accept the Soviet Union's conquest of Eastern Europe, the quarrel in which the East-West conflict had originated. The only added element, beyond an impatient desire for action, was the conviction that under the Democratic Administration, the United States had not radiated a sufficiently powerful ideological message.

In a speech in December 1952, Mr Dulles said: 'During the recent political campaign, there was discussion about a policy of "liberation". Some were frightened by this idea feeling that it meant war. That fear illustrates the degree to which even free people have come to think in governmental and military terms. Our nation from its beginning has stood for libera-tion . . .' (Here there followed a passage about the Declaration of Independence). 'Once men who are free demonstrate that freedom produces the qualities of mind which solve human problems, then the influence of freedom cannot be contained. It is all-pervading. No iron curtain of the despots, no cringing policies of the fearful can prevent moral and spiritual forces from penetrating into the minds and souls of those under the ruthless control of the Soviet Communist structure. They will inevitably subject that structure to new thoughts, new hopes, new purposes, new standards which are bound to change the mood of the captives and to diminish the imperialist capabilities of the Soviet Communist dictators.'[18] 'Liberation' was thus the Republican version of an idea which had been commonplace at least as far back as Mr Kennan's article *The Sources of Soviet Conduct*: that high *morale* and high ideals were the one positive contribution which the United States could make to the process of change in the internal nature of Soviet power.

In all other respects too the policy of containment was continued and intensified. The mood of the Republicans was such that the idea of a struggle against Communism, of two worlds and only two, of total, linear, military defence to which economic and political action was subordinate became more powerful than ever. The tone of policy, at least up to 1955, became more and more military. Military policy itself laid more and more stress on atomic weapons.

It was one of the major paradoxes of postwar American affairs that while the dominant factor in the Republican electoral victory of November 1952 was the personality of General Eisenhower, the personality of General Eisenhower was only a very limited factor in the determination of policy thereafter. On the foreign policy side, the leading influences were the personal ideas of Mr Dulles and a variety of ideas more or less widely diffused throughout the Republican Party and the electorate which had chosen them.

The strongest of these ideas was economy. From first to last, the Republican Administration of 1953-60 was haunted by the desire to return to economic virtue, to halt the surge forward of government expenditure on domestic and foreign programmes, to balance the budget. How much virtue and how much myth there was in this is not our concern, but certainly it was an ever-present influence on the course of American foreign policy and in particular on defence policy.

Next there was the image of a world struggle against Communism which we discussed in the last chapter. This rose to a paroxysm in the period preceding the Republican victory with correspondingly strengthened effects on the temper and methods of foreign policy. Finally, and closely connected, there was a welter of ideas, all in one way or another expressive of anxiety and impatience at the course of world events in the two years before the election.

In the early fifties there was an increase of suggestions from all sides for reform of the United Nations Organization but simultaneously, among the Republicans, there was a growing irritation with the Organization in entirety. It suffered from the unpopularity of the Korean War since this was a United Nations war. It did not work; it was full of foreigners; its agencies, particularly UNESCO, were full of Reds and Pinks. Closely linked with this irritation was the return of isolationist sentiment in a new form, the idea of 'fortress America'.

Throughout 1950 more and more Americans began to feel that the United States was carrying too large a share of the free world's burden. They noticed the slowness of continental Western Europe to rearm, and that at the same time the United States, in addition to the Korean War, was committed by NATO plans to increasing its troops in Europe. On 20 December, a broadcast by former Republican President Herbert Hoover sparked these suspicions into public controversy, passionate among statesmen and commentators and widespread among the public at large. United States policy, Hoover declared, should focus on holding the Pacific and the Atlantic with the aid of

Japan, Formosa, the Philippines, Britain and the Commonwealth. 'Not another man or another dollar' should go to Western Europe until it had produced 'combat divisions of such huge numbers as would erect a sure dam against the Red flood.'

In January, Hoover was joined by Robert Taft in a major speech in the Senate. 'Our first consideration must be the defense of America', he declared. This could not be achieved by armies stationed overseas. The Russians could not be matched in numbers and the only result would be a disastrous Dunkirk. The defence of America must rest on sea and air power. This was not isolationism but realism, for America was 'the citadel of the free world'.[19] In a further broadcast address on 9 February, Hoover argued that it was positively unnecessary for America to try to match Soviet armies for it was 'still surrounded by a great moat' for its protection. Truman had called for new taxes, but the country would not be able to withstand the strain over a decade or so. It was therefore necessary to concentrate on essentials: sea and air power.

The editorial comment of the *New York Times* on this second broadcast is a representative summary of the views of the other side: 'In his general thesis, Mr Hoover proceeds from an assumption which we believe to contain a fundamental fallacy. This assumption is that Communist numerical superiority makes war inevitable and that since Europe and Asia cannot be defended except by whatever strength they may themselves develop, the United States should withdraw from the indefensible first line to the defensible second line, from which to carry the war to the enemy. In contrast, the policy he opposes is based on the assumption that by bolstering up Europe's spirit and military strength by *immediate* aid, not only in munitions but also in divisions, war can be averted, and in time a balance of power can be restored in Europe adequate to establish real peace and enable us to reduce our contribution and therewith our burden.'[20]

The controversy had the constitutional edge that the NATO

treaty did not explicitly commit the United States to stationing troops in Europe and it was therefore arguable that to do this required a further sanction by the Senate. After fifteen weeks of dispute, 'the great debate' was settled by a Senate vote, 69-21, on 4 April 1951 which re-affirmed the involvement of the security of the United States in the security of its NATO partners and approved the commitment of troops to Europe.

No sooner was this controversy dying, however, than another, closely related as regards popular and particularly Republican moods, burst out. On 11 April, after months of increasing friction on the conduct of the Korean War, Truman relieved General MacArthur of his command. The last straw had been the repetition by MacArthur of his public demands that, unless North Korea surrendered, the scope of the war should be widened, just at a time when the Administration's policy was moving towards a negotiated settlement. Returning to New York to an unprecedented hero's welcome, MacArthur declared a week later to a joint session of Congress that, whatever his dislike of war, 'once war is forced upon us, there is no alternative than to apply every available means to bring it to a swift end. War's very object is victory, not prolonged indecision. In war there is no substitute for victory.'[21] The wave of support for MacArthur was not sober support; it was based more on hero-worship and on frustration with the war than on lucid approval of his views, and hence the issue soon died away. Still, some approval there certainly was, linking with the Taft-Hoover thesis in 'the great debate'; there was the same impatience with a long drawn out commitment to an overseas struggle, the same desire to cut the knot by recourse to sure if extreme solutions.

Though these controversies of 1951 died down, the moods behind them smouldered on to become an element in the Republican victory of 1952 and subsequently in Republican policy. Mr Dulles's view in 1950, which became his policy later, that it was useless to try to protect every country by static defence forces and that what was needed was a capacity to counter-attack from an 'arsenal of retaliation', plainly came from the same stable as the strategic views of Taft, Hoover and Mac-Arthur. Mr Dulles did not agree with neo-isolationism, with the concept of 'fortress America' or with the suspicion of NATO as an entangling alliance; but he did share the common wish of Republican circles to break through stalemates, to roll back the enemy, to adopt swift, decisive methods.

This mood, added to the search for economy, can be read in and between every line of the statements on defence made by the new Administration in the spring of 1953. A 'new look' at defence was promised but in essence the decision was already taken. Broadcasting to the nation on 19 May, President Eisenhower declared that the Russian threat 'is more than merely a military threat. It has been coldly calculated by the Soviet leaders – by their military threat they have hoped to force upon America and the free world an unbearable security burden leading to economic distaster . . . Prolonged inflation could be as destructive of a truly free economy as could a chemical attack against an army in the field. If, in today's continuing danger, we were ever to strain our capacity until rigid governmental controls, indefinitely or permanently continued, became mandatory – where then would be the freedom we defend? . . . With all this in mind, we are putting major emphasis on air power . . . Almost 60 cents out of every dollar for defense next year will be for air power.'

Beyond these moods and arguments, two other factors contributed to the trend towards heavy reliance on air power for defence against the Soviet Union. The first of these was the successful testing of the hydrogen bomb in November 1952 and Britain's explosion of an atomic bomb the previous month. The Western powers, it seemed, were successfully 'keeping ahead'. It might be an appalling policy to threaten to destroy the Soviet Union should it invade Western Europe; but it appeared to be a justifiable policy and also a workable one. The decision after all lay with the Russians; the likelihood was that they were sufficiently far behind to be deterred; the strain on the United States of any other deterrent policy would be great. There were snags, of course. Would the new Administration be prepared to meet a Korea-type outbreak with an atomic attack, and would the Russians believe this? What would happen when the Soviet Union developed the hydrogen bomb? The answers to these questions lay partly in the use of troops produced by allies and partly, as before, in optimism.

The second factor was that America's allies were faltering in their progress towards the Lisbon targets for conventional forces. Though the United States now favoured reliance on atomic power so far as its own efforts were concerned, joint defence of the West could still have rested on a balance of atomic power and conventional forces, the former supplied by the United States, the latter mainly by the European powers. This indeed was the solution to which the United States tended; but it was not to be.

In 1952, there was a growing mood of reappraisal in Europe as well as in the United States. Even before the Lisbon meeting, the new Conservative government in Britain had decided that the economic strain of the Labour government's £4,700 million defence expenditure programme for the three years 1951-4 was too great. In France, four days after the Lisbon meeting, the government of M. Faure fell, primarily because it proposed a 15 per cent tax increase to meet increased defence expenditure. At that time, the burden of the Indo-China war was growing rapidly. Both France and Germany had political difficulties in the way of rearmament. Even if the allies agreed to a peace treaty and the rearmament of Germany, Chancellor Adenauer had to pick his way gingerly amidst strong sentiment against re-armament among sections of his electorate; and, of the allies, while the United States was insistent from late 1950 on a

German contribution to defence, Britain was lukewarm and French opinion either sought elaborate safeguards or sought to avoid it entirely. Once France had secured an American guarantee of Western Europe through the NATO treaty, the appointment of an American supreme commander and the commitment of American troops, it was in no hurry to face the economic and political problems involved in further progress towards rearmament.

There was, however, a still more basic reason for these falterings in the Western Alliance. The basis of NATO rearmament as stated in the Council's communiqué of 18 May 1950 had been that the combined resources of the alliance, 'if properly co-ordinated and applied', were sufficient to ensure 'the progressive and speedy development of adequate military defence without impairing . . . economic and social progress.' The practical meaning of 'properly co-ordinated and applied' had been further worked out by the December 1950 communique; it meant 'balanced collective forces' or, in other words, the contribution by each country of parts to a united defence structure. But the European powers were not in fact sufficiently united politically to accept such a degree of military dependence on each other. They were willing to ally and, to some extent, to co-operate, but not to integrate. This was equally true of the relationship between these powers and the United States. The whole NATO alliance found dependence on Amercan atomic power an attractive and adequate alternative.

The Western European powers felt themselves confirmed in their belief in the adequacy of atomic power to deter the Soviet Union by the news in March 1953 of the death of Stalin. Since the Western European powers were on the whole inclined to visualize the Soviet Union more in terms of men than of ideologies, the replacement of Stalin by a 'collective leadership' of lesser men raised their hopes of a new and less hostile period in East-West relations. These hopes gained some support from the comparative mildness of bearing of the Soviet leaders and in particular from Mr Malenkov's emphasis on 'peaceful coexistence'. Throughout 1953 an atmosphere of 'thaw' developed both inside the Soviet Union and, scarcely interrupted even by the suppression of the popular rising in East Berlin in June, in East-West relations.

In consequence, belief in the likelihood of armed aggression by the Soviet Union waned among the Western European powers and this chilled still further the enthusiasm for burdensome rearmament. Britain and France took their belief in new men and new possibilities still further. On 11 May, Winston Churchill suggested new discussions with the Soviet Union 'upon the highest level' and from the three-power Washington talks of July onwards, France joined Britain as a still stronger advocate of a new four-power conference; for if such a conference eased tension still further, German rearmament might become less necessary and might even be postponed indefinitely. The United States resisted the idea and pressed for the completion of the European Defence Community and the attainment thereby of more or less balanced collective forces in continental Western Europe, including German forces. But by 1953 the new atmosphere had brought progress on EDC to a standstill.

European attitudes thus did much to justify the American mood of impatience with Europe in the early fifties. 'Europe must realize' wrote the *New York Times* editorially on 31 January 1953, 'that this is a new Administration, that it was elected at least in part because of growing American impatience with the slow progress towards our unchanged foreign policy goals.' The occasion was Mr Dulles's mission to Europe immediately after the Inauguration to find out the position on the European Defence Community. Throughout the year, Western Europe was inclined to resent Mr Dulles's lecture tours and was dismayed by the ironclad tone of many American defence policy statements and deplored their effect in Asia; but it had to some extent provoked the frustration and impatience of which these were the manifestations. A tendency developed from this time onwards to criticize the ruthless American emphasis on the atomic deterrent; but this limelight on the atomic bomb was the inevitable result of the fact that the West had little else for its defence. And for this situation, the Western European governments and their electorates were at least as responsible as the United States.

As a result of the new attitudes in the United States and Western Europe, the basis of NATO defence policy changed radically during the course of 1953. Various euphemisms were adopted; targets for conventional forces were not overtly abandoned; hope was pinned on the attainment of a German contribution. Unmistakably, however, the idea of the containment line in Europe ceased to be that of a strong bulwark of conventional forces in readiness or in reserve to check any Soviet action; it became that of a trip-wire for the atomic bomb.

The first stage was the NATO meeting in Paris in April 1953. A *New York Times* editorial of 27 April summarized its atmosphere and its results in these terms: 'There are too many indefinite, inconclusive and confusing elements in the international atmosphere these days to set official targets that might prove too high. The experience that followed the famous and over-ambitious meeting in Lisbon in February 1952 is too fresh in all our minds. Lisbon showed that economics could play havoc with military goals, although it has to be noted that the objectives of fifty active and reserve divisions, 4,000 tactical aircraft and 1,612 naval vessels by the end of 1952, were met, at least approximately. What has been knocked away is the continuing program, which originally had 1954 as its target date. We are to have a "stretch-out" and sensibly so.' The NATO statesmen appreciated that the West must remain on its guard. 'However it would be unrealistic for them or for any of us to ignore the popular and political pressures to ease up on defense expenditure which the Russians have cleverly set in motion. The French are naturally inclined to think more of Indo-China and less of Western Europe in the light of the new Viet-Minh offensive in Laos. The Germans are showing less enthusiasm for the European Defense Community, and they and we know that the next really great move of the Russians on the European and world stage may well be a bid for German unification and "neutrality". The United States for its part is preparing to reduce its defense expenditures.'

The strength of the forces available for the defence of Western Europe was not in fact as high as this pleading implied. The active and reserve divisions which had been formed could not be said to meet even the guarded Lisbon formula of '50 divisions in appropriate conditions of combat readiness'. The 'stretch-out' of further rearmament over a greater, unspecified number of years was in fact an euphemism for its abandonment. There was admittedly no overt abandonment; there was always the elusive vision of Germany's divisions; but abandonment in practice so far as the other Western powers were concerned.

On the following 8 August, in the midst of the American and NATO 'new look' at defence, the Soviet Prime Minister Malenkov made an announcement in the course of a speech to the Supreme Soviet which the Council on Foreign Relations chronicle called 'the most shattering news of the entire year': 'The government considers it necessary to report that the United States has no monopoly of the production of the hydrogen bomb.'

On the face of it, this news might have been expected to produce a reversal of the trend towards Western reliance on the atomic deterrent. A situation was now in prospect in which there would be mutual atomic deterrence, a 'nuclear stalemate', in which the side with dominant forces of other types would be in a commanding military and diplomatic position. The announcement did not in the event have this effect for several reasons. It would take some time for the Soviet Union to develop a delivery capacity equal to that of the United States. The three or four years of grace might see new weapons developments whereby the United States could continue to 'keep ahead' in atomic striking power. In any case, by that time West Germany would have produced its twelve divisions. Beyond that, serious troublemaking by the Soviet Union did not seem in prospect. The East German rising of June 1953 suggested that the satellites were unreliable and that this would confirm Soviet passivity.

In January 1954, therefore, undeterred by the Soviet achievement, the Administration formally announced the long-foreshadowed results of its 'new look' at defence. First, in Mr Dulles's words, the aim: 'We want for ourselves and the other free nations, a maximum deterrent at a bearable cost.' Then the method: 'Local defenses will always be important. But there are no local defenses which will contain the mighty man-power of the Communist world. Local defenses must be reinforced by the further deterrent of massive retaliatory power. A potential aggressor must know that he cannot always prescribe battle conditions which suit him. Otherwise, for example, a potential aggressor who is glutted with manpower, might be tempted to attack in confidence that resistance would be confined to manpower. He might be tempted to attack in places where his superiority was decisive.' If the enemy were to be allowed to pick his means and point of attack, the West would have to confront him with means of resistance at all points, and the burden would be too great. Therefore some fundamental decisions had to be made. 'This has been done. The basic decision was to depend primarily upon a great capacity to retaliate, instantly, by means and at places of our own choosing.'[22]

Mr Dulles's statement was greeted with some revulsion in Western Europe. By clarifying existing policy so starkly, the statement allowed doubts about it to focus; the sheer phrase 'massive retaliation' created dismay. One doubt was whether the threat of retaliation was a workable deterrent now that the Soviet Union was approaching nuclear equality; however, this was not widespread since the belief was that the United States was still ahead. A more serious doubt, affecting even American popular opinion, was whether any 'local war', any Korea-type crisis would now necessarily be converted into a general, nuclear war. Attention naturally centred on Mr Dulles's treatment of the current local war. 'I have said in relation to Indo-China that, if there were open Red Chinese army aggression there, that would have grave consequences which might not be confined to Indo-China.' Technically, this view was well-guarded and unexceptionable but its spirit was alarming. It seemed that the United States would no longer accept a Korea-type war if such was forced upon it. In an article in April Mr Dulles reasoned that while an aggressor might risk considerable damage to his homeland in order to capture Europe and therefore comparatively large 'local defensive strength' was needed there, most other areas 'offer less value to him than the loss he would suffer from a well-conceived retaliatory attack.'[23]

Over the following year, Mr Dulles developed his view on the right response to 'local wars', simultaneously modifying his original concept of 'massive retaliation'. So, in a speech of December 1955, he said: 'We have developed, with our allies, a collective system of great power which can be flexibly used on whatever scale may be requisite to make aggression costly. Our *capacity* to retaliate must be, and is, massive in order to deter all forms of aggression. But if we have to *use* that capacity, such use would be selective and adapted to the occasion.'[24]

This conception of a spectrum of force, only so much being used as was essential to repel the enemy's attack, was both militarily and morally perfect, but unfortunately it was an ideal and not a reality. In Western Europe, there was nothing but a modest 'shield' of conventional forces and thereafter the 'sword' of atomic weapons. Since 1953, smaller or 'tactical' atomic weapons had been tested, but by the time they were available for use, the fear had developed that they would provide not so much a spectrum of force as an 'escalator' to total nuclear war. Still more as regards Asia, the inadequacy of local forces, the manpower situation of the allies, the American revulsion from a Korea-type war, all combined to suggest that the West would have no recourse in face of a determined enemy thrust save atomic retaliation. In the more likely event of a slow and comparatively quiet erosion by infiltration and support of rebels, the choice of the West would lie between screwing up its courage to a sudden, dramatic ultimatum threatening all-out war or long drawn out but inevitable defeat.

The final comments which may be made on the trend of American military policy differ between the case of Asia and the case of Europe. In Asia, the United States, in drawing a rigid containment line on the borders of the free world, had undertaken a political commitment which it did not have an adequate range of military power to fulfil. The classic case was the war throughout the fifties in Indo-China where the political commitment was complete and diplomatic compromise was excluded and yet where atomic action was impracticable and conventional military power was inadequate or ineffective.

In Europe, the containment line was not an American construction but a fact of political geography; at the same time, there were certain manifest dilemmas in a policy which had converted this line from a bulwark of conventional forces into a trip-wire for the atomic bomb.

Debate on East-West deterrence admittedly had a certain air of unreality; the stakes were overpowering and the factors involved were usually imponderable; the idea of the 'Atomic Bomb' probably had a deterrent effect on both East and West which trivialized the nice calculations of political intention and military potential. But this element of unreality in debate increased rather than lessened three serious effects of the Western theory of defence by threat of atomic attack.

In the first place, the United States had apparently swung

from repugnance for the use of the atomic bomb save in self-defence to readiness to use it in defence at least of its NATO allies; but was this change credible to these allies? Collective security was hard enough to live up to when the stake was only conventional warfare; it would be immeasurably harder when the stake was atomic warfare. Reliance on atomic weapons for defence suggested that each power could rely only on its own atomic weapons and should therefore, so far as military considerations went, seek to acquire them.

Reliance for defence on atomic retaliation also had effects on the *morale* of America's allies. Popular defence analysts and propagandists gained an easy audience for the argument that the West was attempting to deter an enemy equal in nuclear strength and superior in conventional strength by threats which it would be suicidal to carry out. Anti-Americans were the better able to characterize American policy as militarist and recklessly militarist. This picture worked like a leaven in European populations as the fifties progressed and as Soviet atomic parity became more and more clear, gradually spreading unease, guilt and fear and contributing perhaps the greatest element in the growing sense that the Soviet Union held the initiative in world affairs. The courage and vigour of the Western powers was sapped by constant doubt and questioning on their security position, in a word by insecurity. This atmosphere was for the most part inherent in the very existence of atomic weapons; but it was significantly strengthened by the limelight which Western defence policy cast on them.

In the nature of Western policies and of public diplomacy, Western statesmen were unable to combat this situation by giving effective reassurance to their populations. From a purely military point of view, Western defence policy was indeed open to all the doubts and anxieties expressed against it; it took greater risks than were naturally inherent in the atomic age. Western statesmen were prepared to take these risks because they believed it unlikely that the Soviet Union wished to attack and that the economic strain of any other defence policy, with its national and international consequences, was unnecessary. But they could not of course publicize this calculation. On the contrary, if their defence policy was to carry conviction both at home and with the enemy, the starkest of declarations of readiness to begin an atomic exchange were required.

Finally, Western defence policy, as we have said, depended heavily on a belief that the Soviet Union, quite irrespective of Western deterrent measures, did not want a European war. To this extent, the policy was built on a factor entirely outside Western control and to this extent it was a weak policy. The Soviet Union had only to hint at a change of attitude for a tremor to shake the West. This situation was only potential in the trends of Western defence policy in the period of which we have been speaking. But once the Soviet Union attained sufficient nuclear power parity with the West, as it inevitably must, and, in consequence, overall military superiority, its power to threaten would become significant in East-West diplomacy. The Western powers were not willing to match the Soviet Union in conventional forces and were not in the event able to 'keep ahead' in nuclear power and missiles development. The effects of this were to be particularly clear in the exchanges on a German settlement in the late fifties.

5

Collective Security:
Europe and the Atlantic

The growth of the system of alliances through which the United States pursued the policy of containment began in the summer of 1947. By that time, incident after incident had almost destroyed American faith in the possibility of co-operation with the Soviet Union. The Moscow Conference on Germany in March-April, largely fruitless, had given added impetus to this loss of faith. Proclaimed in the Truman Doctrine, the interpretation was rapidly strengthening that the Soviet Union was a relentlessly hostile power with the unlimited ambitions of Communism and that the governing idea of American policy should be resistance in concert with Britain and other free nations. In facing the problems of the postwar world, the United States was thus no longer in a mood to delay or to compromise for the sake of co-operation or agreement with the Soviet Union. On his visit to Europe for the Moscow Conference, the new Secretary of State, General Marshall, was powerfully impressed by Europe's economic distress, and he returned convinced that this problem required immediate action. But by this time, America's conception of the Soviet Union had altered and its patience was exhausted. A great period of decisions opened on entirely new lines.

In a broadcast report to the nation on the Moscow Conference, Secretary Marshall said: 'The German negotiations involved not only the security of Europe and the world but the prosperity of Europe. While our mission was to consider the terms of a treaty to operate over a long term of years, we were faced with immediate issues which vitally concerned the impoverished and suffering people of Europe who are crying for help, for coal, for food and the rest of the necessities of life and the majority of whom are bitterly disposed towards the Germany that brought about this disastrous situation. The issues also vitally concern the people of Britain and the United States who cannot continue to pour out hundreds of millions of dollars for Germany because current measures are not being taken to terminate expeditiously the necessity for such appropriations.' In a conversation during the Conference, said Marshall, Stalin had remarked that with patience, compromises could be reached. In this, the clash of American and Soviet temperaments was naked. In Marshall's view, 'We cannot ignore the factor of time involved here. The recovery of Europe has been far slower than had been expected. Disintegrating forces are becoming evident. The patient is sinking while the doctors deliberate. So I believe that action cannot await compromise by exhaustion. Whatever action is possible to meet these pressing problems must be taken without delay.'[1]

From this mood, there followed in turn from the summer of 1947 actions whose inevitable effect was to widen and consolidate step by step the division of East and West: the Marshall Plan, the particular form adapted for it, the Soviet rejection of it and the bitter quarrel which developed, drew a sharp line between the Western and Eastern *bloc* of nations, between those which participated and those which did not; in this way, it helped to precipitate the crisis in Czechoslovakia; it also required the economic recovery of West Germany and so West German autonomy; the Western moves to this end were met by the Soviet blockade of Berlin; the Czechoslovak crisis and the blockade lead to NATO and eventually, Western rearmament; Western rearmament required German rearmament.

Before entering into greater detail on these events, the two main ideas which governed American policy throughout may be noticed: the idea of 'collective security' and the idea of 'Western Europe'. United States membership of NATO is sometimes said to have been a revolutionary step in that membership of a military alliance in peacetime was unprecedented. Such a view needs qualification, however, partly because the late forties were not considered by Americans to be genuinely peacetime but mainly because NATO was the application on a narrower front of a revolution already broadly accepted in 1945 with American membership of the United Nations Organization. Significantly, the NATO 'revolution' roused little opposition in the United States at the time and when serious discontent did develop in the 'great debate' of the spring of 1951, it was not just NATO but the whole principle of collective security and the whole postwar policy of internationalism which were under fire.

Admittedly, the scope of NATO collective security was perhaps less self-evident. The United States apparently felt itself equally involved in the fate of all its Western European allies; all of them were apparently willing to support and if necessary to fight for any of the others; the smallest like-minded power had the right to the equal protection of the alliance. This wide and indiscriminate commitment is on the whole explained by the fact that the United States saw the Western Alliance as a coming together of men of common ideals and circumstances and not as a privileged group whose members it had the right to pick and choose on other grounds. The spirit in which the United Nations Organization had been set up, the repugnance for exclusive alliances, the idea of co-operation, continued so far as was possible in the setting-up of the Western Alliance.

At the same time, to revert to a point noticed in the last chapter, such indiscrimination was also comparatively easy in 1949 at the foundation of NATO because of the feeling of

America's basic overwhelming superiority over the Soviet Union. It seemed likely that an American guarantee of Western Europe, if only it could be secured, would deter any form of Soviet attack, and, even if it did not, very unlikely that the NATO commitment might involve the members in total annihilation in the cause of one of their number. Only later, in the late fifties, when the Soviet Union had actually attained sufficient nuclear equality with the United States did it become seriously questionable whether collective security was a realistic principle in the nuclear age: realistic, that is, on the old basis of a mere *ad hoc* alliance of separate states with, in the last resort and at the moment of critical decision, separate obligations to separate populations.

In the early fifties, when Soviet nuclear equality was still only foreseen, the United States made little attempt to transform NATO from an *ad hoc* alliance into a community which might seriously be expected to hang together in the face of nuclear crisis. The countries of continental Western Europe sought a defence commitment from the United States but, beyond this, they believed that the unit for the building of a community was Western Europe, not the Atlantic. They believed that the solution of Europe's problems, and particularly of the old problem of Germany, was to be found in Western European unity and not Atlantic unity, and they believed this through a complex of aspirations for Europe more or less relevant to the mid-twentieth century.

The United States accepted this approach partly no doubt through the persuasiveness of Western European statesmen, but basically because the spirit of its postwar foreign policy was defensive. For the security of Western Europe against the old internal wars, for the security of Western Europe and the Atlantic region against the Soviet Union, all that seemed necessary was the growth of Western European unity, backed by Atlantic military co-operation. There seemed to be no reason why the great difficulties of building an Atlantic community, of overcoming the tepidity or resistance of continental Western Europe, of harmonizing policies, economies and eventually institutions, should be faced. The progressive union of nations was not, that is to say, an objective in its own right.

The United States did not clearly foresee how fragile the Atlantic military co-operation would be without a basis in a political and economic community. Nor was there much discussion of the implications of Western European unity rather than Atlantic unity for the future of Europe as a whole and of the world at large. In retrospect, the absence of such a debate is one of the most remarkable features of the nineteen fifties and must be mainly ascribed to preoccupation with the defensive aspect of the Cold War.

In those years, the deadlock between the great powers was such that it was probable that a solution to the division of Germany could not be found directly but only through a general relaxation of hostility and suspicion and the gradual growing-together of Europe as a whole. Yet the United States did not even consider that of the two possible frameworks for Western unity, the rise of a powerful, independent Western Europe in which West Germany shared the leading role might most strengthen those forces in Eastern Europe and the Soviet Union which feared or hated the West and which would resist the growing together of Europe. On the contrary, it was fundamental to the policy of containment that the problem of the division of Germany and of Europe should be shelved until the Eastern bloc came to its senses. In Chancellor Adenauer's view the Eastern zone and Eastern Europe would one day succumb to the power and prosperity of Western Europe as to a magnet.

For the world at large, the United States was encouraging the unity of a group of countries which had been humiliated in the War and further humiliated in the peace by the overshadowing power of the United States and the Soviet Union and by the break-up of their empires overseas. It was at least to be feared that as the strength of this group of nations grew, its tone would change from dependence, co-operativeness, and defensiveness to assertiveness and a European nationalism. Though there were strong liberal and outward-looking currents in Western Europe restraining any such development, an Atlantic framework for the growth of unity might well have greatly furthered them. In sum, if the idea of Western European unity was on balance good, it might well have been considered that the idea of Atlantic unity was better. As it was, the world was treated to the unprecedented spectacle of a great power single mindedly encouraging the growth of another great power almost equal to itself without discussion, at the crucial, formative stage, of the wider implications of this for the whole future of world affairs.

So far as American initiatives are concerned, the story of these events began with Secretary Marshall's speech at Harvard on 5 June 1947, foreshadowed in his broadcast on the Moscow Conference and elsewhere.

In considering the requirements for the rehabilitation of Europe, the physical loss of life, the visible destruction of cities, factories, mines and railroads was correctly estimated, but it has become obvious during recent months that this visible destruction was probably less serious than the dislocation of the entire fabric of the European economy . . . the rehabilitation of the economic structure of Europe quite evidently will require a much longer time and greater effort than had been foreseen . . .

Aside from the demoralizing effect on the world at large and the possibilities of disturbances arising as a result of the desperation of the people concerned, the consequences to the economy of the United States should be apparent to all. It is logical that the United States should do whatever it is able to do to assist in the return of normal economic health in the world, without which there can be no political stability and no assured peace. Our policy is directed not against any country or doctrine but against hunger, poverty, desperation and chaos. Its purpose should be the revival of a working economy in the world so as to permit the emergence of political and social conditions in which free institutions can exist . . .

. . . It would be neither fitting nor efficacious for this Government to undertake to draw up unilaterally a program designed to place Europe on its feet economically. That is the business of the Europeans. The initiative, I think, must come from Europe . . .

The intention of this speech was clear and its impact on European governments, enormous. The piecemeal loans to Western European countries which seemed all that was left after America's withdrawal from the United Nations Relief and Rehabilitation Agency, were now to be superseded by a broad programme for recovery which America would help to finance. 'This is the turning point,' Ernest Bevin said. As to the motives behind the offer, it seems equally clear that the first of these was friendship towards Europe and generosity. Coupled with this was awareness that the health of Europe's economy deeply affected the health of America's economy. If there had been no East-West struggle, there would still have been a Marshall Plan, twelve and a half billion dollars would still have been given or lent to Europe.

In this sense, the most famous sentence in Marshall's speech was true. 'Our policy is directed not against any country or doctrine but against hunger, poverty, desperation and chaos.' At the same time, as was reflected in the patchwork texture of the passage, because the offer was in fact made in the circumstances of an East-West struggle, its motives were deeply influenced by that struggle. 'The near collapse of Europe', said

Marshall in a speech that autumn, 'has left weakness where once there was strength and has created in effect a political and economic vacuum. It is certainly not our purpose to exploit the situation by filling the vacuum with American power.'[2] But though the American motive was not offensive, it certainly was defensive; the United States was determined to resist any attempt by the Soviet Union to exploit the power vacuum. Throughout the sessions of the Congressional Committees on the European Recovery Programme a constantly recurring theme was the threat of a Communist victory in the countries of Western Europe and the danger to the United States if the economies of those countries should be closed to the United States and harnessed to that of the Soviet Union. How this might come about was expressed lucidly by the President's Committee on Foreign Aid, the Harriman Committee: '. . . if these countries by democratic means do not attain an improvement in their affairs, they may be driven to turn in the opposite direction. Therein lies the strength of the Communist tactic; it wins by default when misery and chaos are great enough. Therefore the countries of Western Europe must be restored to a position where they may retain full faith in the validity of their traditional approaches to world affairs and again exert their full influence and authority in international affairs.'[3]

In this conception of Marshall Aid there lay the germ of later, cruder theories of economic aid as a weapon against Communism. There was some tendency in the discussions of Marshall Aid to exaggerate the influence of postwar poverty on Communist electoral strength and to underestimate social and political aspirations and causes, some of them deep-rooted as in France and Italy. Later, much discussion of aid programmes in Asia and elsewhere was permeated with gross forms of the idea that Communism was the product of poverty and that the aim of economic aid was to immunize populations against it.

However, so far as Marshall Aid was concerned, it was true in a wider sense that economic dislocation had a large bearing on the prospects of Communist victory. It eroded the *morale* of governments, it restricted their resources in resistance to strikes and agitations, it weakened the loyalty of those who believed in democracy, it fostered instability and recklessness. In this sense, Marshall Aid could reasonably be seen as a method of preventing Communism. It aimed to remove a sudden destitution which, if unchecked, might revolutionize traditional political and social ways. It was a very different matter later in the southern world to seek to remove vast traditional destitution as a means of combating one aspect of a political and social revolution.

Despite the background of the East-West struggle, it was clearly grasped in the planning of Secretary Marshall's Harvard speech that the offer of aid could not be made to Western Europe alone. This would be hailed as an attempt to divide Europe and to organize an American sphere of influence. At the same time, it was felt that there could be no question of American aid to the Communist régimes of Eastern Europe. To resist Communism in the West and to aid it in the East was an absurd notion. The decision therefore was that the United States should not suggest a plan but should make an offer, guardedly and to the whole of Europe and then wait and see what happened. If the Soviet *bloc* refused, the way would be clear. If it accepted, then, the argument ran, some joint American-Soviet scheme would have to be worked out.

However, it seems clear that the Administration had some confidence that the Soviet Union would not accept; and whether or not there was co-ordination between the Administration and the British and French governments, the type of plan insisted on by these governments ensured this. When Bevin, Bidault and Molotov met in Paris on 27 June, the opening remarks of the two Western statesmen at once made it clear that they meant Europe to act as a unit and not as separate nations in developing and carrying out a plan. They urged this method partly on the grounds that it was technically the most simple and that it maintained Europe's self-respect, and partly because the whole trend of the European movement conditioned them to think in collective terms.

This approach was totally unacceptable to Molotov. On the grounds of non-interference in the internal affairs of sovereign states, and, no doubt, because a united plan would tend to draw Eastern Europe from Soviet control, Molotov's counter-suggestion was that each European country should separately assess its needs and separately administer its share of the aid. This proposal was in turn rejected by Bevin and Bidault. Because of the urgency of the economic crisis, they were not willing to delay action on the American offer in a further search for Soviet co-operation. The conference ended in disagreement after six days. The Marshall Plan was, as a result, a Western European plan.

The outcome of this and of the bitter East-West quarrel which developed over the Plan was a great stride in the consolidation of Eastern and Western Europe as two units, separate from each other. In Western Europe in the summer of 1947, though working co-operation of governments with the United States was increasing continuously, left-wing and 'third force', neutralist sentiment was strong. 'In any prudent estimate of our world position', wrote Walter Lippmann in a book which popularized the phrase 'the Cold War', 'they (the countries of Western Europe) are no longer to be counted upon as firm members of a coalition led by the United States against the Soviet Union . . . The aim of the leading democratic states of Europe and probably also of the Americas is at best to hold the balance of power between Russia and America, and thus to become mediators of that conflict. At worst, their aim is to isolate themselves in some kind of neutrality which will spare them the dual catastrophe of being overrun by the Red Army and bombed by the American air forces.'[4]

In this atmosphere, the ideological language of the Truman Doctrine had roused dismay or hostility. To many in the European left-wing, the choice posed seemed to carry the overtones of Capitalism or Communism and they disliked both almost equally. Moreover, as Hamilton Fish Armstrong wrote of the Truman Message: 'The hopes of European democratic leaders leapt up at seeing the United States preparing to stay in Europe and contribute to the stabilization of nations threatened with social disintegration. At the same time, they could not help being worried at the intention that everyone must now take sides in an ideological battle . . . many of the millions who had simply registered protest votes for Communist candidates and even some others could logically be expected to drift back to Socialist or various Liberal parties whenever the economic situation improved and the social structure became more stable . . . Various leaders of tested devotion to democracy therefore hoped sincerely that the United States would not press for a showdown until economic recovery was on the way; and in the spring of 1947 it patently was not.'[5]

In this situation, the language and the substance of the Marshall offer were by contrast a shrewd stroke. 'Our policy is not directed against any country or doctrine but against hunger, poverty, desperation and chaos.' As one American comment put it, 'neither the French nor the Italian Communists can afford to be against food, clothing and jobs; they cannot keep their mass support on the basis of any such programme'.[6] In the event, the Communist parties and the Soviet Union were forced into the position of opposing these things. They fought them in Western Europe with the slogan 'Marshall Aid is martial aid'; they denied them utterly to the destitute in Eastern Europe. This in itself did much to consolidate opinion against them. The gradual return of prosperity and the progress of social reform through Socialist or Liberal parties converted waverers and buttressed the *morale* of governments against Communist-inspired strikes, particularly dangerous in France and Italy in the autumn of 1947 and later. In Belgium, Denmark and Norway, the Communist vote was reduced by nearly two-thirds in 1949-50 compared with 1945-6.

In France and Italy the voting strength of the Communists was less seriously affected. Largely for historical reasons, Socialist parties were not considered by many to be adequate alternatives to the Communist parties. Moreover, social reform was impeded in part by the very strength of Communist parties. Fear of Communist extremism forced the moderate parties into ramshackle and indecisive coalitions in order at all costs to govern without them. The result was that the major source of European reform, the direct governmental action of representatives of the poorer classes, was unable to operate and political life, particularly in France, easily tended to become an artificial game among politicians.

Despite this, Communist strength in the two countries received a severe check and Marshall Aid played its part. In the famous Italian elections of April 1948 in which Americans from Ambassador James Dunn to Rocky Graziano played their part and which revolved round the Marshall Plan and the Interim Aid already flowing in, the combined Communist-Nenni Socialist vote sank from 40 to 31 per cent. Eight million Italians had voted for the *bloc* and more than nine millions were to do so in 1953; but there was still no disguising the fact that they had been defeated in what Togliatti himself had called an event of decisive significance not merely for Italy but for the whole world.

The Marshall Plan began the consolidation of Western Europe on a more fundamental level. In 1947 the European movement was strong but still incoherent. The Marshall Plan gave it its first framework. It was implicit in Marshall's offer that Europe should act as a unit and this was readily accepted by the Western governments. 'The yeast in Secretary Marshall's words', wrote one American observer 'lay in the promise of American aid to an indigeneous European Recovery Program designed not merely to reconstitute the state of unstable equilibrium which had preceded the last war, but rather to establish a solid economic foundation of mutual collaboration and interdependence that would preclude the recurrence of armed conflict such as had engulfed Europe and involved the United States twice in a single generation.'[7] Americans were confident on the analogy of their own country of the benefits of economic federation and a free market. They were also as convinced as many Europeans that an end must be made to war within Europe by amalgamation. By the time of the Congressional amendement to the Economic Co-operation Act of April 1949, formally declaring that it was America's policy to encourage European unity, another motive, still greater solidarity against the Soviet Union, had for many months joined with these.

Beyond the co-operation between Western European governments directly required by the Plan, the United States Economic Co-operation Administration entered with missionary zeal into the task of reducing trade and payments barriers in Western Europe. In particular, it arranged a series of bilateral Payments and Co-operation Agreements, converted in 1950 into the European Payments Union, the most significant of the monuments Marshall Aid left behind it.

On the other hand, while the Organization for European Economic Co-operation, set up by the Western European countries in April 1948 to work with the ECA, had American and Canadian associate members, it was never intended by the United States as a step in the formation of an Atlantic economic community. It gradually fell into the background in the fifties. On a wider scale, the International Monetary Fund, one of the United Nations institutions unhampered by the presence of the Soviet bloc, made only sluggish progress, far short of the original wartime vision. In American economic predominance in the postwar world, in particular in the Marshall Plan, there may have been the makings of an Atlantic economic community; but the attempt was not made.

So soon as major plans were drawn up for the economic re-building of Western Europe, a role had necessarily to be given to the Western zones of Germany. Already in March 1947, the Hoover Report had given authority to the growing belief that Germany must be allowed to recover not only to relieve the economic burden on the Western powers but in the interests of European recovery. Then followed the failure in April of the Moscow Conference on the German peace settlement. As a result of the 'cooling-off period', the four powers were now in varying degrees less inspired by hostility towards Germany; but they now inspired by mounting hostility towards each other.

The quarrel over the Soviet Union's continued refusal to treat Germany as an economic unit gradually centred on the reparations issue, the Soviet Union seizing on the tentative Yalta figure, the Western powers insisting on no more than was surplus to the Levels of Industry Agreement of March 1946. The Soviet Union was determined that Germany could pay and, before anything else happened, should pay; the Western powers refused to adopt a retributive attitude to German destitution, were in any case coming to the conclusion that German recovery must be promoted and were unwilling to see the results of this flow to the Soviet Union in reparations.

There was a minor quarrel over the Soviet Union's claim to share in the control of the Ruhr and a complete deadlock over the constitution of Germany. The Western powers wanted a federal régime, the Soviet Union a centralized régime, at best a paradoxical and more likely a disingenuous or even sinister proposal. The whole conference was characterized by diatribes from Molotov, particularly by grossly exaggerated accusations that Nazis were being employed and armed German units maintained in the British and American zones.

By the end of the conference, Marshall was unwilling, as we saw, to wait for 'compromise by exhaustion'. The Marshall offer was made in June. In August, Britain and the United States announced a new Levels of Industry Plan, revising the permitted levels upwards. Though this now gave a basis for dismantling the surplus for reparations, dismantling was controversial from the outset as contradicting the general trend of policy and was half-hearted to the end in the autumn of 1949. At the London Conference in November 1947, the last of the postwar series, the same ground was again covered fruitlessly. In that month, against the background of the now raging struggle over the Marshall Plan, Marshall openly declared: 'The restoration of Europe involves the restoration of Germany'.[8]

The decision that autumn to include the Western zones of Germany in the Marshall Plan necessitated the restoration of administrative autonomy to the Germans. The Western powers had in varying degrees encouraged democratic political and industrial movements in their zones and these had soon built up pressure for increasing self-determination, pressure which the United States in particular found it hard to resist. In addition, the provincial governments and the Economic Council in the Bi-zone increasingly disputed the economic edicts of the Anglo-American authorities, who in any case were becoming increasingly dependent on German officials and experts. When now the economic recovery of Germany and its co-operation in the Marshall Plan were decided on, the fact had to be faced that, in plain terms, the Germans could manage affairs in Germany better than the allies could.

So it was that in February 1948 a new London Conference opened of the three Western powers and Belgium, Luxemburg and the Netherlands. When the conference ended on 1 June, it was revealed that a federal republic was to be set up in the western half of Germany. The State Department commented on the agreement: 'The three Western powers have for some time been deeply concerned that there is no political organization in Germany capable of regulating economic matters and serving as a focus for the revival of democratic political life. It is moreover clear that the European Recovery Program for West Germany can only be administered successfully by a competent German government."[9] It was on these grounds that after fifteen months of further negotiations, the Federal Republic of Germany was established, primarily as an administrative expedient and without formal sovereignty, on 7 September 1949.

The Soviet response to these successive steps from February 1948 to September 1949 was one which popular opinion in the West tended to see as a new challenge rather than as a response: the Berlin Blockade. As the London Conference opened, the first traffic incidents began in Berlin. In March, the Allied Control Council finally broke up on the refusal of the Western representatives to give an account of the London discussions. Regulations tightened throughout April and May until finally on 24 June, all rail traffic between the Western zones and Berlin was stopped by the Soviet authorities and the heroic Western airlift began. The blockade and airlift, interspersed with Soviet demands for a four-power conference to discuss the London decisions, continued through the winter of 1948-9 and until the summer of 1949.

A further event of February 1948 aroused still greater alarm in the West: the *coup d'état* in Czechoslovakia. In all the belt of countries bordering on the Soviet Union, Czechoslovakia had retained the greatest independence. It still had two leaders of European stature, President Benes and Foreign Minister Masaryk. It had decided, it seems, to take part in the conference to draw up the Marshall Plan and had only reversed this decision under Soviet pressure. The democratic tradition was stronger there than in any other Eastern *bloc* country and this, reinforced by current events, seemed to ensure that the Communists would not win the elections of spring 1948 as they had those of 1946. The Communists, abetted by the Soviet Union, decided not to risk the issue and a *coup d'état* was carried out.

Though this event may seem in retrospect part of the postwar series of violent blows by which the Soviet Union consolidated Eastern Europe, in Western minds at the time it aroused exceptional dismay and anger precisely because of Czechoslovakia's stronger democratic tradition, its stronger links with Western Europe, and the element of independence which it had retained. It no longer seemed possible to excuse the Soviet Union on the plea that it sought friendly régimes on its borders; no régime, it was argued, could have been more friendly. Against the background of antagonism over Germany, the Truman Doctrine, and the Marshall Plan, of the appointment of a Soviet Commander to the Polish forces, of the pressure on Finland for a treaty of friendship and, above all, the retention by the Soviet Union of large armed forces, the *coup d'état* in Czechoslovakia aroused widespread fear that the Soviet Union was not closing an old chapter but opening a new chapter of postwar conquest.

This fear and its restraining effects on the recovery of Western Europe were the origin of the North Atlantic Treaty Organization. Already the Labour Government in Britain had begun to abandon hope that a crystallization of the division of Europe could be avoided. In a House of Commons speech of 22 January, Bevin declared: 'I believe the time is ripe for a consolidation of Western Europe'. He went on to suggest a Western Union of Britain, France and the Benelux countries covering military and many other forms of co-operation akin to the Commonwealth. This was the nearest that Britain was to come to the European movement for many years, but whether or not the idea could have been carried through, in the eyes of Bevin, and of Spaak, its other main progenitor, it was partly a bait for a United States commitment, and the immediate success in this respect submerged the wider vision. In answer to inquiries from Bevin before his speech, Truman replied that 'We agreed with them on the urgent need for concerted measures by the nations of Western Europe. As in the case of the European Recovery Program we welcomed European initiative and would give their undertaking our wholehearted sympathy . . .'[10] Following the signature of the Brussels Treaty of Western Union on 17 March 1948, the State Department submitted to the National Security Council a draft plan for NATO.

The Administration did not on balance believe that the Soviet Union was planning war in the summer of 1948. Though Western propaganda stressed the size of Soviet armed forces, it was estimated that the Soviet Union had reduced its forces from twelve and a half million to three and a half or four million, and its military budget by about half between 1944 and 1947.[11] A conference of the ambassadors of the Brussels Pact signatories and America and Canada in Washington in July affirmed that there was no evidence of a Soviet timetable for armed aggression.

On the other hand, the statement also spoke of the constant danger of incidents which might explode into war. In particular, in those months, military intelligence estimates from Berlin veered nervously back and forth. There was, in general, a strong and oppressive if vague dread abroad in Western Europe. The Marshall Plan, wrote Truman in his memoirs, had brought relief to Western Europe but 'the constant threat of unpredictable Soviet moves resulted in an atmosphere of insecurity and fear'.[12] This factor of fear, the need to bolster the *morale* of Europe was described by Truman as the 'key point' behind the planning of NATO.[13] Not only was insecurity bad in itself, but as James Reston wrote in October 1948, 'the more ERP was debated, the more people recognized, even on Capitol Hill, that unless the fear of aggression were removed in Western Europe, economic recovery could not be achieved.'[14] None of the various forces making for European recovery and unity could work with full effect without confidence in the future. The NATO Treaty was put forward as the complement of the Marshall Plan and of the accompanying political and spiritual revival. It was intended to create confidence that all this effort would not suddenly be destroyed and was worthwhile.

Great care was taken over the presentation of the Treaty to the American people though, in the event, while attracting great interest, the measure was not, in principle very controversial. The *coup d'état* in Czechoslovakia and the Berlin Blockade were compelling arguments for a further step in collective security. The Treaty seemed a logical guarantee of Marshall Aid, an investment in success. Though the world situation was dangerous, policy was moving confidently and successfully. It was only later under the shocks and frustrations of the Soviet atomic explosion, the Korean War, the slowness of Western Europe to rearm that a delayed reaction against international involvements began in the 'great debate' of 1951.

Still, there were aspects of the American temper which needed to be watched by the Administration. One was dislike of helping those who would not help themselves. This was covered by the European initiative, the Brussels Pact. Then there was suspicion of unilateral action. This was covered by the co-operative nature of the commitment. Again, closely related, there was United Nations sentiment. The Treaty would have to be reconciled with the Charter. In this respect, as in the whole of its nature, there was a fortunate precedent for NATO: the Organization of American States finally established at Bogotá that April.

All these precautions, with an eye to both home and world opinion, were taken in Resolution 239 which the Administration inspired Senator Vandenberg to introduce in the Senate in the spring of 1948 and which was passed on 11 June. The resolution began by reaffirming that it was the policy of the United States to achieve international peace and security through the United Nations. It then endorsed current efforts to strengthen the effectiveness of the Organization by again recommending the abandonment of the veto on the pacific settlement of disputes and on admission of new members, maximum effort to equip the Organization with armed forces and to achieve regulation of armaments, and, if necessary after adequate efforts to strengthen the Organization, review of the Charter 'at an appropriate time'.

Only after thus satisfying the various currents of opinion about the United Nations did the resolution move on to devices to supplement it, to the recommendation that the United States Government should further 'the progressive development of regional and other collective arrangements for individual and collective self-defense in accordance with the purposes, principles and provisions of the Charter' and should promote 'the association of the United States, by constitutional process, with such regional and other collective arrangements as are based on continuous and effective self-help and mutual aid, and as affect national security'.

When the North Atlantic Treaty was concluded the following year on 4 April 1949, the Bill passed rapidly through Congress and was signed by the President on 25 July. However, the complementary measure to put teeth into NATO by rearmament, the Mutual Defence Assistance Bill, introduced that same day, had an uneasy passage. Congress was becoming querulous at the number of new, separate programmes presented to it. It was also averse to any shift of emphasis from the economic recovery of Western Europe to military rearmament. The Soviet atomic explosion announced at the end of September eventually speeded the Bill through but, afterwards, progress was equally hesitant in the field, in the setting up of the NATO command structure and in getting rearmament under way, and remained so until the galvanizing shock of Korea.

Even then and throughout the nineteen fifties, NATO never became more than an American guarantee of Western Europe and an American commitment to Western Europe. It was, as we saw in the last chapter, never more than the American atomic bomb. A large infra-structure programme was implemented and a huge command network was established; but the troops to be commanded and to use the installations were never provided in worthwhile numbers; only the runways and the launching pads signified. The necessary basis for a wider spectrum of strength, co-operation in 'balanced collective forces', was not achieved. In contrast to the Marshall Plan on the economic front, the United States Mutual Defence Assistance Programme was not designed to exert pressure towards integration. The weight of the programme lay on bilateral arms agreements.

NATO was equally unsuccessful in armaments co-operation. The outstanding example was the Atomic Energy Act of 1946, the MacMahon Act, which had the effect of ending the wartime collaboration of the United States, Britain and Canada. After the new Act of 1954 relaxation still came only slowly. The American attitude was easily explicable by the treason cases among the allies in 1946 and later, by reluctance to encourage the spread of atomic potential, and by considerations of national power over the ultimate weapon. The failure to co-operate in other fields was less understandable. Since France could get information neither from the United States nor Britain, it spent enormous financial and technical effort in developing types of rockets which they already had. Years of negotiation were needed to agree even a standard rifle for the Western European armies, to say nothing of more complicated military equipment. Under the shock of the launching of a Soviet intercontinental missile and an earth satellite in the summer of 1957, NATO statesmen began to stress to each other and to the world at large how much was being lost by duplication of effort. But even then, concern for national sovereignty, for separate national interests and for national armaments industries made progress in co-operative weapons development and standardisation very slow.

If NATO was scarcely a military community, this was basically because it could not be so without being a political and economic community. In the fifties, little progress was made towards remedying this. Through the NATO Council and by everyday means a great effort was made to ensure a common policy towards the Soviet Union. This was on the whole successful in the early fifties because the heart of this policy was the strengthening of Western Europe and this was manifestly in the common interest. But great discrepancies of interests and policies remained and these became increasingly apparent as the focus of problems widened from Western Europe to much larger areas of the world. It was not part of the conception of NATO that its members should co-ordinate or even discuss their interests and policies in Africa and Asia and elsewhere. Co-operation was sought whenever the problem was a direct threat from the Soviet Union or China but this was only moderately successful because a basis was lacking; it was an attempt to create unity in a crisis which had never been decided upon in principle. No basic decision was involved in NATO that it should grow into a total community, gradually co-ordinating policies, economies, defence arrangements in all aspects and areas. Because the essence of NATO was simply a guarantee, a static thing, not the idea of growth, there was the likelihood from the outset that it would not outlast the particular set of circumstances and dangers in which it had been formed.

The growth of a community, first internally and then increasingly towards the outside world, was confined to Western Europe. The first step, apart from the Marshall Plan, was the Council of Europe. This never found much favour with governments, however, and from 1951, symbolized by the departure of M. Spaak, it fell into the background. The next step was the Schuman Plan of May 1950 for a common market in coal and steel and common organization of production. Its motives were to make internal conflict in Western Europe impossible and to enhance Western Europe's strength in the world, including, a constant theme in successive French plans, the united pursuit of the development of Africa. At the heart of the Schuman Plan lay a new solution to a problem unsolved at the last conferences with the Soviet Union, control of the industry of the Ruhr. The solution proposed at the London Conference of the Western powers on Germany in February 1948 had been an International Authority composed of the five Western European powers, West Germany and the United States. The new solution equally did not include the Soviet Union; but neither did it include the United States.

It was also agreed at the London Conference, with particular regard to the nervousness of the continental allies, that the new Federal Republic of West Germany should remain disarmed and that the occupying powers would not withdraw until 'the peace of Europe' had been secured. However, just as in the case of the Marshall Plan, so soon as Western rearmament was decided, the issue of a German contribution arose. The first public hint of American thoughts in this direction was given in a speech by the American High Commissioner McCloy in May 1950. It was met with angry protests by France and by serious misgivings in Britain and among the other allies.

A deadlock might have resulted but for the outbreak of the Korean War the following month. The common mood was now one of serious rearmament and at the three-power conference and the NATO Council meeting in September 1950, the United States insisted on a German contribution. The United States had to some extent weakened its bargaining position in advance by the existence of the NATO guarantee and by President Truman's announcement early in September that the American commitment of forces in Europe would be increased; these were the key requirements of the Western European nations. However, rearmament enthusiasm was high, the Americans were insistent, and the additional American commitment had yet to be endorsed by the Senate. Accordingly, France put forward a solution of its own, the Pleven Plan, based on a suggestion by Churchill at the Council of Europe that August. German rearmament should take place in the context of a European Defence Community, a Western European force, in which national units would be fused, directed by a European Political Community. Separate overseas interests would be covered by maintaining other separate national forces as required.

The United States was reluctant to accept this plan, considering it a complicated and doubtful method of attaining the required end. However, the United States allowed itself to be persuaded, partly in deference to French fears and partly because of the great step towards Western European integration involved. Nineteen-fifty saw a high tide of federalist enthusiasm in Western Europe and the circumstances as a whole seemed propitious. Accordingly the plan was adopted in principle that winter. The following spring, after the 'great debate' in the United States, touched off by eighteen months slow progress in Western European rearmament, the Senate endorsed the increase of American troops in Europe. An American general was appointed NATO Supreme Commander in Europe. The American commitment to Europe was sealed and delivered.

Obstacles then began to appear to the progress of the Pleven Plan. It was established that Germany, though cool towards rearmament and the plan and determined on sovereignty as the price, would join in, but that Britain would not. France was thus to integrate the bulk of its military power with that of its two former enemies, Germany and Italy, with only the Benelux added. There was also the distraction of the prolonged Palais Rose talks with the Soviet Union; France still cherished the hope that agreement might be reached with the Soviet Union, removing the necessity for German rearmament. Then followed twelve months of technical haggling, casting serious doubts on the will of the participants to succeed. The Treaty was finally signed in May 1952, but it still needed ratification and by the end of the year, the French government had still not found it expedient to face the Assembly.

By January 1953, the exasperation of the United States under the new Administration had reached the point of threats. In his first public broadcast as Secretary of State, Mr Dulles said: 'The United States has made a big investment in Western Europe on the theory that there could be unity there. Of the 40 billion dollars which we have sent abroad since the end of the Second World War, 30 billion dollars have gone into Western Europe. If however, there were no chance, and that I just refuse to believe, but if it appeared there were no chance of getting effective unity, and if in particular, France, Germany and England should go their separate ways, then certainly it would be necessary to give a little re-thinking to America's own foreign policy in relation to Western Europe.'[15] By the end of the year Mr Dulles had had no more success in the maze of French politics and diplomacy than his predecessor. He could do no more than repeat his warning in more dramatic terms at the Paris NATO meeting in December. 'If however the European Defense Community should not become effective, if France and Germany remain apart, so that they would again be potential enemies, then indeed there would be grave doubt whether continental Europe could be made a place of safety. That would compel an agonizing reappraisal of basic United States policy.'[16]

By this time France and Germany were at loggerheads on the Saar and the Italians were anxious for a solution to the Trieste question as their price for co-operation in EDC. Enthusiasm for rearmament had waned rapidly in 1952 and the following spring with the death of Stalin, Western European hopes for a settlement with the Soviet Union leapt high. The outcome of their pressure on the United States was the Foreign Ministers Conference of January 1954 in Berlin which at least seemed to offer to France prospects of Soviet assistance in an Indo-China settlement. The following August, the Mendes-France government finally submitted the EDC Treaty to the Assembly. It was rejected on 30 August by a vote to suspend discussions, 319 for, 264 against, with 46 abstentions, including the French cabinet.

At this juncture, with flying visits to London and Bonn but not to Paris, Mr Dulles set off for South-East Asia, to the conference on SEATO. A lightning round of diplomacy by Anthony Eden produced agreement on German membership of a Western European Union, an expansion of the Brussels Treaty, containing limitations on German armaments and a formal commitment by Britain to maintain troops on the continent. On these terms, sovereignty was to be restored to Germany, and it was to rearm and join NATO. Agreement was also reached on the Saar and on Trieste.

The comparatively smooth ratification of the London and Paris Agreements by the French Assembly had an element of paradox. The Western European Union of the Six and Britain contained little of the basic idea of Western European politics that the solution to the old problem of Germany was integration with its neighbours. Western European Union was largely a diplomatic device; as an institution, it was overlaid by NATO.

The paradox arose mainly from French internal politics, but there was also a general realization that EDC had failed because the necessary basis was lacking. It had been an attempt at international unity at the summit, security, when the groundwork of unity in policies and economies was still weak. There was a lesson here for the Atlantic Alliance also, but it was still not taken. Instead, a conference was held at Messina in June 1955 which began the building of a European Economic Community.

6

Korea

The Korean War which began on 25 June 1950 was the great caesura in the course of postwar history. At one level of events, the North Korean invasion of South Korea was the outcome of the threats and counter-threats of two rival governments in an obscure Asian peninsula. Perhaps, had the Western powers been so minded, the conflict need never have attained any other significance. Action by the United Nations might have been invoked simply to repel the aggression of one government, to restrain the almost equal belligerence of the other and to maintain the peace between the two. As it was, the Western powers led by the United States, while determined to confine the scope of the war, did nothing to minimize its significance. On the contrary, rightly or wrongly, they automatically interpreted the North Korean invasion as the explosion of a far greater conflict, the world-wide struggle between East and West, between Communism and the free world.

In consequence, the Korean War caused drastic developments across the whole field of world politics. Thanks to a global view of events, an invasion six thousand miles away brought urgent action on rearmament for the security of Western Europe. In Asia, American policy, hitherto neglected and diffuse compared with policy in Europe, crystallized overnight into the ideological and strategic pattern developed in Europe. Not only was this pattern largely unsuited to the different circumstances of Asia, resulting in a period of trials and frustrations in marked contrast to the successes of the forties in Europe; in addition, America's ideas were barely shared by its allies, resulting in tensions and weakened confidence in America's leadership in all aspects of world affairs.

Before discussing the two most far-reaching decisions of the Korean War, the decision to neutralize Formosa and the decision to conquer North Korea, something should be said of the greatest American decision of the war, the decision to fight it. The conduct of the war by the United States and the conclusions which it drew from it for general policy, damaged the standing of the United States whether in the Western Alliance or in Asia; but the basic decision, to fight, was essential to all of them. It was essential to the influence of the United States whose client South Korea was, to the security of Japan, to the influence of the United Nations Organization which might not have survived inactivity, to the security of all countries against the idea of aggression. It was thus one of the harsher facts of postwar history that three years of courageous warfare, brilliant military campaigns, some fifty thousand American dead in a vital cause aroused little sense of achievement in the American people and gained America little credit in the world. The idea that the Korean War expressed a global struggle for Freedom against Communism and the decisions which followed from this, then and later, were too inflated, too unrealistic and too sure of failure either to sustain the enthusiasm of the American people, to confirm the *morale* of their soldiers, or to impress allied and neutral opinion. The Korean War was, in any positive sense, strikingly unprofitable for the United States and in large part, this was the fault of its own policy: but it was, for all that, a necessary and an heroic war.

FORMOSA

Even before the failure of the Marshall Mission of mediation in China in 1945-6, American attention to postwar problems was focussed on the European, not the Asian theatre. In Marshall's decision on becoming Secretary of State in January 1947 to promote a vast European programme, there may have been an element of choice between Europe and Asia. Truman, Marshall, Acheson and most of the other leaders of American opinion knew more and cared more about Europe, the origin of America's culture and of the overwhelming majority of its people. American policy was still made on the eastern seaboard; America was still primarily an eastward-looking power.

Beyond this, the elements of the problem of restoring Western Europe and saving it from Soviet Communism seemed clearer than those of the problem of saving China from Mao Tse-tung's Communism. Nothing in the results of the Wedemeyer Mission of July 1947 changed the essentials of the China situation as they had appeared to the Marshall Mission. There was a vocal 'China lobby' in the United States, strong in California. To secure its assent to the economic programme for Europe, the Aministration decided in the autumn of 1947 to give some economic aid to the Kuomintang. The result was the China Aid Act of 1948. On the whole, however, the United States simply waited, working in Europe.

With the collapse of Kuomintang resistance in the summer of 1949, American opinion awoke violently to the realization that the most populous country in the world had fallen to the Communists. The world situation no longer disposed Americans to see Mao Tse-tung's rebels as 'agrarian revolutionaries', as first and foremost, Chinese; they were first and foremost, Communists, the same monstrous breed of men as controlled the policies of the Soviet Union. China was no longer China; it was a Soviet satellite or, at least, part of the Communist world in the great struggle of East and West.

Everything that followed strengthened this interpretation. The revolutionary government's expressions of solidarity with the Soviet Union were given full weight. A speech by Liu Shao-ch'i to the Trades Union Conference in Peking in November, a paen of victory which called upon all Asia to imitate China's example, was taken as a programme for expansion, a manifest expression of the limitless aims of Communism. Confirmation of this lay in the Chinese advance into Tibet. The treatment of American consular staff and American property was not the traditional behaviour of the Chinaman to an American, but very much the behaviour to be expected of Communists. Americans were not disposed to make much allowance for the history of China before the coming of the West, for the jubilation of victory, for the ending of a generation of civil war, for the final ejection of the foreigners who had humiliated China for more than a century. They remembered rather the efforts of generations of Americans to 'civilize' China. They remembered most sharply of all twenty years of support for China against Japan, paralleling their support for the Soviet Union against Germany. The one ingratitude was as black as the other. The cause was the same. They were Communists.

To Americans in this mood the plain necessity was to apply to China those same attitudes and policies which had been applied to the Soviet Union in Europe and which should be applied to all Communists. Specifically, recognition of the Nationalist Government which had fled to Formosa must be maintained and the island supported against further Communist advances. In the view of former-President Hoover in a public letter to Senator Knowland of 2 January 1950, this was essential on seven counts: '(1) a wall against Communism in the Pacific; (2) the defense of Japan and the Philippines; (3) the prevention of Chinese legations and consulates in the United States (and such countries as agree with us) becoming nests of Communist conspiracies; (4) the prevention of another Communist permanent member of the United Nations Security Council with its dangerous implications for that body; (5) the dangers of Chinese Communist participation in formulating peace with Japan; (6) by maintaining at least a symbol of resistance, we would have a better basis for salvation of south-eastern Asia; (7) there would be at least a continued hope of sometime turning China in the path of freedom again.'

The rising popular clamour, the Republican pressure for action on Formosa received support from the Administration's military advisers. They insisted on the danger to Pacific, and particularly, Japanese security if Formosa should fall. The strategic reasoning behind this is not clear to the layman, but at all events, General MacArthur and others, like the Republicans, urged the necessity of a continuous Pacific defence perimeter.[1]

The reaction of Truman, Acheson and the State Department to the events in China was, however, cautious. In August 1949, as part of the growing battle of the scapegoats, the State Department published a massive White Paper explaining and justifying policy towards China in past years. When asked what he intended to do now, Acheson's reply aroused widespread mockery or fury: 'Let the dust settle.' In response to Hoover's letter, Truman contented himself with the re-affirmation that, in America's view, Formosa was part of China, but in a speech of 12 January, Acheson was more forthright. He sketched America's 'defense perimeter' in the Pacific from Japan to the Philippines, (omitting South Korea as his opponents pointed out during the Korean War) and omitting Formosa. He argued, furthermore: 'The Soviet Union is detaching the northern provinces of China and attaching them to the Soviet Union. This process is complete in Outer Mongolia. It is nearly complete in Manchuria and I am sure that in Inner Mongolia and in Sinkiang there are very happy reports coming from Soviet agents to Moscow . . . I should like to suggest at any rate that this fact that the Soviet Union is taking the four northern provinces of China is the single most significant, most important fact in the relations of any foreign power with Asia.' The United States must not by any 'ill-conceived adventures' deflect the righteous wrath of the Chinese people from the Soviet Union to itself.

Hopes in the Administration that a rift might develop between the Soviet Union and China survived the Sino-Soviet Treaty of February 1950. On the face of it, the Treaty and the accompanying Soviet loan appeared favourable to China, but expert commentators were inclined to emphasize Soviet retention of Outer Mongolia, of a foothold in Manchuria at least for the present, and the virtual sharing of rule in Sinkiang. It was argued that these and other aspects of Soviet activity in China might well become irksome to China. As a more general hope, now and throughout the fifties, though the China lobby thought all Communists were alike, scholars were doubtful whether Chinese civilization could be cast in a universal Communist mould. China might produce its own form of Communism.

On such grounds as these, until the outbreak of the Korean War, the Administration would not commit itself to the policy of the China lobby. Congress attempted to force the Administration's hand by resisting aid to South Korea until the bill was recast as a Far Eastern Economic Assistance Bill for the general area of Korea and Formosa, passed on 14 February. However, though the aid to Formosa had symbolic significance, no guarantee of Formosa was given.

At the same time, despite its caution, the Administration already to some extent deferred to or shared popular interpretations of the China situation. It showed this first of all by its delay in recognizing the Communist Government. At the turn of 1949-50, India, Pakistan, Burma and other Asian countries gave their recognition. Acheson urged delay on the Western countries, but on 6 January Britain followed suit as did other European countries at later intervals, the notable exception being France with an eye to Indo-China and American assistance there. To the extent of his hopes about China, Acheson envisaged eventual United States recognition; but the delay was ominous and the more so as those hopes could scarcely be speedily fulfilled and America's attitude was not likely to help matters.

The delay in recognition was coupled with a far more serious source of friction: American resistance to the admission of the Communist government to China's place in the United Nations and on the Security Council. From the point of view of China's leaders, representation of their country on the international scene was no doubt one of the main prizes of victory in the civil war. The denial of this prize by the United States, supported by its clients in Latin America, in favour of the beaten rival was a serious affront. The United States had an historic doctrine of recognition and there were various criteria in the Charter bearing on admission to the United Nations of which one, the idea of 'peace-loving nations', subsequently became more or less relevant and was much cited. But the plain fact was that America, like any other power, gave recognition or supported admission in the light of its interests and policies. America's delay in the winter of 1949-50 was a tentative declaration of hostility towards China and of resistance to its influence.

This issue was not the root of American-Chinese hostility in the early months of 1950; the root was the contrast of traditions, brought to the pitch of active hostility by the element of brutality in the one and of impatience and lack of understanding in the other. On the other hand, the issue was the key to the general international crisis which developed at that time.

By the spring of 1950, the accumulated heat of action and reaction between the great powers in Europe, the Middle East and Asia, seemed to be nearing explosion point. The Soviet delegate had walked out of the Security Council on the China issue. The United Nations Secretary General was keenly aware of the wider danger of the situation: tension, hostility, impasse, lack of contact between the great powers in the United Nations or in conference across the whole field of world politics. On his return from a tour in May 1950 in which he had urged on the powers a 'peace programme' of ten subjects for negotiation, Trygve Lie reported to the United Nations on 6 June: 'It is evident that no significant progress can be made while the members of the United Nations remain sharply divided on the question of the representation of one of the permanent members of the Security Council – the Republic of China. It is necessary that this question be settled.' Trygve Lie also said on his return: 'My trip has confirmed my belief that no government wants war'. It was an ominous comment.

On 25 June North Korea invaded the South. The United States promoted a resolution in the Security Council calling for a cease-fire and a North Korean withdrawal. Two days later, 27 June, on the failure of North Korea to comply, the Administration announced armed assistance to South Korea. That evening, the decision was supported by a further Security Council Resolution recommending general armed assistance.

The American Administration did not, however, simply take the decision to fight. In those hectic hours, it adopted the idea of events in Asia which had for the past months been urged on it by popular opinion, the China lobby and by its military advisers. In the face of a military crisis, the views of the military took precedence over the views of the diplomatists. But far more important, the Administration was itself convinced that this aggression was not an aggression by North Korea, nor even by China, nor even by the Soviet Union and China; it was an aggression by Communism.

For months, even years now, the Administration had conditioned itself to the possibility of a new thrust by international Communism. It might have followed the *coup d'état* in Czechoslovakia, it might have arisen from the Berlin Blockade, it might have arisen anywhere through Communist subversion and incitement. Recently, the alliance between the Soviet Union and China had grown, tension had mounted ominously, had centred on the China issue, was only too likely to explode in the Far East. The North Korean invasion was that explosion. It was the testing-time in the East-West struggle, now truly global in scope, with the Soviet Union and China now clearly arrayed in the cause of international Communism against Freedom. As President Truman flew back to Washington on 25 June, his thoughts had nothing to do with the venomous quarrel between the leaders of North and South Korea. 'I remembered how each time that the democracies had failed to act, it had encouraged the aggressors to keep going ahead. Communism was acting in Korea, just as Hitler, Mussolini and the Japanese had acted ten, fifteen, twenty years earlier.'[2] The detail of Korean affairs, even of world affairs was as nothing against the vision of a world struggle between Communism and the Free World.

In his plane on 25 June, in Washington in the two days that followed, President Truman and his colleagues did not have evidence that the Soviet Union or China had connived at the North Korean attack. There was the possibility to be reckoned with that this was so, on a scale ranging from outright orders to North Korea to a permissive mood; but it was a possibility only, no more and no less. But the Administration did not think that it was a possibility, nor even that it was a probability, but that it was a certainty.

Nor was this all. Not even the fullest and most certain evidence of Chinese complicity, whether with direct objectives in South Korea or indirect objectives in the world at large, would have made it inevitable or even desirable that the United States should now reverse its long-standing declarations that Formosa was part of China, should give its support to a rejected and beaten Chinese government, should commit itself to total hostility to the most populous nation on earth, should cut itself off from all contact with it whether diplomatically or in the United Nations, and should thereby place itself in a position which time was to prove increasingly sterile and which was shared neither by the Asian nations nor by the majority of America's Western partners.

But in his statement of 27 June, President Truman said: 'The attack upon Korea makes it plain beyond all doubt that Communism has passed beyond the use of subversion to conquer independent nations and will now use armed invasion and war. It has defied the orders of the Security Council of the United Nations issued to preserve international peace and security. In these circumstances, the occupation of Formosa by Communist forces would be a direct threat to the security of the Pacific area and to United States forces performing their lawful and necessary functions in the area. Accordingly, I have ordered the Seventh Fleet to prevent any attack on Formosa. As a corollary of this action, I am calling upon the Chinese Government on Formosa to cease all air and sea operations against the mainland. The Seventh Fleet will see that this is done. The determination of the future status of Formosa must await the restoration of security in the Pacific, a peace settlement with Japan, or consideration by the United Nations.'

THE 38TH PARALLEL

Four days after the North Korean invasion, two days after America's decision to aid South Korea, Secretary Acheson said: 'This action pursuant to the Security Council resolution is solely for the purpose of restoring the Republic of Korea to its *status quo* prior to the invasion from the north and of re-establishing the peace broken by that aggression'.[3] In discussions in the National Security Council that day, 29 June, Truman had 'wanted it clearly understood that our operations in Korea were designed to restore peace there and to restore the border'.[4]

This attitude did not outlast the period of retreat in Korea. By the beginning of August, the North Korean attack had been halted and the perimeter around Pusan stabilized. The build-up for a counterstroke began, and decisions on its extent needed to be taken. The decisions in the event taken, while they aroused comparatively little public controversy at the time, were in retrospect momentous. They changed what might perhaps have been a three-month war with the North Koreans into a three-year war with China, and added the finishing touches to China's hostility towards the United States and finally confirmed the United States in a policy of Cold War of the European style towards China.

The decision not merely to restore the border, the 38th parallel, but to cross it and to conquer North Korea was an American decision. This point is worth emphasis not because America was alone in responsibility for what followed; many of its allies gave their support with greater or less conviction. The point is rather that the decision was habitually seen at the time as a 'United Nations' decision, a habit which readily gave rise to serious illusions.

The first hints that the United States foresaw the crossing of the North Korean border were given in mid-August in American statements supporting all-Korean elections. A formal decision appears, however, not to have been taken until 11 September. On that day, Truman approved a National Security Council policy paper which recommended that 'General MacArthur was to conduct the necessary military operations either to force the North Koreans to surrender behind the 38th parallel or to destroy their forces. If there was no indication or threat of entry of Soviet or Chinese Communist elements in force, the National Security Council recommended that General MacArthur was to extend his operations north of the parallel and to make plans for the occupation of North Korea. However, no ground operations were to take place north of the 38th parallel in the event of Soviet or Chinese Communist entry.'[5]

On 15 September a directive in these terms was sent to General MacArthur. On the same day, MacArthur's forces landed at Inchon. Seoul was retaken on the 28th and Syngman Rhee re-established there on the 29th. On 2 October, Republic of Korea units crossed the parallel. On the 3rd, the first definite warnings of possible Chinese intervention reached Washington.

On the 7th, the United Nations Assembly passed a resolution which implicitly endorsed the crossing of the parallel. On 9 October MacArthur's forces began a full-scale offensive northwards.

The United Nations resolution of 7 October in deference to the opposition of such countries as India to the conquest of North Korea, was vague. It recommended that all appropriate steps be taken towards such ends as all-Korean elections and a unified Korean Government. However, this was an implied endorsement of the crossing of the parallel and all knew this. But equally important from an outsider's point of view, that of China for example, the endorsement was one which the United States could readily secure. It could at that time raise the necessary majority in the United Nations Assembly on grounds with only a remote bearing on the Korean issue. The resolution was no more than an American confirmation of an American decision, or, if one preferred, a Capitalist confirmation of an American decision in a Capitalist forum to which China was not admitted. Moreover, as in the Assembly, so in the field, it required adherence to the Western political philosophy to see as a United Nations force, an army almost entirely composed of Americans and South Koreans, commanded by an American general who received his orders from Washington.

These various points are, it is true, no more than a commentary on the nature of the United Nations Organization; it was not a body above the normal forces of world affairs but a microcosm for the interplay of those forces. However, American opinion in particular did not fully appreciate this. The fact that the action in North Korea could be described as a United Nations action rather than as the invasion of North Korea by America, South Korea and their supporters, gave it a degree of naturalness and righteousness in American eyes which helped to blind them to the likely reactions of other powers who did not see the matter in this way. It is true that Americans contrived simul-

taneously to see the United Nations action as an action of the
free world against Communism, and that this more pugnacious
view of the matter might have been expected to arouse awareness of the likely reactions of the free world's opponents. In the
event, however, it simply led to still greater indignation when
those reactions duly occured.

Though the United Nations Organization had committed itself by a resolution of November 1948 to the principle of a re-
unified Korea, a principle re-affirmed in the resolution of 7
October, it seems unlikely that this fact figured among the
motives for the crossing of the parallel. United Nations resolutions were subject to Western policy, not the reverse. The argument was raised in the debates of the time but probably only as
a piece of pleading. The motive for crossing the parallel seems
to have been simply the wish to settle the Korean question once
and for all. There appeared to be an excellent prospect, especially
after the brilliant success of the Inchon landing, that MacArthur
could rapidly conquer the north. If, on the other hand, North
Korea were left unconquered, there was every prospect that
it would repair its forces and at very least continue to harass
South Korea, requiring a continued heavy American commitment.

The crucial question was the attitude of the Soviet Union and
China. Their intervention might well transform this calculation.
The National Security Council's policy paper of mid-September
had made operations by MacArthur north of the parallel conditional on there being 'no indication or threat of entry of Soviet
or Chinese Communist elements in force'. On 30 September,
such a threat was made, if in veiled terms, in a speech by Chou
En-lai. 'The Chinese nation will by no means suffer foreign
aggression and cannot remain indifferent to the fate of its neighbour, subject to aggression from the side of the imperialists.' A
more explicit warning was given on 3 October when, so far,
only ROK troops had crossed the parallel. The Indian ambassador

in Peking, K. M. Pannikar, took steps to inform Washington that Chou En-lai had sent for him and had told him that if United States forces crossed the parallel, China would send troops into North Korea; however, if only South Korean troops crossed, this action would not be taken.

President Truman records that these warnings were treated as doubtful on two grounds. Pannikar 'had in the past played the game of Communist China fairly regularly, so that his statements could not be taken as the view of an impartial observer'. Second, the vote was due on the United Nations resolution which, if adopted, would be 'a clear authorization for the United Nations Commander to operate in North Korea; it appeared quite likely that Chou En-lai's "message" was a bald attempt to blackmail the United Nations by threats of intervention in Korea'.[6]

China's interest in the fate of North Korea had next to be taken into account. Though North Korea was in the world's eyes Russia's *protegé* rather than China's and though diplomatic relations between China and North Korea were not good, ideological solidarity might count for something. The root of the matter was likely to be, however, the degree of China's strategic interest. There were, in particular, the hydro-electric installations in the far north, on the Korean side of the Yalu River, which supplied power to North Korea but also to Manchuria. In general, North Korea bordered on Manchuria and this, for a century the focus of Chinese, Russian and Japanese rivalry, was one of the most important industrial areas of China. China might, in sum, attach as much importance to the fate of North Korea as the United States did to the fate of South Korea.

It may be that the United States underestimated the likely anxieties of China partly because it was not conditioned to think of a Communist power as having legitimate anxieties, and partly because, in any case, China could have nothing to fear from an action undertaken by the United Nations. This second point is

suggested by American comments on the eventual Chinese intervention, quoted later. Certain precautions were attempted but
they seem to have been half-hearted. In a directive of 27 September the Chiefs of Staff charged MacArthur that no non-
Korean ground forces were to be used in the areas bordering the
Soviet Union and Manchuria. Throughout this period of the
Korean War, the Administration may have been bemused by
the speed of MacArthur's campaign; his personality made for
loose control. Whether or not the idea of unconditional surrender
entered into the Administration's motives in invading North
Korea, the idea of total victory certainly entered into the attitudes of the general. However, on this particular point, there
seem to have been good grounds for MacArthur's view that these
nervous, last-minute precautions were not practicable.

The remaining factor in the calculation was whether China
would dare to intervene and what would happen if it did. Military intelligence estimates of China's intentions gave no clear
picture, but as to its effective strength, the Chiefs of Staff
appear to have envisaged that if China intervened, Mac-
Arthur would be able simply to break off his action and hold
the line. In their directive of 27 September they said: 'In the
event of open or covert employment anywhere in Korea of
major Chinese Communist units, without prior announcement,
you should continue the action as long as, in your judgement,
action by forces now under your command offers a reasonable
chance of success.' General MacArthur, according to Truman,
was still more sanguine. He told Truman at their meeting on
Wake Island on 15 October that 'he thought there was very
little chance that they would come in. At most they might be
able to get fifty or sixty thousand men into Korea, but since
they had no air force, if the Chinese tried to get down to Pyong-
yang, there would be great slaughter.'[7]

At about this time, it seems, the first Chinese units crossed
the Yalu River; on 27 October clashes occurred; the Chinese

proved to be backed by a formidable air force; a month later General MacArthur's forces had been driven back behind the 38th parallel. The reaction of American opinion to these events was not that of a gambler who has taken a chance and has lost. There was no inclination to cut losses, to shorten the aims of battle to those declared at the outbreak of the war, the restoration of the border. There was only passionate indignation and strengthened resolve to fight on. America's determination not to negotiate was equalled only by victorious China's insistence on Formosa and entry to the United Nations as the price. Negotiations did not begin until July 1951 when neither side could claim to be victorious. Peace was not reached till July 1953.

The reasons for America's attitude, the reasons perhaps for two years of war, were these. 'Whatever the Chinese purposes may be, however,' said a *New York Times* editorial of 1 November, 'there can be no doubt that any Chinese intervention in the Korean War would represent aggression even more flagrant than the Communist attack on South Korea. That aggression would be directed, not, as Communist propaganda would have it, against the United States but against the United Nations which is conducting its first military peace enforcement action in Korea . . . Even the Chinese Communists must know that the United Nations action in Korea carries no threat to them but rather aims at a stable, independent and democratic Korea that would be both a better neighbor and a better protection for them than a Korea in perpetual dispute.'

By the end of the month, the full weight of China's intervention was clear, and in a speech of 30 November, Secretary Acheson too said: 'Now no possible shred of doubt could have existed in the minds of the Chinese Communist authorities about the intentions of the forces of the United Nations. Repeatedly, and from the very beginning of the action, it had been made clear that the sole mission of the United Nations forces was to repel the aggressors and restore to the people of Korea their independence.' For Acheson too, this was 'a second shocking act of aggression'.

That these sentiments were not mere propaganda is confirmed by the furious determination with which America acted upon them. The wave of sentiment for an attack on China, supported by MacArthur, was checked by Truman, but, short of direct warfare, the Administration was determined on punishment of China. In January, the United Nations Assembly called for a cease-fire but the Administration and Congress browbeat the Assembly until on 1 February a resolution was passed condemning China as an aggressor. In May, economic sanctions were imposed in the shape of an embargo on exports to China.

These events were only symbols of a general consolidation of America's attitudes to China, of America's determination to isolate and contain it until it collapsed. By its intervention in Korea, China had not shown that it resented an attempt to extend the influence of the United States to the Yalu River; it had shown that it was a malignant power, a gratuitous aggressor against the United Nations and the free world. In the Washington discussions of 4-8 December, Prime Minister Attlee argued much as Acheson had argued against Hoover and the China lobby at the beginning of the year. China, Attlee believed, was not a Soviet satellite. 'I think', he said, 'that all of us should try to keep the Chinese from thinking that Russia is their only friend. I want the Chinese to part company with Russia. I want them to become a counterpoise to Russia in the Far East. If we don't accept this theory, if we treat the Chinese as Soviet satellites, we are playing the Russian game.' It must be the primary aim of Western policy in Asia to win the support of Asian opinion; Asian opinion opposed America's China policy. As to the present conflict, since it was to be confined to Korea, it would be impossible to beat China into submission; therefore in the end there would have to be a negotiated settlement with her; therefore overtures might as well begin immediately. As to

China and the United Nations, 'The British', he said, 'had found out that it did not pay to pretend that the "nasty fellow" on the other side was not there.' It was not possible, in any case, to use the arguments of the principles of the United Nations in dealing with China so long as she was not a member.

In reply, Secretary Acheson now argued thus. 'First of all, it had to be remembered that the central enemy was not China but the Soviet Union. All the inspiration for the Korean action came from Moscow' . . . 'We ought not to try to prove that we were more friendly to them (the Chinese) than the Russians. After what they had done to us, it seemed to him that the Chinese would have to prove that they were *our* friends. Our position now, Acheson went on, was that we ought to get the military power and strength to stop this sort of thing happening in the future. We had to have a policy that would keep going on the basis of strength.' He was not optimistic about the prospects of negotiating with the Chinese Communists. In cease-fire negotiations the Chinese would probably ask for diplomatic recognition and admission to the United Nations. To accept would be to buy off aggression. 'It would be a very confusing thing to try to get the American people to accept aggression in the Far East and not to accept it in Europe.' Chiang Kai-shek, 'rightly or wrongly, had become something of a symbol'.[8]

7

Collective Security : Asia

When in 1949-50, at the fall of China and the outbreak of the Korean War, the United States began to give urgent attention to the security of areas of Asia bordering the Soviet Union and China, its approach differed in one fundamental respect from the approach which had served it so well in Western Europe. The origins of the Western European security system lay in a Western European initiative, the Brussels Treaty, and not in an American initiative. The system, that is to say, was chosen by the countries of the region themselves. America's role was to support, join and guarantee. In the case of Asia, on the other hand, America's approach was not to ascertain the ideas of the region, to follow them and to make what it could of them; rather, it sought to introduce in Asia its own ideas of security: collective security, containment and the whole outlook involved in the phrase, the Cold War between the free world and Communism.

These ideas, transferred from Europe, were on the whole unacceptable and unsuited to countries in Asia. The experience of world affairs of some of the most important countries of Asia was of course almost as recent as their independence; for the most part, they had few clear ideas of security of their own and still fewer in common. It was thus tempting to seek to impose ideas, to try to make Asian countries see sense. But, however tempting, the pursuit of ideas which required the co-operation of Asian countries but which were alien to them inevitably proved in the end to have been wasted effort, contributing nothing to security.

It proved, indeed, on balance to have been harmful effort. A variety of countries enrolled themselves behind America's ideas. Many of them did so, however, with an eye in great part to their own purposes: Pakistan to its quarrel wtih India, Iraq to its rivalry with Egypt, Thailand to its traditional balancing act between the great powers, France to its position in Viet-Nam, Britain to its influence in Iraq and Egypt. None of these countries could offer much to collective security and containment by miltary means; few of them believed in the American-Russian idea of two worlds, the free world and the Communist world, except as a slogan of current expediency. On the other hand, their use of Western ideas for their own purposes alienated their rivals from the West, with especially significant consequences in the cases of Iraq and Egypt and Pakistan and India. Egypt's reaction to the British and American ideas was an understanding with Russia; India was allowed to substitute criticism of American ideas for debate on ideas of its own. In sum, America's guarantees and arms programmes may have contributed to the security of some Asian countries; but its more esoteric ideas increased the insecurity they were intended to remove.

The widest reason for the transference by America of ideas from Europe to Asia in the crisis of 1949-50 was that reactions were called for at great speed and until that time comparatively little attention had been given to Asian affairs outside Japan. In mid-1948, of 336 State Department officials working on political affairs, 100 were concerned with Europe, eighty-three with the Americas, ninety with the Near East and Africa and fifty-five with the Far East. European affairs and European posts traditionally had the highest prestige in the Foreign Service and, generally speaking, received the best men. Europe was traditionally the focus not only of its own affairs but of those of most of Asia as well. The great development of Asian political studies in American universities and institutes had not yet begun; there too, there was preoccupation with the urgent crisis in Europe.

If American policy until 1949 was generally confined to routine diplomacy, the cause was the quiescence of the Soviet Union and the weakness of China and Japan. There was no great need for an active policy. The burden of the independence movement was carried by the European powers; little more was needed from the United States than exhortation and encouragement. The Soviet Union was as little interested in Asia generally and as preoccupied with Europe as was the United States. The Soviet Union did not and probably could not make much use of the major movement on the Asian scene, the nationalist movement for independence.

It is sometimes said that Stalin underestimated Asian nationalism and dismissed the nationalist leaders as imperialist stooges because he clung to Marxist-Leninist doctrines of the inanity of *bourgeois* nationalism. Perhaps a better way of expressing the point is that Stalin was interested in power in Europe; he was not interested in influence in Asia. Such parties as the Wafd, such leaders as Gandhi, Aung San and Sukarno were of no use to the extension of Soviet power and were indeed on the long term its most bitter enemies. No doubt some of these leaders were influenced by Marxist social theories; no doubt there was a parallelism of interest in breaking the European empires. But the nationalists were generally the rivals of the Communist parties for the leadership of the independence movement and were, in the last resort, the enemies of Russian or any other imperialism. Stalin had had bitter experience of these truths in the onetime alliance with Chiang Kai-shek. It was not until the Soviet Union seriously desired an increase in its influence in Asia that an understanding with Asian leaders seemed worthwhile and was pursued by the Soviet Union and was subsequently sanctified by Communist theorists.

In the Middle East in 1946-7, one of the main focuses of American concern was Iran. Iranian hopes of sustained American interest, particularly in the shape of economic aid, were, however disappointed. To quote an American comment, if perhaps a somewhat harsh one, 'Ample reserves of Iranian friendship were thus frittered away in 1947-50. If United States generosity failed to catch up with Iranian need, it was perhaps because of the prevailing feeling that with the defeat of Soviet designs, the Iranian situation was no longer urgent.'[1]

The attitude was similar as regards the Arab Middle East. There was a standing awareness of the instability and weakness of the region and the consequent danger to the oil companies and other Western interests. Some in the State Department like Loy Henderson urged a forward policy, paralleling the acceptance of responsibility for Greece and Turkey. However, it seems that no basic decision of this sort was taken. Soviet activity in the region was slight; the Administration was preoccupied; responsibility for Middle East politics could still, after all, be left primarily to Britain. In any case, Henderson and his Middle East specialists were at odds with the President on the Palestine question and the Middle East countries themselves would listen to little else until this question was settled.

According to Truman, the main anxiety of his State Department and military advisers on the Palestine issue was two-fold: the effect on Arab opinion and the possibility of an opening for Soviet influence. He was reminded of Roosevelt's promise to Ibn Saud early in 1945 that Roosevelt 'would make no move hostile to the Arab peoples and would not assist the Jews against the Arabs'. Saudi Arabian opinion was of particular importance in view of America's oil interests, but, more generally, in the State Department's view, 'Great Britain has maintained her position in the area by cultivating the Arabs; now that she seems no longer able to hold this position, the United States must take over, and it must be done by exactly the same formula; if the Arabs are antagonized, they will go over into the Soviet camp'. Similarly, the Joint Chiefs of Staff 'were primarily concerned about Middle East oil and in long range terms about the danger that the Arabs, antagonized by Western action in Palestine, would make common cause with Russia. The second argument in particular was one that I had not lost sight of at any time . . .'[2]

Truman was not convinced that these dangers need necessarily outweigh his sympathy for the Jews, and the Administration's attitude throughout the prolonged controversy was on the whole favourable to their cause. However, it avoided any direct American responsibility in the Palestine question until after the armistice of spring 1949 when the United States became a member of the United Nations Conciliation Commission and a major participant in the relief agency for Arab refugees. The United States annoyed most of the parties to the dispute most of the time by withholding outspoken support and permanently alienated nobody. Even Truman's snap decision to recognize Israel on Britain's withdrawal in May 1948 had no disastrous effect on Arab opinion. It was not followed by pronounced official support for the Israeli cause, and, as regards the East-West aspect, the Soviet Union, which had taken little part in the whole affair, also decided to recognize Israel.

In the Far East at the same period, America's policy towards Japan followed the same trend as its policy towards Germany. However, the process was slower. The burden on the American taxpayer was considerable in this case also but the need to enlist Japan's strength for wider economic recovery and in resistance to the Soviet Union was not so acute. Unlike the new directive of July 1947 to General Clay in Germany, the new statement of policy on Japan by the Far Eastern Commission on 19 June was on the whole a re-affirmation of existing policy. Admittedly, most of the hesitation to turn from reform to recovery lay with America's allies; for some months General MacArthur had been speaking of recovery; Secretary Acheson referred in his Cleveland speech of 8 May, foreshadowing the Marshall Plan, to the reconstruction of both Germany and Japan. However, the Johnson Committee's report which urged the same arguments as the Hoover Committee's report on Germany, did not appear until April 1948. Thereafter developments in Japan, the removal of economic restraints and the handing over of government functions, roughly kept pace with developments in Germany. There was still not the same urgency for the Administration as in the case of Germany and even less for the allies; but General MacArthur had his own views.

In South and South East Asia, America's strongest sentiment was sympathy for the struggle for independence against the European powers. Cold War considerations and the threat of Communism began to raise increasingly strong cross-currents in the late forties but they were not as yet dominant. The immediate postwar enthusiasm of Americans for the Viet-Minh in Indo-China cooled in 1946-7 as the international situation developed; their Communism seemed to have more bearing on the matter and so equally did support for France in Europe. From the time of the quarrel in the Security Council in January 1946, the State Department was increasingly inclined to favour the Dutch in Indonesia in view of the need to strengthen the Netherlands in Europe. However, at no time up to 1949 did American opinion favour the French and the Dutch and at no time did the Administration give direct support to them.

The friendship of France and the Netherlands was almost as important to the United States as that of Britain in the light of the European situation, but the contrast of American attitudes to the conflicts in Indo-China and Indonesia and the Malaya emergency of 1949 was very marked. No doubt the Malayan rebellion, unlike the other two, was only marginal to the genuine independence movement; but this dissimilarity only reflected another, that, in American eyes, the British were repentant imperialists, intent on eventual independence in Malaya as in India, Burma and Ceylon, whereas the French and the Dutch scarcely seemed to be so. When in the first months of 1949, the

United States decided to put heavy pressure on the Dutch to withdraw from Indonesia, the motive was partly fear that if the nationalist leaders were thwarted, the population might turn to the Communist rebels, but partly also the strong popular revulsion in the United States against the 'second police action' of the Dutch, powerfully expressed in the Brewster resolution in the Senate. At the turn of 1948-9, imperialism was still on the whole the most important yardstick in American attitudes to Asia.

When in early 1949 eventual victory for Mao Tse-tung in the Chinese civil war began to seem certain, the State Department began urgent studies of United States policy in Asia. In the following months, as Nationalist resistance rapidly collapsed, the attention of the American public swung to the Asian scene with alarm and anger. In October, the Chinese Peoples Republic was proclaimed. America's attitudes now had to be decided.

Not until the Korean War did American attitudes finally solidify into the belief that China was an enemy in Asia of the same type as was the Soviet Union in Europe, that it was a powerful satellite of the Soviet Communist empire. Only then was the full apparatus of European-style containment brought into action, the iron-clad military resistance on the free world's borders with China, the buttressing of China's neighbours with economic and military assistance, the building of perimeter alliances, the rejection of diplomacy. Earlier however these policies were foreshadowed by the delay in recognition of the new Chinese régime and in its admission to the United Nations Organization. They were also foreshadowed by the decision in February 1950 to send aid to the French in Viet-Nam.

One element in this decision to support France was the need for French co-operation in other areas of policy, notably the consolidation of Western Europe against the Soviet Union. The dilemma of needing to show sympathy both to nationalists and to the colonial powers with an eye to the struggle with the

Soviet Union was one with which the United States was to become very familiar throughout the fifties. Except in the case of Cyprus and to some extent in Middle East policy in general, Britain rarely confronted the United States with this problem; France did so perpetually, especially in North Africa. In Morocco in August 1953, the French exiled the Sultan for his nationalist leanings; the shock to the Arab world was immense; but the United States felt obliged to vote with France and Britain against debate on the issue at the United Nations Assembly session that autumn. The United States followed a similar policy on Tunisia and on the Algerian war from its outbreak in 1954. These decisions were, however, painfully difficult. Could Arab opinion or at least the nationalist leaders, be placated by mere behind-the-scenes sympathy? How important was their friendship compared with the friendship of France?

The balancing-act of America in the face of French colonial policy was summarized by Assistant Secretary Byroade, speaking of the 1953 crisis in Morocco and Tunisia, in these terms: 'The United States Government believes that this complicated problem must be resolved primarily by the parties concerned ... We know of the delicate problem that the Government of France confronts in view of the large French population in this area. We agree that the local system of government in North Africa needs change before it can cope with present world conditions or guarantee social progress. We have important security interests in the strength of the French nation, as well as deep friendship for the French people. We also have a firm policy of supporting the right of dependent peoples to self-determination. We therefore understand the desire of the Tunisians and Moroccans for self-government. It is no secret that these problems confront America with a dilemma. The present situation therefore calls for a middle of the road policy which will permit us to determine our position on practical issues on their merits as they arise.'[3]

These considerations also applied to American policy in Indo-China in the fifties. The situation was one in which France was able to manœuvre with great astuteness. As its position steadily deteriorated, the need for its co-operation in the European Defence Community, and thus its ability to insist on aid, steadily grew. Moreover, at the very outset of the American intervention in February 1950, France was able to produce persuasive evidence of constitutional advance, the Elysée Agreements establishing governments of Laos, Cambodia and Viet-Nam within the French Union.

However, in the case of Indo-China, considerations of the East-West struggle and of friendship produced more than a balancing-act between the colonial power and the nationalists; they produced intervention on the side of the colonial power. The decisive factor was that in the winter of 1949-50, the United States suddenly made up its mind that the Viet-Minh rebellion was no longer a genuine independence movement. In January 1950 the new Chinese Government like its predecessor recognized the Viet-Minh government and the Soviet Union hastily followed suit. The Viet-Minh offensive was strengthening and assistance from across the border, begun by the Kuomintang, was increasing. American policy-makers now decided that the relevant way of considering a possible Viet-Minh victory was no longer that it would mean independence from the French but that it would mean a triumph for Sino-Soviet expansion against the United States and the free world. Accordingly, in February the United States recognized the three governments of Indo-China and announced that Viet-Nam could expect economic and military aid in combating 'internal dissension fostered from abroad.'[4]

On the widest view, the most remarkable feature of this American plunge into the revolutionary movements of Asia was that it was apparently made without any preliminary consultation with those who might be expected to have some valuable views on the matter, the Asians themselves. Quite unilaterally, the United States decided that the revolution in China was a disaster for China and a danger to Asia and thus indirectly to itself; that the best way to deal with the matter was to isolate and blockade China; that the character of the war in Viet-Nam had changed radically; that Chinese influence there was unacceptable.

Even if Asian views on these issues were valueless, even if India, Burma, Thailand and the rest knew as little about China and Viet-Nam as did the United States, even if America's views on Asian security were right, was it feasible to be right alone? It was ironical that it should be Britain which insisted from the fall of China to the formation of SEATO that the indispensable requirement for a successful Western policy was the support of the Asians themselves; and that it should be the United States, the critic of colonialism, which preferred to impose its own views in a style which it would never have considered in Europe.

America's radical reappraisal of the Viet-Minh rebellion in the light of events in China was to a very great extent the product of purely American points of view. Preoccupied with its quarrel with China, the United States assumed that, for the whole world as for itself, the important fact about a Viet-Minh victory would now be that it was a Sino-Soviet victory in the struggle of the free world with Communism. In fact, however, no such change of appearances had taken place for people in Asia or indeed for many in the West. In their eyes, the important fact about a Viet-Minh victory would still be that it was a victory for independence against colonialism. People in Asia did not naturally see events in terms of the free world against Communism; they saw events in terms of nationalism against colonialism; thus, little had changed. If the independence movement in Viet-Nam happened to be Communist-led, this was exceptional and not altogether pleasing but largely irrelevant;

if China, first Nationalist and then Communist, gave assistance against the colonialists, this was natural and understandable. Only to the extent of America's feud with China, only to the extent that America injected this feud into the independence struggle in Viet-Nam, would a Viet-Minh victory with Chinese support seem a Chinese victory over America and the free world.

A subordinate cause of American alarm was the effect of a Viet-Minh victory with Chinese support on Viet-Nam itself. The issue here was not so much that Ho Chi Minh was a Communist; this had always been so; as such he had become President with French recognition in 1946; the prospect of a Communist régime was unpleasant and was brought much closer by Chinese Communist support, but this was not in itself decisive for intervention. The issue was rather the effect of Communist China's influence. American policy-makers no doubt appreciated that a strong China of any complexion would naturally exert deep influence over Viet-Nam in the absence of the French; but the outcome of an alliance between Ho Chi Minh and a Communist China would almost certainly be a much tighter closure of Viet-Nam to the outside world than would otherwise have been the case.

One possible reaction to this aspect of the struggle was simply to hope that the leaders of the Chinese and Viet-Namese peoples would one day see better reason in the running of their countries. An even-tempered attitude on the part of the outside world would do something to assist this. It was at least worth bearing in mind that just as China and the Soviet Union were strange bedfellows, so traditional Annamese policy had been to resist Chinese influence, a tradition which Ho Chi Minh continued in his balancing-act between Soviet and Chinese influence. But, for American policy-makers, alarmed by the spectre of a triumphant Communist China, taking decisions in an atmosphere of popular anger and demand for action, such a reaction was impossible. The need of the hour was for resistance, for support of those

M

already engaged in stemming the Red flood. So it was that in February 1950, America set out to overthrow the leaders of the Viet-Namese people, to give security to Viet-Nam and indirectly to the whole of Asia, against a danger in which these peoples did not believe and by actions to which they were opposed. America set out, that is, apart from France, alone.

The tragedy of America's approach was that in going forward alone, it could never go far enough. Though the United States could spend millions of dollars and could thoroughly identify itself with the cause of France, international and domestic attitudes were such that it could never bring its full power to bear on the struggle. It could not possibly win the small war and it could not make a large one. The international tension which built up over Indo-China in 1953-4 was heightened by such statements by Secretary Dulles as that open Chinese armed intervention 'could not occur without grave consequences which might not be confined to Indo-China.'[5] It may be that these warnings had a useful deterrent effect on the Chinese, though at the time they were generally held to be unnecessary. The only positive effect of America's intervention, at all events, was to prolong the agony for four years with the most harmful effects on France, Indo-China, opinion in Asian countries and the confidence of the Western powers in American leadership.

Though unable to attain the security of Indo-China by military means, the United States was unwilling to supplement them with diplomatic means. Indirectly, it is true, the United States made a contribution to the success of the Geneva Conference of May-July 1954 where the principle of the settlement was the security of Indo-China by neutralization. At the final crisis of Dien Bien Phu, Mr Dulles sought to organize allied intervention, and it seems clear from Eden's memoirs that the basis of Anglo-Soviet co-operation in arranging the conference and during it was Soviet fear of a full-scale clash between the United States and China.

However, the United States did not accept the Geneva settlement or the idea of neutralization. 'I will not be a party to a settlement which makes anyone a slave,' said President Eisenhower of the Geneva discussions.[6] Later the President stated: 'The United States has not itself been party to or bound by the decisions taken by the conference, but it is our hope that it will lead to the establishment of peace consistent with the rights and needs of the countries concerned.'[7] This statement was in fact a prelude to mounting activity by American organizations in Indo-China in the following years, particularly in Laos. The American determination that Laos could not be saved by neutralization but only by aid, armaments and intrigue was matched only by Ho Chi Minh's support of the Pathet Lao and his determination to unify Viet Nam under his rule as it had been in 1946.

During the Geneva Conference, America's main preoccupation was first to arrange a collective Western intervention and later to arrange a collective security treaty to guarantee the area. The idea of Far Eastern collective security treaty began, however, in 1949-50 at the fall of China and the outbreak of the Korean War.

Suggestions in 1949 by the President Syngman Rhee and President Quirino for such a treaty met with little enthusiasm in the American Administration, and the only step was an investigatory mission in the spring of 1950 on aid to South East Asia. The Korean War transformed America's attitude. The immediate reaction was piecemeal aid to Korea, the Philippines, and Viet-Nam, and, for the first time, to Formosa. In the autumn, an arms agreement was signed with Thailand, 'made in the knowledge', said the American Ambassador, 'that aggressive forces are rampant in the Far East today and appear to be looking hungrily towards Thailand and her neighbors'.[8] That September, Mr Dulles accepted an assignment to arrange a Japanese peace treaty, with or without the Soviet Union, coupled the following January with an assignment to arrange a Far East collective security treaty.

The attempt failed at that time. What was achieved was a series of separate treaties, with Formosa in April 1951; with the Philippines in August; with Australia and New Zealand, the ANZUS treaty, on 1 September; and with Japan, accompanying the peace treaty, on 8 September. Thereafter, there was a lull in the development of collective security. The United States was preoccupied with Korea and was, moreover, reluctant to extend its commitment from the Pacific into South East Asia. It was particularly with regard to Hong Kong and Malaya that the United States resisted British requests to be included in the ANZUS treaty. As late as 1953, President Eisenhower gave the impression that the United States considered South East Asia marginal to its interests.

With the ending of the Korean War, the shift of attention to Indo-China and the final, acute crisis there early in 1954, United States interest in a security treaty covering South East Asia suddenly became intense. The arresting but always nebulous idea was propounded that the fall of Viet-Nam could topple the successive countries of South East Asia one after the other like a row of dominoes. 'The propagandists of Red China and Russia make it apparent', said Mr Dulles in a speech of 29 March, 'that their purpose is to dominate all of South East Asia. South East Asia is the so-called "rice bowl" which helps to feed the densely populated regions that extend from India to Japan . . . The area has great strategic value . . . Communist control of South East Asia would carry a grave threat to the Philippines, Australia and New Zealand . . . The entire Western Pacific area . . . would be strategically endangered . . . Under the conditions of today, the imposition on South East Asia of the political system of Communist Russia and its Chinese Communist ally, by whatever means, would be a grave threat to the whole free community. The United States feels that the possibility should not be passively accepted but should be met with united action.'

The immediate aim behind Mr Dulles proposal for a collective security treaty seems to have been to make a demonstration of unity to influence events in Indo-China and at Geneva. On the longer term, his aim was the security of South East Asia including Indo-China. Though Indo-China was neutralized at Geneva, a striking feature of the eventual Manila Treaty was that the treaty covered not simply the signatories but included Indo-China.

Anthony Eden's outlook on Mr Dulles's proposal was that it might possibly be made into a way of bringing in the Asian countries to guarantee the Indo-China settlement. During the Geneva Conference, the Prime Ministers of India, Pakistan, Burma, Ceylon and Indonesia met at Colombo to consider the Indo-China question and their co-operation in the outcome of the Conference was an important objective for Eden. As to the wider aims of a security treaty, here too, in Eden's opinion, no permanent South East Asia Organization could be 'fully effective without the understanding and support of the Colombo Powers'.[9]

Unfortunately such understanding and support were very unlikely to be achieved. The whole trend of American thinking on Asian affairs was at complete cross-purposes with that of the Colombo powers. During the struggle for independence, there had been considerable mutual respect and goodwill. After independence, as preoccupation with economic development grew, there was pressure on the United States for economic aid, and some disappointment at the modest scope of the programme which eventually resulted from point four of Truman's Second Inaugural Address in January 1949. The $34·5 million allotted in May 1950 under the Act for International Development did not seem much compared with the $12 billion of Marshall Aid to Western Europe. However, relations remained, in general, good during the quiescent period of American policy up to the Korean War. Thereafter attitudes rapidly diverged.

India supported the United Nations decision to defend South Korea, but opposed the invasion of North Korea and equally the United Nations decision of May 1951, brought about by American Congressional pressure, to impose economic sanctions on China. It continued to advocate the admission of the Peking Government to China's place in the United Nations. These attitudes led to a vigorous dispute in Congress in the same month on the despatch of two million tons of surplus wheat to relieve India's food shortage. If India wanted American wheat, it should support America's policies. This attitude in turn aroused indignation in India.

When the Republican Administration took over, it was made clear that economic aid was to decline. So far as Asia was concerned, there was thus not only to be no major economic aid programme but simultaneously America poured out large sums in military or para-military aid to South Korea, Formosa, Viet-Nam and to its other clients in its struggle with the Soviet Union and China. $2 billion were spent in aid to Viet-Nam from 1950-54. It seemed that America's only use for Asia was as a battleground in a struggle from which most people in Asia wished above all to be isolated.

The new Republic Administration, by 'unleashing' Formosa in February 1953, by repealing President Truman's undertaking of June 1950 that the Seventh Fleet would prevent action by Formosa against the mainland, appeared to be deepening tension to the point of permitting war. Distaste was further increased by the bomb-rattling tone of America's defence pronouncements and its growing belligerence in the Indo-China conflict. As the final irritant to India, in May 1954, in the midst of its attempts to win support for a security treaty, America announced a Mutual Defence Assistance Agreement with Pakistan. The focus of Indian and Pakistani 'foreign' policy was their own Cold War centring on the Kashmir issue. Both of them, the one publicly and the other privately and despite the assurances extracted from Pakistan by America, saw America's military aid to Pakistan in the light of this quarrel.

When on 8 September 1954, the South East Asia Collective Defence Treaty was signed at Manila, the signatories were the United States, Australia, Britain, France and New Zealand and Pakistan, the Philippines and Thailand. Quite apart from other arrangements, a five-power Staff Agency had been in existence since January 1953 so that for the Western signatories, the new treaty was superfluous. The point of a new arrangement lay in the participation of Asian countries and an increase in their security, and in this respect SEATO was a failure.

Pakistan, the Philippines and Thailand already had defence assistance agreements with the United States. The United States was already committed to them and they were already as committed to the United States as they wished to be. The American conception of military defence in Asia was that the countries of the region should provide conventional forces backed by the massive retaliatory power of America. Because of the economic strain and the political and social effects, there was some question whether the maintenance of large forces with American aid would not increase the instability of Asian countries rather than strengthen their security. But, in any case, SEATO added nothing to this conception.

A novel and much-emphasized aspect of the Manila Treaty was its provision for co-operative action not only against direct aggression but against subversion. The main target of this provision in America's eyes was Indo-China. But whether America's approach to the problem of Indo-China was correct or the Geneva formula of neutralization, here too SEATO added nothing. It was scarcely necessary to set up SEATO to exchange information about guerrilla warfare.

As a guarantee of Indo-China and of South East Asia in

general, the Manila Treaty like the earlier bi-lateral treaties was based on what Mr Dulles called 'the Monroe formula'. To avoid any recurrence of the constitutional dispute over NATO, there was a declaration of common interest in resisting aggression but the commitment to action was explicitly subject to the necessary constitutional processes. In effect, therefore, the Manila Treaty went no further than existing well-known American commitments to the signatories and was a mere addition of paper so far as the attitudes of the signatories to involvement in Indo-China were concerned.

There was, however, the collective aspect of the SEATO guarantee to be considered. No longer was the United States alone committed to the signatories; Pakistan was committed to Thailand and Thailand to the Philippines and so on. But the fact was that in the event of trouble between, say, China and Thailand, the intervention of the Philippines would be likely to raise dangers far outweighing any practical armed assistance it would be able to give. Military collective security was excellent as a principle in Western Europe where aggression against one country was bound to involve all and where each could genuinely add strength to the others. But these conditions did not exist in Asia. The existence of a collective military commitment by Asian countries would simply be an additional force tending to inflate a local conflict into an ominous international struggle without any countervailing gain. It was no doubt fortunate that so few Asian countries were drawn into the SEATO fold.

The idea of collective security in Asia did not, in sum, arise from an estimate of the conditions in the region. American bi-lateral assistance may in some cases have increased the security of individual Asian countries; the general United Nations guarantee under which America and anyone else could act was valuable to them all; but the only worthwhile collective security arrangement for Asian nations lay in quite different directions.

The American idea of collective security represented, as did most of America's Asian policy, a simple transference from Europe.

America, in Dewey's words in the autumn of 1951, 'must draw a line in the Pacific and put it in a treaty for all to see – just as we have done in the Americas and just as we have done in Europe'.[10] The decisive impetus to the Manila Treaty was given by Mr Dulles's anxiety in 1954 for collective action in Indo-China, collective intervention at Dien Bien Phu or later, a collective guarantee, or later still, collective measures against subversion. But in this too the basic inspiration was that just as in Europe, the nations who stood for Freedom against Communism must be banded together and must buttress the common frontier of the free world with armaments. The idea of collective action for the free world entirely overrode analysis of the Asian situation. In consequence, SEATO had little significance beyond the further irritation of some of the most significant countries in Asia by the further appearance of importing the East-West struggle into Asia.

Most of these considerations also applied to British and American efforts from 1950 onwards to arrange a collective security treaty in the Middle East. In the case of the Middle East, however, there were notable differences in the relations of the great powers. First, in the Far East, China was already active militarily, however this was to be interpreted, whereas the Soviet Union was on the whole inactive in the Middle East. The question therefore arose in a more pointed form in the case of the Middle East, whether it was better for the United States to move into the area with security precautions in advance and run the risk of provoking the Soviet Union; or whether it was better to avoid provocation but to run the risk of unpreparedness.

American policy-makers had little difficulty in answering this question. The Soviet Union was seen far less as a country which could be provoked than as a country which was essentially an aggressor. Its whole record in Eastern Europe, its whole theory of Communism supported this. As Assistant Secretary McGhee said at the time of the publication of the Middle East Command proposals in October 1951 : 'It would be a dangerous mistake to see Russian moves as merely a revival of Tsarist aims and methods . . . At least the old Russian Empire set itself relatively limited aims in the Far East, in Iran, in the Middle East, and for control of the Dardanelles . . . There are no limits to the new Russian expansionism. The all-encompassing aim of the Soviet Union is world domination.'[11]

From this point of view, it was only a question of time before the Soviet Union erupted into the Middle East. Precautions as swiftly as possible seemed essential. 'A traditional objective of Russian expansionism,' wrote one American observer of the 1950 Middle East scene, 'the region seemed almost to invite a Soviet push that would split the free world along its North-South axis, deny it the abundant oil resources of Iran, Iraq and the Arabian peninsula, and open a path for the extension of Soviet influence westward across Africa and eastward into Pakistan and India. This was a region which seemed to call pre-eminently for creating a "situation of strength"; yet the actual situation was one of notorious and dangerous weakness. Great Britain held only shreds of its former prestige and influence in the area; the United States had not come in to fill the vacuum effectively; and the capacity of local governments to fend for themselves in such troubled times was doubtful to say the least'.[12]

Having decided rightly or wrongly that the need for action outweighed the risk of provocation, it was essential to the British and American purpose that the action taken should win the support of the peoples of the area and genuinely lead to additional defensive strength. Otherwise, of course, nothing at all would be gained in return for the risks. It is unnecessary to set out the reasons why a Middle East collective security system was extremely unlikely to do any of this; nor the reasons why the United States nonetheless favoured the idea. The reasons were the same as in the case of SEATO.

The significant difference in the Middle East situation was the reversal of the roles of Britain and the United States. Britain was on the whole the leader, the United States the follower. Britain was prepared to show considerable disregard for Middle East opinion or at least important sections of it; the United States in the last resort was not.

The explanation of this was that for British policy, a collective security system was not primarily a device for direct defence against the Soviet Union. It was primarily intended to encourage at least some form of co-operation among the Middle East countries, to attract the United States into a more active partnership with Britain in the area, and to make a respectable way of perpetuating Britain's old security arrangements and influence. The United States, on the other hand, also had its interests in the Middle East. Torn between the idea of collective security and the realities of its interests, the United States at last came down on the side of Middle East opinion, Saudi Arabia and oil. By this time, however, the joint policy had come to fruition, had outraged Middle East opinion and was leading to the increased Soviet influence which the whole scheme was supposed to prevent.

After the Palestine armistice of spring 1949 and America's acceptance of membership of the United Nations Conciliation Commission, the next significant step in America's movement in to the Middle East was the Tripartite Declaration of May 1950, primarily directed at preventing an Arab-Israel arms race. However, to set beside the Israel issue was the growing dispute between Britain and Egypt on the 1899 Sudan Condominium Agreement and the 1936 Treaty on the Suez Canal base and zone. On 16 November 1950, King Farouk finally made a definite threat to abrogate these. The following day, Nuri es-Said declared Iraq's solidarity with Egypt and described the 1930 Anglo-Iraqi treaty as equally outdated.

The United States had kept clear of the postwar Anglo-Egyptian exchanges on the matter. Now, while avoiding general identification with Britain's cause, it joined in attempting to persuade Egypt to accept Britain's proposals for a collective security arrangement which would include Egypt and suitable Arab and outside powers. Egypt resisted the idea, but Britain was adamant that without some such new arrangement, it would not budge. In September 1951, the support of the NATO Council was sought, won and announced. Finally, on 13 October 1951, Britain, the United States, France and Turkey formally proposed a Middle East Command which was to be a regional security arrangement under the United Nations Charter, composed of 'countries able and willing to contribute to the defense of the area', including the sponsors and Australia, New Zealand and South Africa. Speaking three days before this, Secretary Acheson said: 'The United States considers the new proposals shortly to be presented to the Egyptian Government should serve as a sound basis for an agreement which will not only satisfy the interests of all parties concerned but also contribute to the defense of the free world in which the Middle East plays such an important role'.[13] Two days after the proposals were published, Egypt replied by abrogating the Agreement and the Treaty.

Though the sponsoring powers announced that they would nonetheless continue with their plan, this was a little beside the point for Britain and in fact a lull ensued. The United States rejected a British suggestion in January 1952 that the sponsoring powers should all station troops in the Canal Zone as evidence of their unity of purpose. Throughout 1952, Anglo-Egyptian relations were progressively embittered by incidents in Cairo and in the Zone.

By the time of Mr Dulles's tour of the Middle East in the spring of 1953, the major preoccupation was the Iranian oil

crisis. It had arisen as long ago as April 1951 with the nationalization of the Anglo-Iranian Oil Company but it was now threatening to develop an East-West aspect. Originally, the United
States and the Soviet Union had remained neutral, but now,
under Malenkov, the Soviet Union expressed friendship for Iran
and offered Mossadegh its support. Mossadegh refused, but un-
mistakeably his position was becoming desperate. By the time he
appealed once again for American support in May 1953, a take-
over by the Tudeh Party, the Iranian Communist Party, whether
by alliance with Mossadegh or by *coup d'état*, was a clear possibility.

In the event, the United States stood firm. The major elements
in this decision appear to have been friendship with Britain and
disapproval of the original Iranian action; the success of Britain in
gradually cementing a working partnership with the United
States and the American oil companies on the issue; and calculations of the forces at work in Teheran and particularly of the
attitude of the army. Eventually, in mid-August, Mossadegh was
overthrown by an army *coup d'état* and the way to the solution
of the oil question was opened.

Stabilization in Iran also cleared one obstacle to renewed
attention to the security of the region, apparently all the more
vital in view of the recent alarm. In his broadcast report in June
on his Middle East tour, Mr Dulles had re-stated the permanent
American cause of anxiety. 'It came as a surprising shock when
the 450 million Chinese people, whom we had counted as
friends, fell under Communist domination. There could be
equally dangerous developments in the Near East and South
Asia. The situation calls for urgent concern.'

However: 'In Saudi Arabia we were received by King Ibn
Saud, one of the great Near Eastern figures of this century,
conspicuous in his dignity and singleness of purpose. He is a
good friend of the United States, as he has shown by deeds.
Our policy will be to reciprocate this friendship. In Saudi Arabia,

Americans and Arabs are working together in good fellowship in the vast oilfields of the country.'

Mr Dulles was almost equally concerned to cement a friendship with the new, strongly anti-Communist military junta in Egypt. In general: 'We cannot afford to be distrusted by millions who should be sturdy friends of freedom. They must not further swell the ranks of the Communist dictators.' In consequence: 'A Middle East Defense Organization is a future rather than an immediate possibility. Many of the Arab League countries are so engrossed with their quarrels with Israel or Great Britain or France that they pay little heed to the menace of Soviet Communism. However, there is more concern where the Soviet Union is near. In general, the northern tier of nations shows awareness of the danger. There is a vague desire to have a collective security system. But no such system can be imposed from without. It should be designed and grow from within out of a sense of common destiny and common danger.'[14]

The initiative was eventually taken late in 1954 by Iraq. At the time of Mr Dulles's tour, Iraq had requested a Mutual Defence Assistance Agreement, but the United States, aware of the likely effects on the attitudes of other Arab countries, had not agreed. On the other hand, the United States had welcomed the Agreement for Friendly Co-operation between Turkey and Pakistan in April 1954 and had backed this approval with a Mutual Defence Assistance Agreement with Pakistan in May. Iraq now seems to have believed that it could take the same route as Pakistan to American arms, especially if the whole matter was placed in the context of a 'northern tier' collective security system. Accordingly towards the end of 1954, Iraq began negotiations with Turkey and in February 1955, a Pact for Mutual Co-operation was signed in Baghdad.

Britain may have encouraged Iraq's initiative and certainly approved of it. The Anglo-Iraqi Treaty now had only three years to run; Nuri es-Said wished for its replacement forthwith; new arrangements were essential. Admittedly it was known that Egypt was pressing Iraq to withdraw from this line of development, and in February 1955, Eden discussed the matter with Colonel Nasser in the hope at least of overcoming his opposition and if possible of drawing Egypt in. However, Nasser, while stressing his goodwill towards Britain, would have nothing to do with the Turco-Iraqi pact. 'No doubt jealousy plays a part in this', Eden noted, 'and a frustrated desire to lead the Arab world.'[15] Regrettable as Egypt's attitude was, it was not allowed to impede developments. In April, Britain acceded to the Baghdad Pact, followed by Pakistan in September and Iran in October.

To the consternation of the signatories, the United States refused to join. 'Having played a leading part to inspire the project', Eden wrote, 'the United States Government held back while Britain joined in, alone of the Western powers.'[16] There may have been some self-deception in this remark; the ambiguities in American policy were perhaps clear enough to Britain and Iraq; they may have decided to proceed despite these, over-confident that America would be drawn in. As it was, the United States was not prepared in the last resort to alienate Egypt and Saudi Arabia and gave only general approval to the Pact in terms of the external defence of the region.

The damage had, however, been done. Saudi Arabia was merely hostile to the Pact but Egypt was infuriated by the figure cut by Iraq and by the splitting of the Arab front against Israel just at the moment of the damaging Israeli raid of February 1955 in the Gaza strip. Nasser cast quickly around for other support, for the makings of a counter-blow. He found these in the Soviet Union.

In this development, there was an element of sheer bad luck for the Western powers; throughout 1954 and 1955, Nasser frequently emphasized his sympathy for the West. On the other hand, intent on their own lines of policy, the Western powers perhaps underestimated the overriding significance of the Israel quarrel for Egypt, the repeated Soviet warnings from the time of the Middle East Command proposals of 1951 and the Soviet change of attitude to the nationalists rulers from 1953 onwards, all of which made an understanding between Egypt and the Soviet Union at least possible.

Tentatively established in 1954 during the Anglo-Egyptian negotiations on the Suez Canal base, interrupted by the Agreement reached in the autumn, this understanding strengthened rapidly from the beginning of 1955. The Gaza raid led to urgent Egyptian requests to the Western powers for arms. Britain, it seems, was inclined to make supply conditional on Egyptian membership of the Baghdad Pact; the United States hesitated. As Iraq's alliance grew further in April with Britain's accession, Nasser's plans for a counter-organization of Syria and Saudi Arabia developed apace. The Bandung Conference may have stirred Nasser to the possibility of a middle way for Egypt between the great powers, using either as suited the turn of his plans for leadership towards Arab unity. In the summer, the United States offered armaments with the condition that similar quantities would go to Israel. But Nasser now had a more attractive possibility to hand. In August, a trade agreement was signed with China and on 27 September, an agreement was reached with Czechoslovakia for the exchange of cotton for armaments.

This bargain, causing shock and dismay in the West, was followed by the establishment of an Egypt-Syria-Saudi Arabia Joint Command in opposition to Israel and the Baghdad Pact, and by the swift forging of commercial and armaments links between Egypt, Syria, Yemen and the Soviet Union. The pattern was now firmly established which was to lead to the upheavals of 1956 and thereafter: to the struggle between the two alliances for the alleigance of Jordan; the swelling confidence of Nasser, conscious of Soviet support, and the panic of Israel; the

Western decision in response to withdraw promises of finance for the Aswan Dam; the Suez crisis.

This was a tragic outcome to the idea that a collective security arrangement in the Middle East could convert a situation of weakness into a situation of strength. In the event, the Baghdad Pact, like SEATO, contributed nothing except increase to the problems it was designed to solve. The same was in many cases true even of the military aid which the United States gave bilaterally to the countries on the Sino-Soviet perimeter. It was in theory very desirable that every country in the world should have its own first line of defence and that the United States should help to make this possible. In practice, unfortunately, in many cases, the conditions did not exist for the building of a convincing first line of defence. The political tensions and economic strains which were created, on the other hand, were usually grave. In some cases, it might have been unwise on political grounds for the United States to reject requests for military aid; but deliberate encouragement and impatience with other countries for not joining in seems to have had very little justification.

There was an overall consideration bearing strongly on such assessments. No doubt, in the postwar and post-independence world, the Middle East, South Asia, South East Asia and the Far East, could be seen as a series of power vacuums. The European powers were withdrawing; the countries themselves were preoccupied, inexperienced and weak. The situation might well seem to invite the expansion of an aggressive Sino-Soviet *bloc*. But what was the evidence and what was the likelihood that the Soviet Union and China wished to and could invade these areas? There was much against the idea and little for it except the dubious analogy of Eastern Europe, presuppositions about Communism and the consequent assumption that the Soviet Union and China had inspired the attack on South Korea as part of an expansionist campaign against the free world.

193

There could be little doubt that the Soviet Union and China would seek influence in the areas adjacent to them, just as would any great power. Historically, south-eastern Asia from Tibet and Nepal to Indonesia was overlaid by Chinese and Indian culture. It was essential not to underestimate the disposition of the Soviet Union and China to control adjacent areas and the leverage, resources and skill at their disposal. But it was equally essential not to exaggerate them.

In all these circumstances, unless the United States was capable of total military defence of the whole of Asia, which it was not, it must eke out military defence with all the available tactics of diplomacy. And what contribution could the countries of Asia best make to their own security? Certainly, these countries themselves, whether through blindness or greater understanding than they were often credited with, rapidly concluded that their security must lie primarily in neutrality, diplomacy and in economic progress. The Bandung Conference of the spring of 1955 was a curious meeting with many crosscurrents, but in sum it was a manifestation of this spirit. Typically, the Conference was largely obscured from American attention by the current crisis between Formosa and China.

There was only one country in Asia which was perhaps in part deceiving itself by this approach, a country of giant size, with immense ability and potential, a country which could not avoid rivalries and thus leadership and responsibility, India. But the United States, far from seeking understanding with India as the basis of its approach to Asia, antagonized it with all the rest by its own obsessive vision and the measures which it took in response. Surveying the accomplishments of the containment policy in the conflict of the free world and Communism, Mr Dulles said: 'These treaties abolish, as between the parties, the principle of neutrality which pretends that a nation can best gain safety for itself by being indifferent to the fate of others. This has increasingly become an obsolete conception, and except under very exceptional circumstances, it is an immoral and shortsighted conception. The free world today is stronger, and peace is more secure, because so many free nations courageously recognize the now demonstrated fact that their own peace and safety would be endangered by an assault on freedom anywhere.'[17]

8

Coexistence

The ring of alliances built around the Soviet Union and China in the late forties and early fifties and backed by a ring of American air bases in thirty-one countries, was founded on an idea of resistance wider than that of merely halting Sino-Soviet expansion. In speeches in the winter of 1949-50, Secretary Acheson expressed this wider aspect in a phrase which became well known and which was seized upon by Soviet propagandists to characterize American policy. Experience had shown, he declared, that the only road to agreement with the Soviet Union was that of converting 'situations of weakness' into 'situations so strong that they can be recognized and out of them can grow agreement'. This had been the basis of American policy in Germany, Japan and Western Europe and indeed throughout the world. It demanded 'purpose, continuity of purpose, perseverance, sacrifice and . . . more than anything else, very steady nerves'.[1] 'It is clear', said Acheson in another speech, 'that the Russians do not want to settle these issues as long as they feel there is any possibility they can exploit them for their own objective of world domination. It is only when they come to the conclusion that they cannot so exploit them that they will make agreements and they will let it be known when they have reached that decision.'[2]

These speeches were, however, an attempt to check a modest wave of sentiment in the United States in the winter of 1949-50 for a renewed effort towards a settlement with the Soviet Union. Though this sentiment died away in the United States in the quarrels of 1950, the Communist 'peace campaign', begun in March 1950 and continued intensively throughout 1951, had some success among Western European populations, suggesting a widespread unease. With the death of Stalin in March 1953, a strong current of opinion developed in Western Europe for renewed negotiation. The building of strength was an entirely negative policy. Surely some place must be found for positive initiatives towards a settlement.

The answers of Western statesmen to this question varied considerably. The British answer was the idea of 'negotiation from strength'. This was largely a political slogan and contained in consequence a large element of absurdity. For each measure of strength made negotiation more difficult until in the end in 1955, when the edifice of strength was complete, there was nothing for the West to negotiate about except the very strength which was held to make negotiation possible. Measures of strength were in themselves settlements of a sort, making an overall settlement progressively more difficult. The British disposition from 1953 onwards to look for a settlement in Europe, exemplified in such proposed first steps as control zones and disengagement, involved the weakening of strength and was thus suspect, even to the British. Simultaneously, however, the British believed that the object of negotiation was not really negotiation at all. It was meeting and discussion for the sake of understanding and the relaxation of tension.

The French answer was the more logical one that before taking any new measure of strength, there should be negotiation with the Soviet Union to see whether it could be avoided. However, this view was more logical than practicable. The motive was fear of German rearmament, and there was the danger that if this objective was confused by negotiation, the will to attain it would weaken.

The American answer was the briefest and most coherent of all. It was that, having built up its defences to an adequate level, the West should simply wait behind its ramparts, busy with its own affairs, until the Soviet Union came to its senses, that is, accepted the Western point of view.

At the outset in 1947, America's attitude to negotiation was expressed simply in terms of a concept which had been declared anathema in 1945, the concept of a balance of power as a necessary condition for peace. Speaking of the London Conference of Foreign Ministers of November 1947, the last of the postwar series, Secretary Marshall said: 'There is another and, I think, even more fundamental reason for the frustration we have encountered in our endeavour to reach a realistic agreement for a peace settlement. In the war struggle, Europe was in a large measure shattered. As a result, a political vacuum was created, and until this vacuum has been filled by the restoration of a healthy European community, it does not appear possible that paper agreements can ensure a lasting peace . . . The Soviet Union has recognized the situation in its frank declaration of hostility and opposition to the European Recovery Program. The success of such a program would necessarily mean the establishment of a balance in which the sixteen western nations who have bound their hopes and efforts together would be rehabilitated . . . The issue is really clear-cut, and I fear there can be no settlement until the coming months demonstrate whether or not the civilization of Western Europe will prove vigorous enough to rise above the destructive effects of the war and restore a healthy society.'[3]

The determination to restore Western Europe did not in itself soften the Soviet mood; on the contrary, the quarrel grew fiercer, and that same winter discussions began on a Western European security system. Still, when Bevin took the initiative in January 1948 he thought, as Truman noted, that 'if a collective security system could be built up effectively, it was more than likely that the Russians might re-study the situation and become more co-operative'.[4]

The following March, however, the Soviet Union reacted to the calling of the London Conference on Germany with the first pressure on Berlin which mounted to the blockade of the autumn and winter. Though war-tension relaxed in 1949, the division of Europe deepened with the signature of the NATO treaty in April, the charade of the Foreign Ministers meeting on Germany in May following the lifting of the blockade, and the relentless accomplishment of a West German government in September.

Despite these advances in Western strength, in the winter of 1949-50 the Soviet Union was still not considered to be sufficiently mellow for negotiation. The idea of the neutralization of Germany was revived and discussed in America but was not acceptable to the Administration. Then followed the quarrel over China, the Korean War and urgent rearmament. Accordingly, when in October 1950, the Soviet Union protested against the proposals for West German rearmament, the attitude of the United States, and, with some reluctance, of her allies, was that this step also must be completed before negotiations could conceivably be successful. 'The Soviet Union has made it clear', said President Truman in his 1951 State of the Union Message, 'that we must have strength as well as right on our side. If we build our strength – as we are building it – the Soviet rulers may face the facts, and lay aside their plans to take over the world.'

Soviet protests and demands for negotiations were met to the extent of discussions between the deputies of the Foreign Ministers of the four powers at the Palais Rose in Paris beginning in March 1951. However, after three and a half months, the discussions were abandoned, the decisive obstacle being the refusal of the Western powers to allow NATO to be placed formally on the agenda of a four-power conference. The negotiations for West German rearmament and entry into NATO were at a crucial stage and the Western powers would not allow the whole structure of NATO to be called in question at such a time. Thanks to French delay on EDC, this difficulty continued throughout the remainder of the Democratic term of office and beyond. In reply to Soviet proposals in 1952 for the neutralization of Germany, the United States reaffirmed its faith in the policy of Western European unity and its refusal to be 'deflected from pursuing this path of peace'.[5]

Fundamentally, however, the Truman Administration did not envisage that NATO would become a subject of negotiation at any time, even when German rearmament and the whole structure had been completed. As Secetary Acheson said in July 1951: 'Once a level of defense has been achieved which should deter any power from plunging the world in war, the task will shift from creating defenses to maintaining them'. Behind this 'stout shield of defense', the free world would proceed with such tasks as co-operation in economic development. The ultimate purpose was 'to bring realization in the Soviet Union that no one power is going to dominate this world and that it would be foolhardy to try to do so. When this realization sinks home in Moscow, we can begin to hope for those changes in the Soviet régime which will make for a more peaceful world.'[6]

The death of Stalin in March 1953 and the attitude of the new collective leadership seemed to America's allies as possibly just such changes. In his speech of 8 August in which he announced the momentous news that the Soviet Union had developed a hydrogen bomb, Mr Malenkov referred also to the perils of nuclear war and to the necessity of 'peaceful coexistence' between states of different systems. Despite the suppression of the Berlin riots in June, there were many evidences of 'the thaw' both in the Soviet Union and in its dealings with its satellites.

All this encouraged Britain and France to pursue Churchill's suggestion, made in a House of Commons speech of 11 May, for a new meeting upon the highest level. The meeting would be private and informal without an agenda. It would be a mistake 'to assume that nothing can be settled . . . unless or until every-thing is settled'. 'It may be that no hard-faced agreements would be reached but there might be a general feeling among those gathered together that they might do something better than tear the human race, including themselves, into bits.'

Almost simultaneously with the death of a Stalin, however, the Republican Administration had come to power in the United States, and this Administration was, if possible, still more staunchly opposed to negotiation with the Communists than its predecessor. The American population, like the populations of Western Europe, were discontented by the negativity of con-tainment; but the slogans with which the Republicans appeased their discontent were not so much promises of negotiation as 'roll-back', 'liberation' and a 'positive foreign policy'. An end there must be to the war in Korea, but as to general negotiation in the Cold War, one of the choice weapons in the Republican campaign armoury was the myth of 'Yalta'. The third point in President Eisenhower's foreign policy address to Congress on 2 February 1953 was: 'We shall never acquiesce in the enslavement of any people in order to purchase a fancied gain for ourselves'.

A ratification of the *status quo* in Europe was anathema. It would be a settlement by surrender. Citing the dead Stalin on strategy and tactics, Mr Dulles said in April: 'The free peoples are susceptible to Soviet guile because they so passionately want peace that they can readily be attracted by illusions of peace. One such illusion is a settlement based on the *status quo*.' It was of the utmost importance that the West should make clear to the captive peoples that their captivity was not accepted. If they thought otherwise, if they abandoned hope, the West would unwittingly become a party to the forging of a hostile power so vast as to encompass its destruction.[7]

If acceptance of the *status quo* was excluded, what alternative proposal for Europe did the Western powers have? At talks in Washington in July 1953, the United States submitted to British and French pressure for a Foreign Ministers' Conference, but simultaneously reassured West Germany, in a letter of 23 July from President Eisenhower to Chancellor Adenauer, that American policy was determined on a Germany, reunited by free elections, rearmed and free to enter any alliance it chose. With this as the Western negotiating position, the President felt free to inform a somewhat mystified American public in his 1954 State of the Union Message that the West had attained 'a position of strength', and that month, January, the Foreign Ministers met in Berlin.

So far as negotiation was concerned, the Berlin Conference was mere shadow-boxing. The Western and Soviet attitudes to the problem of Germany and of Europe were hopelessly far apart. 'It was not after all our fault', wrote Eden in his memoirs, 'if the result of freedom of choice would be to align Germany with us.' Molotov, on the other hand, 'tried to argue that in insisting upon taking the problem of all-German elections first, I was overlooking the wider issues of European security'.[8] The fact was that Britain and France had agreed with the United States not to pursue a German settlement and European security by an agreement with the Soviet Union. They were all in varying degrees mistrustful of the Soviet Union and of its motives in seeking negotiation. They were all more or less determined to achieve European security by a Western system into which West Germany would be integrated.

On the other hand, the Berlin Conference was at least a resumption of face-to-face contact between East and West. An understanding was reached between Eden and Molotov which led to the Geneva Conference on Indo-China in July. Other signs of better intentions, which President Eisenhower had long demanded before going to a conference at the Summit, appeared early in the following year. With the slogan 'relaxation of tensions', the Soviet Union in February 1955 suddenly revoked its long-standing opposition to an Austrian peace treaty, and in

May, buried Stalin's quarrel with Yugoslavia. The Paris agreements on West German sovereignty, rearmament and entry into NATO were now signed in the West; the Warsaw Pact was concluded in the East; and the heads of the four powers met in July in Geneva.

The Geneva Summit Conference was far from being the quiet meeting without an agenda which Churchill had originally envisaged, perhaps with the misleading memory of wartime conclaves. Indeed, the limelight and drama which could be expected to and did surround it perhaps did more than anything else to reconcile Americans to its taking place at all. As to negotiation, the Conference entirely justified American scepticism; there was by now nothing to negotiate about.

A European settlement which ratified the *status quo* or in any way hinted at this was quite unacceptable to the United States and West Germany and apparently, if with less fervour, to Britain and France. Still less were the Western powers prepared to negotiate away their strength. The alternative of allowing Germany, or still more Eastern Europe, to choose its future for itself was quite unacceptable to the Soviet Union. Eden tried to ease this alternative for the Soviet Union so far as Germany was concerned by linking to it a proposal for a 100-150 mile zone of controlled armaments limitation centring on Germany's eastern frontier, topped off with a mutual security pact against German aggression. But this was not enough for the Soviet Union and was probably too much for Britain's allies. All the proposals including President Eisenhower's striking plan for 'open skies' were remitted to the follow-up conference of the Foreign Ministers in Geneva in October-November. There, disagreement on all of them was publicly admitted.

The Geneva conferences were, it is true, a success for Britain's concept, or one of Britain's concepts, of the meetings. The 'Geneva spirit' at its headiest, the wave of hope in America that the Soviet Union might be 'abandoning Communism' did not outlast the Foreign Ministers' Conference. Still, the East-West dialogue, begun at Berlin, was continuing. Even the public correspondence between the heads of the four powers, begun in 1953 and sustained with occasional intermissions to the end of the decade, filled with propaganda though it was, was markedly better than the tense and angry breach of earlier years and exemplified Churchill's point that 'jaw-jaw' was better than 'war-war'. Even American opinion, at heart, acknowledged this.

On the other hand, the failure of the Foreign Ministers' Conference to make any advance towards a negotiated settlement was taken as additional evidence for an interpretation of the changing scene to which Western, and particularly American, opinion was anyway inclined. In his speech at the 20th Party Congress in February of the following year, Mr Krushchev did not merely deliver his momentous onslaught on Stalin and Stalinism; he specifically abolished the Leninist doctrine which Stalin had re-affirmed at the 19th Party Congress six months before his death, the doctrine of the inevitability of war between the Soviet Union and the Capitalist states. Such a war, Mr Krushchev declared, was not a 'fatalistic inevitability'. His declaration was not, he said, put forward 'merely out of tactical considerations, considerations of expediency' but from the historical fact that 'there are only two ways, either peaceful coexistence or the most destructive war in history'.

Americans did not however interpret this, as perhaps they might have been expected to, as heartening evidence that the Russians shared the common anxieties of mankind. They did even hail it as a triumph for the policy of containment of the Soviet Union until it mellowed and came to its senses. They greeted it, in perhaps the most marked of all the detailed tributes to the grip of Communist ideology on the American mind, as a mere change of Communist 'tactics' in the grand 'strategy' for the destruction of the free world.

All that had happened was that the Communist world had at

last realized that militarily it was checked, that direct aggression would be a suicidal path to its goal. But this meant no diminution of its relentless enmity. The war would continue by other tactics. 'The chief feature of our epoch', Mr Krushchev declared at the 20th Party Congress, 'is the emergence of Socialism from the confines of one country and its transformation into a world system . . . Our certainty of victory is based on the fact that the socialist mode of production possesses decisive superiority over the capitalist mode of production.' Immediately after the Foreign Ministers' Conference, Bulganin and Krushchev set off on a tour of India, Burma and Afghanistan, proclaiming the Soviet Union's friendship for the countries of Asia and its sympathy with the anti-colonial struggle, and making genial offers of Soviet economic aid. It was clear that an economic competition with the United States was to be the Communist line of advance and, still more, an economic, diplomatic and subversive offensive among the Asian countries to detach them from the free world.

In the autumn of 1956, the savage repression of the revolution in Hungary sickened the hearts of Americans and all others in the West. The retreat from the Stalin era in the administration of the Soviet empire was only a tactical change; in the last resort, the ruthlessness of that empire was as great as ever. Towards the outside world also, the old spirit was still there, as was shown by the crude diplomatic attempts in 1956 to lure France and Germany into separate treaties with the Soviet Union and by the still cruder threatening letters of 1958 to various of the allies. Mr Kruschev himself confirmed the matter in many a much-publicized remark in the winter of 1956-7. At a New Year reception in Moscow he said: 'When it comes to fighting imperialism, we are all Stalinists'.

The Soviet economic challenge was accepted by President Eisenhower and Mr Dulles with confidence. In the weeks before the Summit Conference, Mr Dulles had interpreted events as suggesting that the Soviet Union was over-extended and had hinted at the possibility of economic collapse. Now, in the early months of 1956, in speeches and testimonies, the President and the Secretary of State argued that this was a form of struggle which the West ought surely to be able to win. Economic aid programmes now assumed an ever increasing prominence in the Administration's policies. The aid race in Asia began.

In this way, with the idea of a swing of Communist tactics from a direct military threat to economics, diplomacy and subversion, the old imagery of containment and of the free world's struggle with Communism continued as before and continued indeed to the end of the fifties. The idea of a 'bi-polar' world was, it is true, weakening; it had become clear that not all the world outside the Sino-Soviet empire was in the same camp; there was a neutralist group. But still the idea was that of a struggle between East and West for the alleigance of these neutral countries. They were still considered, more or less, as members of the free world.

At the same time, though the old imagery continued to the end of the fifties with no radical modification, the American people became increasingly aware that it was inadequate. The convention continued but the facts no longer fitted as readily as before. The Soviet change to 'peaceful coexistence' and the rise of a neutral world could at a pinch be accommodated to the old picture. But one by one, not just some but all the elements in the old picture seemed to be shifting. The old certainties were no longer so certain. The mercurial Mr Krushchev was a harder puzzle than the iron Stalin. The race to build defences against the tide of Soviet postwar aggression had been easily comprehensible. Now, crisis followed crisis anywhere in the world and no overall progress seemed to be made. The weapon of economic aid did not stir the imagination. From 1957 there was drama enough in the 'space race' but it was accompanied by a growing awareness of Soviet equality and also by a vague feeling that the new dimension of space and weapons in space were dwarfing

the old terms of the East-West conflict and perhaps the conflict itself.

Moments of special crisis and special interest apart, there seems
to have been a decline in popular attention to foreign policy
in the middle and late fifties. The leaders of the Administration
sought hard to rally interest and to catch the imagination of the
people. In speech after speech in 1956-7, President Eisenhower
stressed the idea of freedom as the great world revolution, and
Lincoln's faith that the Declaration of Independence had given
'liberty not alone to the people of this country but hope to all
the world for all future time'. 'These ideals of freedom are still
the truly revolutionary political principles, abroad in the world.
They appeal to the timeless aspirations of mankind. In some regions they flourish; in some they are officially outlawed. But
everywhere to some degree they stir and inspire humanity.'[9]

In the last years of his life, Mr Dulles spoke increasingly of
a problem that had concerned him all his life, the problem of
peaceful change. But he was also the great bastion of the old
convictions of the East-West conflict, giving an heroic touch
even to the uncertainties and set-backs of the current years.
'Materialistic despotisms', he said once in 1958 'with their iron
discipline, their mechanistic performance, their hard and shiny
exterior, have always seemed to have the advantage over democracies which visibly stumble and falter, which advertise their
differences to all the world, and which seem to survive only by
good luck. The fact is that the despotisms are always weaker
than they appear and the democracies are usually stronger than
they seem.'[10]

But the challenge still did not seem quite the same for the
American people as in the heroic days. Neither was it for those
who made policy. In these years, until his death in May 1959,
Mr Dulles was, directly or indirectly, a source of strength to
officials and statesmen at home and in the Western Alliance.
Whatever their feelings at his methods and attitudes, he was

at least a man of conviction. The feeling of loss at his death, even among those who had opposed him, was a tribute to this.

Yet, even Mr Dulles could not quite impose the old ideas, however modified, on the new facts. Nor were these new facts sufficiently clear themselves to impose a new idea. More fundamentally, perhaps, the American spirit in world affairs was still too traditional, too defensive to sustain the initiative beyond the period when the need was for restoration and the building of defences into the period of consolidation and of creative advance. American policy-makers, having, unlike many of the countries of Asia, Africa and continental Western Europe, no imposing idea, were left to a greater degree to interpret and react to events.

In these events, certain lines of change seem in retrospect clear. Above all else, the United States and the Soviet Union had reached a stage of mutual deterrence on an alarming level of destructive power. This situation appears to have led to an understanding between them, apparently unspoken or at least informal, that in any crisis, high priority, perhaps the highest, must be given by both sides to limiting its extent.

At the same time, this same situation, coupled with the restoration of Western Europe's strength and self-confidence, was also the basis of divisions in the Atlantic Alliance. There was growing pressure from some of the allies for a settlement of the standing crisis in Europe. Some sought to assert their independence in their overseas policies. Some saw a need for more control over their own military security.

Closely corresponding to these divisions, there was also a growing unity in the Atlantic Alliance, but confined to a part of it. Attempts to sustain the dynamic of the Alliance as a whole beyond the heroic period had little success. American policy-makers, and Americans generally, gradually began to discover at the end of the decade that the development of Western Europe which they had for so long encouraged under the idea of the East-West struggle, had other implications and was threatening to disrupt the Atlantic Alliance itself.

The first great manifestation of these changes was the Anglo-French invasion of Egypt in October 1956, following the nationalization of the Suez Canal Company in July and the Israeli attack on Egypt in October. The ambiguities in American policy during the summer apparently encouraged the two powers to believe that the United States would at least not strongly oppose their action. Granted this, however, the neglect of communications with the United States in the early autumn and the decision to take drastic armed action without positive American approval showed a marked change of spirit, particularly on the part of Britain. It reflected, in addition, a marked clash of temperament between Mr Dulles and Mr Eden.

Since the United States had a far smaller direct interest in the Suez Canal than Britain and France but had, on the other hand, a very strong interest in Arab friendship with an eye to the East-West conflict and the oil question, Mr. Dulles was at liberty to give comparatively full play to his widest principles of international affairs. At a news conference on 2 October, after the stage of direct negotiations with Egypt, Mr Dulles said: 'There were, I admit, differences of approach by the three nations to the Suez dispute, which arise perhaps from fundamental concepts. For while we stand together, and I hope we shall always stand together in treaty relations covering the North Atlantic, any areas encroaching in some form or manner on the problem of so-called colonialism find the United States playing a somewhat independent role.'

Commenting on these words in his memoirs, Mr Eden said: 'The dispute over Nasser's seizure of the canal had of course nothing to do with colonialism but was concerned with international rights'.[11] In point of fact, Mr Dulles also took the view that an essential aspect of the Suez issue was legality. But Mr Eden was primarily concerned with the maintenance of international agreements; Mr Dulles, on the other hand, was primarily concerned with the peaceful settlement of disputes.

'It seemed to us from the beginning', Mr Dulles said on 27 October, 'that any solution should take account of two facts. One is that an international waterway like the Suez Canal which has always had an international status, cannot properly be made an instrumentality of any government's national policies so that equal passage may depend on that government's favor . . . The second basic proposition is that the economic interdependence between Europe, Asia and Africa such as is served so indispensably by the Suez Canal, cannot be made truly secure by coercion and force.'

In attempting to reconcile these two propositions Mr Dulles swayed back and forth throughout the summer between firmness and conciliation towards Egypt; in the final crisis, he chose the second. This vacillation and the final decision caused deep bitterness in Britain and France among those who supported the action of their governments and concern among many who did not. There was loud protest in Britain against the 'dual standard of morality' of the United States and the United Nations whereby they enforced the rule of law on Britain, France and Israel in the case of Egypt but not on the Soviet Union in the case of Hungary. This thought did not greatly impress Americans who habitually divided the world into two, and for whom it was a commonplace that the rule of law was confined to the free world. Another Anglo-French objection to the American approach was much more formidable: that it simply did not work.

The American answer to this dilemma was indeed extremely feeble and had, in the final logic of the argument, to be buttressed with large drafts of belief that Egypt had some right to the Suez Canal. At a news conference of 26 September after the second London Conference, Mr Dulles said: 'Some may ask what are the inducements for the kind of settlement that we seek if force is not to be used. How can a nation be brought to accept a settlement which recognizes the rights of others? The answer is that no nation can live happily for long or live well without accepting the obligations of interdependence.' Mr Dulles specified that Egypt's tourist trade might end, that produce and capital markets might be denied to her, that financial assistance for widening the Canal might be refused, and that schemes might be devised for by-passing the Canal entirely.

Similar attitudes governed America's policy on Israel's conditions for withdrawal from Egypt. 'If the United Nations once admits', said President Eisenhower in a broadcast address in February 1957, 'that international disputes can be settled by using force, then we will have destroyed the very foundation of the organization and our best hope of establishing a world order.'[12] In the protracted negotiations, the United States pressed Israel to rely, not on coercion, but on the sense of justice of the world for the attainment of such aims as equal passage for Israeli shipping through the Suez Canal. In the end, Israel withdrew, and the sense of justice of the world failed to operate.

The objection to Mr Dulles's approach to the Suez crisis, and indeed to his whole approach to world affairs, was in effect that his range was too long to cover immediate targets. Mr Krushchev once complained to Walter Lippman, apparently referring to Europe, that the United States would not accept the *status quo*; and then added that by the *status quo*, he meant the world revolutionary process.[13] Mr Dulles's refusal to accept the *status quo* in Europe was, however, in reality the outcome of an equivalent paradox, an equivalent disbelief that there could any longer be in the world a static *status quo*. To the stagnation of the Communist revolution, he opposed the idea of liberation, the revolution of freedom. He brought the same vision of the dynamic nature of world affairs to bear on the Suez crisis, on the dilemma of old rights and new aspirations. 'His primary dedication was to peace', wrote Thomas E. Dewey, 'a peace based on the concept that life is fluid and that, if civilization is to survive, there must be a means of achieving change without war.'[14] Inspired by this ultimate necessity, Mr Dulles was relatively impervious to the arguments of others based on immediate dangers and necessities.

A further, if in practice minor factor, in America's reaction to the Anglo-French invasion of Egypt was anxiety that the affair should not grow into a major East-West clash. This anxiety was almost certainly shared by the Soviet Union. There were other, more marked examples of this common concern in the mid-fifties. It is hypothetical but it may be indicative to suggest that the crises of those years, against a background of perpetual tension, would in an earlier century almost certainly have resulted in a war between the leading powers. As it was, the United States made no attempt to meddle in the Berlin uprising of 1953; the Soviet Union was patently concerned to prevent an overt Sino-American clash in Indo-China in 1954; the United States took no advantage, beyond heavy propaganda, of the Hungarian rebellion of 1956; the Russians appear to have been alarmed at the bellicosity of the Syrians in the summer of 1957 and to have restrained the Chinese in the off-shore islands crisis of autumn 1958.

Though some of these decisions by the United States and the Soviet Union may have been comparatively easy, there was growing awareness in the United States of an acute potential danger in the military situation of the two powers. The capacity for mutual annihilation and yet the necessity even within this fearful framework to continue to identify and defend vital interests might at any time lead to miscalculation, followed either by catastrophe or surrender. Mr Dulles said in January 1956: 'The ability to get to the verge without getting into the war is the necessary art. If you cannot master it, you inevitably get into war. If you try to run away from it, if you are scared to go to the brink, you are lost.'[15]

In the course of 1956, United States policy-makers seem finally to have begun to base their planning on the actual or imminent existence of a capacity for mutual annihilation, that is, of the sufficient equality of the Soviet Union not merely in nuclear bombs but in delivery systems. This was not held to mean that if a nuclear war was enforced, it could not be fought, and on the military and civil defence levels, the debate on methods of nuclear war was continuous over the following years. But it did mean that on the political level, interest in reducing the level of risk was greatly intensified.

Nineteen fifty-six saw the high tide of hope that nuclear weapons and nuclear war could be reduced in size to within the limit of total annihilation, to a 'tactical' size, but manœuvres and tests that year and discussions of 'escalation' undermined this hope. Emphasis on the limitation of any outbreak of war was as old as the Korean War and Truman's breach with Mac-Arthur on the issue, but now in 1956-7, symptomatically, there was a wave of discussion in academic and official circles of techniques of limitation, centring on Robert E. Osgood's book *Limited War* and Henry A. Kissinger's *Nuclear Weapons and Foreign Policy*. Above all from the beginning of 1957, the United States began to give serious attention to the question of disarmament.

The years after the Soviet Union's rejection of the Baruch Plan of 1946 were the era of 'comprehensive disarmament', of enormous schemes for stage-by-stage reduction of forces, whether nuclear or conventional, involving great ingenuity, but, in view of the atmosphere and preoccupations of the time, little realism. Even given the new sense of danger in 1956-7, the decision of the United States to make a major effort in the disarmament field was paradoxical. A fundamental belief of Americans about Communists was that they could not be trusted, and this sharpened still further the classic dilemma of disarmament that arms are the outcome of mistrust, or worse, and yet that trust is indispensable to disarmament.

Armaments, it had always seemed to the realist school of

disarmament theory, were the reflection of political situations; to tackle the total problem by beginning with disarmament was like trying to shift the image in a mirror. However, despite these pessimistic echoes from the debates of an earlier generation, it was decided that the attempt must be made. The scale of modern armaments seemed to have increased the common ground between the rivals even if it was only the ground of common fear. At very least, the mere fact of discussions might make some contribution to a relaxation of tension and so, indirectly, to disarmament.

It was recognized that at any rate a comprehensive agreement must depend on political solutions, that, for instance, in the words of the Eisenhower-Adenauer communique of May 1957, it 'must necessarily presuppose a prior solution of the problem of German reunification'. In the eyes of many left-wing observers, this kind of attitude represented an absurd or sinister determination to retain armaments as a means of pressure for political solutions. It is more likely, however, to have been a recognition that in conditions of acute political tension, the indispensable basis for large-scale disarmament did not exist.

For, at the same time, the Western powers were seeking ways of circumventing the problem of mistrust, and they hit upon the idea of 'partial disarmament'. The Eisenhower-Adenauer communique said: '. . . if a beginning could be made towards effective measures of disarmament, this would create a degree of confidence which would facilitate further progress in the fields of disarmament and in the solution of outstanding major political problems, such as the reunification of Germany'.

So in 1957, Mr Dulles, who intervened personally that summer in the disarmament negotiations, was arguing: 'Past efforts have usually proceeded on the assumption that it is possible to establish and maintain certain defined levels of military strength and to equate these dependably as between the nations. Actually, military potentials are so imponderable that this always has been and always will be a futile pursuit. Today there is a new approach. It is proposed to establish a system of international supervision which will make massive surprise attack unlikely. If this happens, then general war becomes less likely and the level of armaments will almost automatically go down . . . That was President Eisenhower's "Open Skies" concept first put forward at the Geneva "Summit" conference of 1955.'[16]

This idea was rejected by the Soviet Union as amounting to licenced espionage and might equally, had it come to the point, have been unacceptable to Western populations. However, by this date, 'open skies' was only one point in a Western partial disarmament plan. Another was the limitation of nuclear tests, and on this point, the disarmament negotiations henceforth focused. Because of the prominence of nuclear weapons and anxieties on the hazards of the tests to world health, international opinion was more stirred by this proposal than it had been even by President Eisenhower's 'Atoms for Peace' speech of December 1953 or than it was to be by American proposals from 1957 for control of outer space.

Even this narrow area of disarmament proved to be beset by the dilemma of disarmament as a whole. The greatest expedient of the West for evading this dilemma, whether in the days of comprehensive or of partial disarmament was 'control'. It was admittedly not possible for East and West to trust each other, but it would not in fact be necessary for them to do so. There would be an organization charged with establishing empirically that an agreement was being kept. One difficulty about this idea was, however, that whatever advances might be made in techniques, there could never be absolute certainty that control was complete. In consequence, in conditions of political mistrust there would tend to be the suspicion, mounting to conviction in moments of crisis, that control was somehow being evaded. The practical reflection of this was that the powers found difficulty in bringing themselves to agree on even the very first implications of a control system. The Soviet Union, in particular, disliked the whole concept of control, whether because of its fear of espionage or because it recognized that to seek to overcome a political problem by mechanical systems was a dubious and typically Western conception.

In an equivalent attempt to reduce the level of risk, various proposals were put forward in 1957 under the general idea of 'disengagement' in Europe. Unlike the American proposals of 1946 and the Eden Plan of 1955, Mr Gaitskell's suggestion in December 1956 for a large neutral zone in central Europe was not dependent on German reunification. It aimed simply to soften the physical confrontation in Europe, so lessening the risk of accidental war and assisting political change in Eastern Europe.

In Mr Krushchev's wider interpretation the following February, 'Soviet troops would be withdrawn to the national territory of the Soviet Union from all the countries where they now stand in accordance with existing treaties and agreements. Meanwhile the Western European countries would also withdraw their troops stationed in the territories of other Western European countries. The United States would also withdraw its troops to American territory from Europe and Asia, and along with that would go the liquidation of all foreign military bases.'[17]

In April, more soberly, the Soviet Union expressed willingness to discuss the Eden Plan of 1955 for a control zone. In October, the Polish Foreign Minister, Mr Rapacki, proposed an agreement banning atomic weapons in West and East Germany, Czechoslovakia and Poland. The idea of 'disengagement' was now fashionable in the Communist world, and was also put forward in 1957 in relation to the Middle East and even by China in 1958 in relation to the Far East. In the West, in November-December 1957, Mr George Kennan, temporarily a private citizen, made a series of suggestions in his Reith Lectures which included the belief that the indefinite retention of American forces on the European continent might be more of a political liability than a military asset.

Whether or not the Soviet Union took these ideas seriously, they were quite unacceptable to the Western powers, especially the United States and West Germany. They did not on balance believe that the prospective gains compensated for the security risk involved in a withdrawal of United States forces to the other side of the Atlantic. More fundamentally, the presence of these troops was symbolic of the total policy on Europe, pursued by the United States since 1947. This policy would be heavily undermined by disengagement. As Mr Dulles reaffirmed to the Senate Committee in 1958, 'I think it is very important, Senator, that a reunited Germany should be integrated into the West through its association with NATO, through its participation in the Brussels Treaty of Western European Union, through its participation in the Coal and Steel Community, Euratom, the Common Market and things of that sort'. A neutral Germany would be 'under an almost irresistible temptation to play one side or the other.'[18]

For Mr Dulles, as for Mr Acheson before him, the West must 'keep going on the basis of strength', the strength of its armaments and of Western European unity. But in the autumn of 1957, the Soviet Union struck a heavy blow at Western leadership in strength, the launching of an earth satellite and of a missile of intercontinental range. Whatever the exact strategic significance of these successes, the Cold War had become, above all, a war of nerves and of competitive achievement, and the psychological and prestige effect was powerful. In the United States, the defence budget, which had sunk continuously since 1952-3, leapt up in 1958-9. 'Our people', President Eisenhower now declared 'will not sacrifice security to worship of a balanced budget'.[19] There was a wave of popular unease about the comparative technical strength of the United States, from its space programme to technical education. In NATO, at the December meeting, the United States offered intermediate range missiles to the Allies with a NATO stockpile of warheads under American control, and promised the amendment of the Atomic Energy Act of 1954 to permit greater supply of nuclear information to them. There was much talk of 'interdependence' and, in particular, of co-operation in armaments.

This outburst of unity scarcely outlasted the immediate sensation. With the launching of an American satellite at the end of January 1958, much of the anxiety subsided; budgetary sobriety returned. The United States was in a new, important and costly race, but it was not far behind. In NATO, America's allies showed themselves less interested in American missiles than in Mr Krushchev's suggestion for a new East-West conference. Once more they began to press a reluctant United States towards the Summit. In all other spheres also, disunity became increasingly apparent, reflecting the failure in the postwar years of common purpose to give economic and political foundations to the Atlantic military alliance.

The American proposal for a NATO stockpile was the first step in a line of policy which was to lead to the Kennedy Administration's proposal for a NATO deterrent. It sought to respond to the fears of Western European countries that the United States would now no longer be prepared to use its atomic weapons in their defence, to satisfy their desire for a greater share in control over war or peace, and to check the spread of independent nuclear weapons. But the trend in the alliance was already otherwise. It had seemed to France, even before the return to power of General de Gaulle in the spring of 1958, that the logic of nuclear defence was national defence. France now refused American missiles; it pressed ahead with its own nuclear programme; it announced that American airbases would have to be surrendered; it removed its Mediterranean fleet from NATO command; it refused to co-operate in the NATO air defence system.

Besides logic there was also resentment in France's policy. The 'Anglo-Saxon' alliance dominated NATO planning and policies. Britain had hastened to repair the breach in its 'special relationship' with the United States caused by the Anglo-French invasion of Egypt, and, to the fury of France, then at the very height of the crisis in North Africa, the two powers in November 1957 sent a token consignment of arms to Tunisia for fear that it should seek these from the Soviet Union. Britain had already accepted America's offer of missiles; Britain alone was elegible for military information under the amended Atomic Energy Act; Britain already had its own nuclear weapons. Indeed, under a new policy announced early in 1957, Britain was to rely for its defence primarily on nuclear deterrence, withdrawing its forces on the continent to the extent of one quarter in 1957-58.

Britain's reason for this course was primarily economic. It would not carry the burden of adequate defence alone and there were not the economic arrangements in NATO for the sharing of a common burden. One symptom of this radical weakness was Britain's wrangle with West Germany for some contribution from its bulging balance of payments surplus to the 'support costs' of British forces in West Germany. The agreement reached in May 1958 included part payment by arms purchases, but in general within NATO, 'interdependence' in armaments limped badly through concern for national armaments industries.

From the autumn of 1959, the United States began to express concern at the outflow of its gold as a result of its overseas commitments. This reversal from 1957-8 of the postwar flow was admitted to be in itself healthy, a sign of the recovery of Western Europe; but the outflow could not go on indefinitely and Western European policies would have to be adjusted to the fact of recovery. The surface difficulties could be tackled by co-operation in exchange rates, such as was secured in 1960. Vigorous attempts were made to achieve a greater share by the allies in aid to the underdeveloped countries, reflected in the setting-up of the Organization for Economic Co-operation and Development in December 1960, as the successor to OEEC. This was the only new move of the time in specifically Atlantic economic co-operation.

These changes, like Britain's agreement on support costs, were mere patches on the problem facing the United States. At the December 1957 NATO meeting, the theme of M. Spaak, then Secretary-General, was the need for an economic equivalent to Western defensive co-operation. In face of the grandiose challenge of the Soviet Union, the West could no longer afford simply to co-operate in one sphere and thus, even in that sphere, weakly. But the United States did not believe that NATO was a proper instrument for economic co-operation. Instead, it was content to leave the initiative in economic co-operation, the great tide of the time within the Alliance, to one part of the Alliance.

The United States watched the growth of the European Economic Community from its origins in the Treaty of Rome of 1956, with strong approval; it viewed the British project for a Free Trade Area, embracing the Community of the Six and other Western European countries, with lukewarmness or impatience, as a half-measure; it watched passively the angry collapse of these negotiations in November 1958, the building of the European Free Trade Association of the Seven in 1959, and in 1960, so far as institutions were concerned, the solidification of Europe into two *blocs*.

In April 1956, Mr Dulles had declared that while NATO was conceived as a military alliance, 'the time has come to advance NATO from its initial phase into the totality of its meaning'.[20] The only significant outcome was the conciliatory role given to NATO in certain disputes between its members, for instance, the Cyprus issue. NATO remained a mere *ad hoc* military alliance. In consequence, when in November 1958, the first serious Soviet challenge in Europe for many years was made, its inadequacy was alarmingly apparent. It was clear that, thanks to the military weakness of NATO, product of its economic and political disunity, if the Soviet Union chose to implement its ultimatum that West Berlin must become a demilitarized free city, the Western powers would have no alternatives but 'suicide or surrender'.

Under this pressure, rationalizations of 'flexibility' were heard even in the highest quarters. Even Mr Dulles toyed with the expedient of accepting supervision by East German officials on Western access routes to Berlin as 'agents' of the Soviet Union, and retreated from the principle that reunification of Germany could only be brought about by free elections. Alarm and suspicion of 'appeasement' shot through the Western Alliance, alarm which produced Mr Macmillan's mission of conciliation to Moscow in February 1959, suspicions which were deeply intensified by it. The crisis and the atmosphere surrounding it waxed and waned intermittently through 1959 and 1960 with nothing between the West and its fearful choice but the hope that the Soviet Union would not enforce it.

The focus of United States policy in those years continued to be the East-West conflict, the perennial search for Western unity against the Sino-Soviet *bloc*, and the more recent search for limits to the conflict. The great concerns of the United States were the Berlin Conference of May-August 1959 on the German crisis, the visit of Mr Krushchev to the United States in September, and the disrupted Summit Conference of May 1960. The United States was at last fully aware that the problem of Communist Russia was not of short and simple duration, that understanding of its mind must be attempted, that there must be a search in Secretary Herter's phrase, for . . . 'ground rules for the great competition which dominates our time . . . to keep it within the bounds set by the conditions of co-survival'.[21]

Despite this awareness of changes in the nature of the East-West conflict, the United States in 1960 seemed to many in Europe to be missing the greatest change. It was now no longer enough to seek collective security against the Soviet Union by mere military co-operation. The military situation and the challenge of the Soviet Union were now such that the need of the time was for a parallel growth of co-operation in every sphere. It was partly on this account that Western Europe was beginning to look less to the Atlantic Alliance and more to its own community.

From another point of view, many felt that the United States was too preoccupied with the East-West conflict, too ready to see changes in the Alliance in that light. The Soviet Union was after all, in the era of 'peaceful coexistence', also at least seeking to avoid war. The 'disarray' of the Atlantic Alliance was fully matched by the problems and quarrels of the Sino-Soviet *bloc*. Other world problems need no longer be seen so exclusively in terms of the East-West conflict. Events in the Atlantic Alliance were as significant in themselves as in relation to Western security against the Soviet Union. The growing disunity could be seen equally well as the reflection of the growing unity of Western Europe, of its strengthening self-confidence and of its struggle to define itself whether in membership or in policies. This unity had implications which would further transform and also transcend the East-West conflict.

In 1960, however, the United States was only just beginning to see matters in this light. Its great concern in the Atlantic Alliance was still the negative one of resistance to the aims of the Soviet Union. The idea of a growing Western community with its own, positive aims was still confined to Western Europe.

9
The Underdeveloped Countries

In the late nineteen forties, when East and West were preoccupied with the conflict in Europe, the countries of the southern part of the world were for the most part almost equally preoccupied with their internal affairs, with the Israel question, and with the struggle for national independence. Only to a very limited extent did the two parts of the world have a common picture of events. In the fifties, when the East-West conflict, moved into the southern world, these countries had two further great concerns, the assertion of their international independence and the building of their national economic strength. They sought freedom from tutelage whether British, as in the case of Egypt, or at the end of the decade, American, as in the case of Cuba. They found that they could achieve this by making use of the divisions of the traditional controlling powers, that is, in practice, by striking up a more or less close relationship with the Soviet Union. They sought to balance themselves in a middle position between the pressures of East and West. They also sought to enjoy the assistance of both sides in the service of their own political and economic aspirations.

The United States, however, had a different picture of events in the fifties. It saw the drift of independent countries not from tutelage but from the free world. Arab nationalism in the mid-fifties was not moving towards the centre but towards the Soviet Union. This alarming idea had lost much of its forces by the end of the decade so far as Asia was concerned. Americans accepted that the ambition of Asian countries was a middle position. Neutralism was a not necessarily disastrous fact. However, the old idea arose as strong as ever when the crisis came in the Western Hemisphere, in Cuba.

Within this general picture, Americans saw three particular dangers. They no longer greatly feared that the southern countries would be drawn into the Communist fold by direct aggression, but they were readily inclined to interpret events as 'indirect aggression' or 'subversion' by the Soviet Union or China. Another danger, slightly exaggerated and apparently greatly misunderstood by Americans, was that these countries might move to the East through the influence of popular Communism. Americans, finally, were deeply alarmed by economic and diplomatic understandings between the southern countries and the Soviet Union and China. They set out to combat them. They tended to be hostile towards the countries which made them.

There was, in reality, in those years, some danger that the southern countries would go too far in reaction against their Western overseers and in pursuit of their own quarrels, and would jeopardize their independence. There was a greater danger simply that their volatility would cause disturbance for their neighbours and the world at large. Correspondingly, because of America's special picture of events, there was some danger that it would push these countries too far. There was a greater danger that by its intervention, it would cause a still worse disturbance than there would otherwise have been.

This situation was exemplified both in the Middle and Far East in the late fifties. The Eisenhower Doctrine of January 1957, framed in terms of a 'vacuum' and 'greater responsibility' for the United States, achieved little more than to arouse Arab fears that the United States was stepping into the shoes of Britain and France. In this way it stoked the already inflamed choice before the Arab countries of Western 'imperialism' or Soviet 'control', an issue which was to play a powerful part in the crises of 1957 in Jordan and Syria and of 1958 in Lebanon and Iraq.

The Eisenhower Doctrine, the Anglo-American intervention in Lebanon and Jordan in 1958 and American policy in general were in part aimed, rightly or wrongly, at the plans of Colonel Nasser but in part also at the supposed eruption of the Soviet Union into the Middle East. To this extent, American policy was the product of an eccentric viewpoint. The Soviet Union from 1954 onwards was not so much erupting into the Middle East as being drawn into the Middle East, more or less willingly, by those who desired a Soviet alliance in defence against the Western powers and in pursuit of their own aims. It was fortunate for the United States that the Arab states had no desire to move so close to the Soviet Union as to incur Soviet control. Its more spectacular actions were those best calculated to promote this.

The United States did not explore the Soviet Union's suggestions in 1957 for 'disengagement' in the Middle East and no more did it explore those of China in 1958 for the Far East. In 1955, there was some talk in the United States of a 'two Chinas' policy, the recognition of both Peking and Taipei, and this strengthened in 1956 and especially in 1957 with the Hundred Flowers period in China. But the Administration had now entrenched itself in a position which it felt it could not abandon without significant loss of face in South East Asia and beyond. Moreover, it believed that recognition of Peking would mean the recognition that the Communist régime was the valid inheritor both of the great prestige of Chinese culture and of the loyalties of the overseas Chinese. In sum, recognition would weaken containment and would be one step towards the loss of South East Asia and its economic resources and market to the United States, Japan and the free world at large. Admission of Communist China to the United Nations Organization would strengthen these dangers and would undermine America's conception of the Organization as not a mere political forum, but an effective agent for maintaining peace.

Suggestions for a 'two Chinas' policy were damped by the off-shore islands crisis of September-October 1958, immediately preceding the crisis over Berlin. The United States made little attempt to thrust economic and diplomatic levers into the cracks which developed from this time in the Sino-Soviet alliance. It tended to take the Sino-Soviet quarrel at its face value, the issue of peaceful coexistence or the inevitability of war. China was irredeemably aggressive. Containment must continue.

In practice, the United States feared not so much Chinese aggression as Sino-Soviet 'subversion', notably in Indo-China. In Viet-Nam, Ho Chi Minh was supporting the Viet Cong rebels with the manifest intention of reuniting the country under his rule. America's response was an increasing commitment to an increasingly unpopular dictator, President Ngo Dinh Diem of South Viet-Nam. This was the extension of the dilemma which the United States had first created for itself in 1950; it could not now withdraw from the war and it could not in the end win it.

In Laos, after the Geneva neutralization, prolonged negoti-ations between Prince Souvanna Phouma and his stepbrother Prince Souphannouvong, leader of the Pathet Lao rebellion against the French and ally of Ho Chi Minh, finally led to agree-ment in November 1957 on a united government. American agencies and officials in Laos, however, were impatient of the local politics of the area; they saw in this arrangement primarily the prospect of Sino-Soviet penetration. Their worst fears were aroused by the strength of the Pathet Lao in the May 1958 elec-tions, and, to the dismay of the French, they began active in-trigue for the downfall of Prince Souvanna Phouma. Early in 1960, an American protégé, Colonel Phoumi Nosovan, achieved control of Vientiane only to be ejected again in August. In the fighting which ensued, the United States supported Colonel Phoumi and the Soviet Union began to airlift supplies from North Viet-Nam to the Pathet Lao. The best that could be said at the end of the Eisenhower Administration was that the Soviet Union evidently wished to confirm the Geneva neutralization and that China had apparently not intervened at all.

Together with Sino-Soviet subversion, the United States in the nineteen fifties was most worried by the possibility that the poverty of Asia would 'breed Communism' and by the allied danger of Sino-Soviet 'economic penetration' of Asian countries by aid and trade. It is, at first sight, odd that America should have discovered the problem of 'the underdeveloped countries', the poverty of the overwhelming majority of mankind, in the spirit of anti-Communism and resistance to the Soviet Union and China. The negativity of America's approach did not escape criticism in Asia and from foreign aid enthusiasts in the West. The greatest single idea which America had of itself in the post-war years and which the world had of America was its economic power and prosperity. With 6 per cent of the world's population, it produced nearly 40 per cent of the world's manufactured goods. Like much of the West, it was embarassed by a new, over-flowing agricultural revolution. It was the largest trading nation. It held half the world's gold. Surely it was possible to launch a great positive programme of aid to the underdeveloped countries?

There were indeed certain criticisms to be made of the defensive aid programme which the United States did undertake. The military aid to Asian countries did not in many cases have the merits claimed for it. The perils which economic aid was designed to combat were exaggerated. It was perhaps inexpedient to invest what needed to be done with ungenerous defensive language. These faults sprang from the very roots of American foreign policy, its whole defensive conception.

At the same time, even if the United States had been inspired by the most positive spirit, even if it had been seized of the problem of the underdeveloped countries only as such, there were sufficient complexities in the situation to give pause to large-scale programmes. The American people were generous by nature but they had a shrewd scepticism of the value of colossal 'hand-outs' to the underdeveloped world. Among economists, administrators and field experts there was great doubt, controversy and fluctuation of theories. The problem had only just begun to be discovered in the late forties. The fifties could be expected to be a decade of hesitant experiment. Not enough was known about the problem. Only enough was known to justify concern, effort, and caution about the more theoretically-based schemes.

Though the idea of raising the material standard of living of the world's peoples appeared in the United Nations Charter, the method was generally thought to be the normal growth of the world economy, and new institutions were set up to assist this growth. In any case, in 1945, the accent was on reconstruction. The first great departure, to some extent inspired by Marshall Aid in Western Europe, was Point Four announced in January 1949. However, Point Four development aid differed radically from Marshall Aid in that it did not for the most part take the form of grants, loans and supplies but was mainly devoted to expanding the United Nations Technical Assistance Programme, notably the agricultural development programmes of the Food and Agricultural Organization and the health programmes of the World Health Organization. It did not as yet occur to many people that the necessary social base existed in the countries of Asia, Africa and Latin America for the artificial acceleration of capital inflow and the promotion of rapid industrialization.

In the early fifties, the aspirations of the underdeveloped countries quickened and correspondingly, their requests for Western governmental capital. The Republican Administration, which had at last to respond to the problem, was, however, sceptical. It was also in a mood of economic sobriety. Its response, in the spring of 1953, was the formula 'trade not aid'. It hoped to promote a greater spirit of trading liberalism in the

United States so that Western Europe and the underdeveloped countries would have a better chance to strengthen their resources through normal commercial effort.

Military aid was in the event increased in Asia in 1953-4, but commenting on a reference in the Manila Treaty to economic co-operation in the SEATO area, Mr Dulles told the Senate Committee in November 1954: 'The possibility of usefully spending vast sums of economic money in this area has not been demonstrated. It is quite different from the situation that existed in Europe . . . People knew how to operate it and were well versed in industrial life and the problem was to re-create something that had been destroyed. In this part of the world, the problem is to create something that is totally new, and I am inclined to think that while the problem certainly needs our best thought, the finding of ways and means to help is the most important first thing. The problem must be tackled from that standpoint rather than from the standpoint of first appropriating vast sums of money and trying to think, later on, how it can be spent with advantage.'[1]

About this time, however, the climate of opinion among specialists in the West began to be favourable to a more adventurous approach. Though far-reaching debate continued, the middle and late fifties were in general a period of heavy emphasis on the role of investment capital in solving the problem of the underdeveloped countries. The ambitions of many Asian countries to rapid industrialization by the direct means of heavy investment in manufacturing industries were widely accepted. So also, though with least enthusiasm among American specialists, was the position of Asian governments as planners and frequently as leading entrepreneurs. There was thus widespread support for aid in the shape of large inter-governmental development loans. The programme was not, however, expected to be of indefinite duration. In some cases, such as India, where a considerable industrial base already existed, a sharply accelerated boost by foreign capital for ten to fifteen years would lead to a 'take-off' into normal growth sustained by local and private foreign capital.

Just as these theories reached their peak in 1959-60, doubts began to strengthen. It began to be recognized that 'the under-developed countries' was too indiscriminate a term. Evidence of large-scale waste even in what aid was given suggested that many countries lacked the political, administrative and social base for the rapid absorption of large drafts of overseas capital. Managerial and technical skills lagged behind capital inflow, particularly in government enterprises. Increased aid was already threatening to throw an increased strain on the external payments position of the developing countries because of interest payments on the aid loans and the rising imports which necessarily attended successful industrial growth. Unless aid was to go on rising indefinitely to meet this strain, the export earnings of the underdeveloped countries would have to grow. But they were not doing so. It was estimated that the fall in commodity prices and the rise in manufactured goods' prices in 1957-8 cost the underdeveloped countries about $1,600 million in twelve months, substantially more than Western development aid.

The scene was thus set in 1960 for a renewed emphasis on trade as well as aid and for other reappraisals of the value of capital aid. This however would not be easy. To give aid was after all easier for the West than to take imports. The recession in 1957-58 strengthened protectionism in the United States and various restrictive steps were taken. The growing European Economic Community, exhorted to be 'outward looking', was as yet more liberal in promises than performance.

This brief summary many indicate that if economic theories and enthusiastic pressure were not the determining factor in the pattern of United States aid in the fifties, they did not altogether deserve to be. At all events, the determining factor was in fact defence. Even of America's $21,000 million bilateral 'non-military' aid to underdeveloped countries from 1945-60, one third went to Greece, Korea, Formosa and Viet-Nam. Even the increasing aid given to neutral countries towards the end of this period had primarily defensive intentions, if of a political nature.

America's interest in the defence of neutral countries was similar to its interest in the defence of its allies: continued freedom of access to them, cultural and commercial. In the case of the allies, there was often the special interest of protecting American military bases; and in the case of the neutral countries, of protecting access to minerals. In both cases, it was important that the strength of these countries should not be added to the strength of another great power. It was equally important that aggression should be resisted, simply as such in whatever form. Suffusing these interests, however, with a red and hazy glow was the idea of resistance to Communism.

One frequently-heard justification of aid to the underdeveloped countries was that 'poverty breeds Communism'. This, however, was a popular notion, with little to support it, and, together with the corresponding fantasy that an aim of Soviet economic aid was to create an urban proletariat, it probably had no great influence on policy-makers. Poverty was doubtless a necessary condition for mass Communism; but where Communist leaders had actually achieved mass support, it was through successful rivalry with other leaders in the cause of nationalism, land reform and such age-old demands as security and justice. Poverty as such, Communism as such appeared to have little significance.

In the fifties, it proved that the main danger to non-Communist nationalist rulers was not the Communists but the soldiers. They were the second most admired and the second best organized body in many underdeveloped countries. The rash of military *coups d'état* in the mid-fifties appears to have caused some uneasiness to American policy-makers. This was partly no doubt because a contribution had been made by American military aid. One of the purposes of this aid, largely unavowed, had been internal security against the Communists. Perhaps these *coups d'état* showed the value of such aid; or perhaps not.

There was certainly the possibility that if the non-Communist leaders and the soldiers failed or seemed inadequate to meet popular demands, populations might turn to the Communists. It was even possible that this danger was increasing now that one of these demands was for economic progress. But, in the view of American policy-makers, there was more to the matter than this. The attractiveness of the Communists could be expected to receive support from the spectacular success of Communism in the Soviet Union in promoting economic growth. The leaders of the underdeveloped countries might themselves find the Soviet model appealing. The Soviet Communist solution was now being drawn to the attention of the underdeveloped countries in the most determined fashion. Beginning in 1955 with the offer of credit for a steelworks at Bhilai in India and with the Bulganin-Krushchev tour, the Soviet Union was now conducting a vigorous campaign of friendship with the neutral countries, confirmed by sizeable offers of aid.

The Soviet leaders, it was true, did not advocate the adoption of Communism by the underdeveloped countries. They confined themselves to expressions of sympathy with national aspirations and to occasional incitement to nationalization of, for example, Western oil companies. The Soviet Union's relations with these countries were manifestly unaffected by the manner in which they chose to deal with their domestic Communist party. However, this was merely in keeping with the Soviet Union's current tactic of 'different roads to Socialism'. There could surely be no doubt of the ultimate intention.

Soviet 'economic penetration' of the underdeveloped countries was frankly alarming. Admittedly, Western aid disbursements in the fifties were thirty to forty times larger than the Soviet Union's. Still, the Soviet Union's aid was very spectacular.

They offered a grand new hotel in Rangoon, a sports stadium in Djakarta; they paved the streets of Kabul, they offered aid for the Aswan High Dam when the West withdrew. And with Soviet aid went Soviet 'technicians'. It was estimated that about 1,500 of them were working in underdeveloped countries in 1957 and 4,000 in 1959. As to trade, about 9 per cent of Egypt's exports in 1950 had gone to the Eastern *bloc* and of Syria's, a negligible proportion; in 1957, the figures were 47 and 37 per cent. Other neutral countries also built up trade with the Eastern *bloc*. It was to be feared that by threatening to break off this trade, the Soviet Union would be able to exert political pressure. The best that could be said in 1958 was that there was no evidence of political influence 'at this early date in the *bloc* offensive.'[2]

Justifying America's aid programme to the American people, the Draper Committee wrote in March 1959: 'Economic assistance serves two main purposes: First, our own military defense requires effective forces in the hands of our friends and allies, which, in turn, depend in large measure on the stability of the underlying economic base of the individual countries. Secondly, our security requires that both out allies and the uncommitted countries have an opportunity to solve their pressing economic problems within the framework of the free world. Without such an opportunity, some of them would offer an easy target for Communism. They are not only being attracted by well contrived offers of assistance by the Communist *bloc*, but they are also impressed by the economic achievements of Russia and Communist China, without always fully understanding the real cost in human misery.'[3]

This whole edifice of American ideas was topped off with concern in the late fifties at the faster growth rate of the Soviet economy than the American. This idea, but still more all the rest, owed much to America's special outlook on world events. The 'attraction' of the Soviet Communist model for the underdeveloped countries was far less significant than the fact that these countries wished to reduce their overwhelming economic and political dependence on the West. The greater their anger with the West, the stronger was this desire. The establishment of trade and credit relations with the Soviet Union was the obvious policy from this point of view but also from another, the maximum increase of resources for economic development.

As to Soviet 'economic penetration', the Soviet Union was certainly seeking to strengthen its feeble diplomatic and commercial position in the southern countries of the world. But because these countries had several alternative sources of support and were more jealous of their independence than of anything else, the amount of harmful political influence which the Soviet Union was likely to gain through its trade and aid was minute. The idea that Egypt, having decided to sell its cotton crop to the Eastern *bloc*, in annoyance at Western dictation, might then accept Soviet dictation was particularly naïve. Soviet aid and trade as such might painfully disrupt old commercial patterns, but they could no more harm the overall commercial interests of the West than Japanese aid and trade. On the contrary, they indirectly furthered Western interests.

Beneath all the drama of attraction and penetration, there lay little more than the exceedingly obvious point that if the whole of the West were to refuse aid and trading opportunities to the underdeveloped countries, the only major recourse of these countries would be the Eastern *bloc*. So unnatural would it be for the West to do this that the point was perhaps scarcely worth making, and the defensive approach could well have been abandoned in entirety. As for centuries, the Western countries had a deep economic interest in the development of the southern countries of the world. This was traditionally least true of America, and it was no doubt fundamentally for this reason that American policy-makers, unlike others in the West, felt that they must justify economic aid in defensive, anti-Communist terms. But it was now to be true for the future. Accordingly, their case might well have carried more conviction with the American people if they had justified economic aid in terms of common economic benefits.

By 1960, American anxiety about Soviet penetration of Asia had become much less acute. In the Middle East, after the violent agitation of the mid-fifties, the pendulum seemed to be more or less central between East and West. Mr Krushchev's tour of India, Burma and Indonesia in February 1960 caused much less alarm than his Asia tour of 1955. Nothing serious, after all, had followed the 1955 tour; moreover, Mr Krushchev's hosts had events in Hungary in 1956 and the recent Chinese reppression of Tibet and encroachment on India to reproach him with. It now seemed less a question of Asian countries drifting away from the West and towards the East than of competition for the goodwill of middle-of-the-road neutralists. It had begun to be appreciated that the majority of Asian countries would not be bound by the issues of the East-West conflict, and that their relations with the Soviet Union and China were part of the politics of independence. Suddenly, however, in 1960, the United States suffered one of the most momentous shocks in its history, a violent blow in the most assured area of American policy, the historic sphere of influence, the inviolate Western Hemisphere. Faced with the monstrous alliance of Cuba with the Soviet Union, it was as though the years of painfully acquired understanding in Asia had never been.

The significance of the Cuban revolution of January 1959 was obscured from most Americans by the conventional idea which they had of Latin America. So far as one aspect of the revolution was concerned, this was very understandable. There was scarcely any precedent in Latin America for a genuinely popular revolution aimed at large-scale social reform. The significance of this aspect of the Cuban revolution for Cuba and for Latin America is even now obscure.

On the other hand, the world over, there was a precedent for the other aspect of the Cuban revolution, nationalism, anti-imperialism, independence. But, Americans did not think of Latin America in these terms. They did not see the United States in relation to Latin America as they saw Britain in relation to the Middle East. They believed in the idea of the Good Neighbour policy and of inter-American co-operation. It was on these grounds, as much as on grounds of commercial interest, that the United States had maintained friendly relations with the dictatorship of General Batista in Cuba. Americans did not realize the extent to which the United States overshadowed the sub-continent and the resentment of 'Yankee imperialism'. Many in Latin America noted the generosity of the United States in Western Europe and Asia and the paucity of aid to Latin America. The $9,000 million worth of American companies were, in their collective image, only another sign of American dominance.

Americans, moreover, had been preoccupied. Latin America seemed immune under the ancient protection of the Monroe Doctrine from the struggles of the outer world to which the United States was now committed. American policy-makers saw the demonstrations against Vice-President Nixon on his 1958 tour as a portent. The request for an Inter-American Development Bank, rejected in 1957, was now hastily conceded. But Americans as a whole ascribed the episode to the work of Communist agitators.

Because of these preconceptions, as Fidel Castro's self-confidence swelled in the months after his entry into Havana, as his tone towards America became more shrill, Americans chose straightway the only explanation which seemed to them possible: Castro was a Communist. It seems probable that from the outset, whether clearly or hazily, Castro hoped to clear the Americans out of Cuba, to nationalize the $1,000 million worth of American property, to hurl defiance at the American imperialists as a messiah of Latin America. Probably America's growing hostility towards the end of 1959 did no more than precipitate the obvious if daring measure of preparation, well-tried by nationalists elsewhere in the world, the economic agreement of February 1960 with the Soviet Union. In July 1960, the United States cut its imports of sugar from Cuba; Castro began to nationalize American property; the Soviet Union proclaimed grandiloquently that it would protect Cuba against aggression with rockets.

The United States, whatever its past preconceptions and mistakes, could not be expected to accept Cuban nationalization with calm reflections on the course of world history. Only one major power had sometimes acted stoically in like circumstances in the postwar years: Britain, in face of massive sequestrations in China in 1949 and in Iran in 1951. But this was in large part simply because it had felt powerless to do otherwise. The clash between the old and the new, the nationalism of the Cuban revolutionaries and the rights of Americans could, humanly speaking, only result in angry chaos.

It was the interpretation of events by the United States on the level of international affairs which was more exceptional. It did not see the Cuban revolution primarily as a Latin American revolution, as a violent symptom of a shifting pattern throughout the sub-continent; it saw events primarily as the incursion of an outside influence into the Western Hemisphere. It did not accept that these events signified the decline of the Monroe Doctrine, that the international relations of Latin American countries were likely to become less and less exclusively inter-American and more and more genuinely international. Its first action was to organize in August 1960 a grand proclamation of inter-American solidarity and opposition to external intervention, the Declaration of San José. Its next, the following month, was the Bogotá Conference and the announcement there of a $500 million economic aid programme for Latin America, excluding Cuba. These were in themselves, no doubt, necessary immediate moves, whatever appraisal was made; but there were no signs of any reappraisal of fundamental policy. America's instinct as regards Latin America was not to set its sail to the wind of change but to strengthen its shelter against it.

America's approach to the international problem of Africa showed the same permanent characteristic of American policy as in Latin America, resistance to Soviet interference, but in a milder form and with, in this case, a strong admixture from experience gained earlier in the Middle East. America had long had reasons for concern with Africa – access to minerals, the repercussion of African problems on Western Europe, the general aim of peace – but from 1957, it showed a marked quickening of interest. The withdrawal of the Western European powers and the rise of a series of new, independent African states was now at hand.

America, long approving of this process, now set out to confirm the bond of sympathy with African nationalism, for instance, by voting in the United Nations Assembly for the first time in 1958 for the discussion of the internal affairs of South Africa. But so far as the vast security problem created by the transfer of power was concerned, America did not make plans for direct responsibility or for the formation of a security system as it once had done in the Middle East. The situation in Africa was too mobile, the mood of the African leaders too averse, the size and diversity of the continent too great for such an approach to seem feasible. On the other hand, the situation in the United Nations Organization and the role which it had recently played in the Middle East offered possibilities. Feeling its way, therefore, America decided that, initially at least, its interests could best be covered by acting through the United Nations Organization.

When in July 1960, M. Lumumba, the Prime Minister of the newly independent Congo, appealed for American assistance against the secession of Kantanga province, he was accordingly referred to the United Nations Organization. The Organization established itself in the Congo with vague terms of reference but with a generally conciliatory intent. The Soviet Union, however, took a different view. Because of its estimate of the Katanga situation and, still more no doubt, with an eye to strengthening its position in Africa, it sided with M. Lumumba and the more stridently anti-colonialist African powers. It urged the immediate eviction of the Belgians from Katanga and the ending of the secession by force. When M. Lumumba was overthrown by a *coup d'état* and his deputy prime minister established himself in Stanleyville, the Soviet Union continued to recognize this government.

The attitudes of the Soviet Union were greeted with indignation in the United States as incitement to bloodshed, as gratuitrous troublemaking, as the deliberate introduction of the Cold War into Africa. At the United Nations Assembly in September, as Katanga strengthened its defences and recruited mercenaries, Mr Krushchev launched a vigorous attack on the Secretary-General, Mr Hammarskjoeld, demanding his replacement by a three-man group, apparently once again seeking to win the good opinion of Africa. In this, he appeared to have been unsuccessful. On the other hand, after two years of crisis and intermittent bloodshed, the United Nations finally decided in December 1962 to fight to end the secession of Katanga by force.

America's support for a wider role for the United Nations Organization in world affairs, notably in the Middle East in 1956 and in Africa in 1960, was mixed with an element of doubt. America had always maintained the idea of the Organization as a body of 'peace-loving states', capable of action to keep the peace, and not as a microcosm including 'aggressor' states. The periodic debates in America from 1947 onwards on how to reform the Organization and the reforms successfully accomplished had all assumed this idea. The 'calculated risk' finally taken in 1950, of shifting power to the Assembly had not in the event jeopardized the idea since America could almost automatically secure a majority there. Now, since the influx of new states after 1955, it could not. Previously, the Organization had been unimpeachably peace-loving but unfortunately incapable of action to keep peace. Now it was capable of action to keep the peace but would it be peace-loving?

In one sense, it was clear that the influx of new states, combined with the onset of coexistence between the great powers, was doing much to make the United Nations Organization effective for peace. In opposition to intervention by the great powers and in fear of conflict among them, the 'Afro-Asian *bloc*' gave strong support to the Organization's pacificatory role in the Middle East and the Congo. But this did not diminish the fact that in their quarrels with a great power, these states had a standing tendency to try to draw in another great power to support them; nor that the tinder for quarrels amongst themselves was immense. Though the danger of deliberate war between the great powers was apparently receding, the possibility of crisis emanating from the small powers was growing with every independent state created, with the progressive 'balkanization' of the world.

No doubt there was also a trend in most continents towards amalgamation. Various attempts by the United States in the fifties to use its economic aid to encourage positive, peaceful co-operation among the underdeveloped countries, such as the Simla Conference of 1955 or President Eisenhower's proposal in August 1958 for a Middle East development institution, had had no success. On the other hand, the Colombo Plan, launched at the beginning of the decade, was producing some co-operation; the Montivedeo Treaty signed at its end might have some meaning, though Americans were commonly sceptical. The decline of the Commonwealth was perhaps balanced by the intended association of many African states with the European Economic Community. By 1960, there was a general fashion throughout the world, in emulation of the Community, for regional economic groupings.

But there were also more ominous groupings, particularly in Africa, and did not all the incipient groupings in the world present the danger merely of larger rivalries? Would the world organization of the United Nations succeed in controlling the new individual quarrels and group rivalries any more than it had succeeded with the quarrel of East and West? These were the kinds of quieter, less-publicized questions about the under-developed countries debated at the end of the fifties. But no one was quite sure of the problem, and still less were they sure of the answer.

10

The New Frontier

It was a natural part of American or any other politics that the Kennedy Administration should take office in a mood of criticism of the past and reform for the future. The Republican Administration had arrived in 1953 denouncing 'the mess in Washington' and proclaiming 'a positive foreign policy'. In the far less bitter campaign of 1960, the Democratic Party castigated complacency, rigidity and drift. The new President arrived in a whirlwind of hope, excitement and new ideas. The image fostered by the public relations campaign was that of youthfulness and vigour. The stories of the President rousing news reporters from their sleep, beating even newsmen to the creation of the news, were a typical stroke. New advisers appeared, notably from the universities. There was to be openness, pragmatism and experiment. Above all there was to be advance.

In his Inaugural Address, President Kennedy gave a sombre description of America's situation, making this the basis, however, of an all the more stirring call to action. Already as a Senator, he had brought a new rhetoric to bear on the scale of world events: 'For the Russian peasant has looked up from his hoe to fling Sputnik into outer space – opening not a new frontier of hope for all mankind but a new and sombre frontier of fear'.[1] In his acceptance speech at the Democratic National Convention on 15 July 1961, the President had adapted this image from the American tradition as a challenge to Americans: 'We stand today on the edge of a New Frontier – the frontier of the 1960's . . . are we up to the task? Are we equal to the challenge?

The spur to this dramatic campaign of challenge was anxiety at the progressive decline of public interest in world affairs in the middle and late fifties, and the inability of the Eisenhower Administration to re-invigorate it and to mobilize enthusiasm for America's programmes. For those who were concerned with foreign policy, 1960 had been an unsuccessful year with the standing Berlin crisis; the disruption of the Summit Conference in May; the riots against the security treaty in Japan in June and the cancellation of the President's visit; the seizure of American property in Cuba, and the Congo and Laos dilemmas in August; the 'disarray' in the Atlantic Alliance. In the late fifties, as the Soviet Union proved to be ahead in intercontinental missile development, there had been stark warnings by Kennedy among others of a 'missile gap' for the years 1960-4, and these anxieties still continued. Three months after the new President took office, in April 1961, the Soviet Union again proved its leadership in the more spectacular side of the 'space race' by launching a manned earth satellite.

In facing the press of problems, in seeking to rouse the apathetic and strengthen the active, President Kennedy offered a shift of perspective to the American people. Not simply because the Soviet Union had proved itself a formidable rival but in the very nature of human affairs, the struggle ahead would be hard and frustrating. From 1945, when America abandoned isolationism, its leaders still often felt the necessity to appeal for support for successive programmes with an implied promise of 'a light around the corner', of a final victory, awaiting perhaps only one last effort. Kennedy instead stressed the immediate difficulties and dangers, and warned that they would continue. Even for the longest term, he muted the promise of a just and lasting peace. In some speeches, he simultaneously pictured and denied 'a final triumph'.[2] His American optimism was blended with his faith that success is not a goal but a quality of spirit and of action. In his Inaugural Address, he said: 'All this will not be finished in the first one hundred days. Nor will it be finished in the first one thousand days, nor in the life of this administration, nor even perhaps in our lifetime on this planet. But let us begin.'

These hints of a more mature philosophy of world affairs could in time work a change in the American people's approach to foreign policy. For the moment, they made a contribution to a greater flexibility in fighting the Cold War. The new policy-makers offered no fundamental changes in the basic ideas of world affairs. Their picture continued to be that of a global struggle between two ways of life, freedom and Communist tyranny. Most of the steps taken in the first two years of the Kennedy Administration were a continuation on lines of policy laid down under its predecessors.

Nonetheless, as a new Administration and as a Democratic Administration, it was relatively unclogged by the accumulated complexities of years of office and less hampered by a conservative wing. It thus greatly accelerated existing trends. Throughout 1961, there were outbreaks of militant right-wing sentiment for 'victory over Communism' and still more dubious domestic objectives. Throughout 1961-2, there was trouble with Congress in many areas of policy. Most of this was reaction to the Democratic victory or was traditional and normal. But there was some element of conflict between old and new. There were, in the phrases of Chester Bowles, two approaches to the three frontiers of the Cold War, military, economic and cultural: the 'maximum rigidity' school and the 'maximum maneuverability' school.[3] To the latter, the President and the Administration as a whole belonged.

President Kennedy did not believe in the possibility of a negotiated settlement of the East-West conflict; but neither did he believe in 'victory over Communism' in the sense meant by the right-wing. He believed in seeking understandings with the Soviet Union to stabilize and, if possible, to reduce the military balance between the powers; and, within the arena so created, to pursue the perennial struggle for freedom by every available means. 'Our greatest challenge is still the world that lies beyond the cold war,' he said in his first State of the Union Address 'but the first great obstacle is still our relations with the Soviet Union and Communist China . . . For if freedom and communism were to compete for man's alleigance in a world at peace, I would look to the future with ever increasing confidence.'

Containment at the outset, in the late forties, had been primarily a territorial conception; it meant above all the barricading of the military frontier of the West against Soviet invasion; the arena for political and economic activity was the free world behind this. By the time of the Kennedy Administration, the whole world, even the world across the Iron Curtain, was the arena for political and economic action. The evocative idea of a frontier was still retained. This was partly because of the communications barrier between the Eastern and Western countries, and, however diminished by intercontinental missiles, the continued military frontier. But it was also partly because of the continuing conception of an all-embracing clash in world affairs between two worlds, freedom and Communism.

President Kennedy and Secretary Rusk sometimes sought to emphasize that there were other enemies in the world beyond Communism, enemies in their own right such as poverty and other tyrannies. They even thought it proper to point out that not all the troubles of the world were the work of Communism. Still, the grand conflict remained the dominant picture and the idea of the frontier with it. All that had changed was that the active frontiers were now economic and cultural. For the 'maximum rigidity' school, 'each frontier is a barrier to be rigidly held, not simply against tanks but against trade, aid, people, and ideas'.[4] For the Kennedy Administration, the military frontier must be held; the others must be crossed.

There were thus for the Kennedy Administration in its first two years, two great areas of policy: concern with the East-West balance and pursuit of the struggle for freedom in the ring thus held. The first of these was a continuation of the search for what Secretary Herter had called 'ground rules' for the Cold War. Kennedy had approved of the meeting between Eisenhower and Krushchev at Camp David in September 1959. It had now become axiomatic that the great powers must ensure that their interests were completely clear and that they therefore could not afford to lose contact with each other. The age-old tradition of breaking-off diplomatic relations at a time of serious crisis was being abandoned.

In June 1961, President Kennedy met Premier Krushchev in Vienna. On his return, the President said:

'Only by such discussions was it possible for me to be sure that Mr Krushchev knew how differently we view the present and the future. Our views contrasted sharply, but at least we knew better at the end where we stood.'

'Neither of us was there to dictate a settlement or to convert the other to a cause or to concede our basic interests, but both of us were there, I think, because we realized that . . . care should . . . be taken to prevent our conflicting interests from so directly confronting each other that war necessarily ensued.'[5]

Among Kennedy's first actions in January 1961 was a decision to try to end the confrontation of the United States and the Soviet Union developing in Laos. Over the eighteen months until the neutralization agreement of July 1962, his efforts were bedevilled by the opposition of American agencies in Vientiane who still believed that the dangers could only be removed by continued American intervention. Curiously perhaps, the President did not take the same view of southern Viet-Nam, but in the winter of 1961-2 made agreements to redouble America's support for President Ngo Dinh Diem's régime. Accepting the Geneva line, the President appears to have pictured South Viet-Nam as a separate nation, the victim of aggression and not of a Viet-Nam civil war paralleling the civil war in Laos.

A second immediate action in January 1961 was an attempt to reduce the confrontation of the great powers overall by a re-doubled attempt at a nuclear test ban. In the late fifties, there had been deep controversy within the Republican Administration on whether such a ban profited America, and the result had been a lukewarm attitude to the Geneva negotiations. President Kennedy seemed convinced that a ban would be in America's interest and represented an area of common interest with the Soviet Union. Such hopes were dashed by the Soviet Union's re-sumption of nuclear testing in August 1961, contradicting its unilateral undertaking of August 1958. But still the President pressed the idea, and, indeed, went further. In his address to the United Nations General Assembly on 25 September he an-nounced a General Disarmament Plan. He cut through the classic question whether armaments were the cause or the symp-tom of tension; on the present-day scale, they must be something of a cause, and this cause must be tackled. The General Dis-armament Plan made no progress, however. The nuclear test negotiations broke up for an interval the following January after the three hundred and fifty-third meeting.

While striving to reduce the level of the military balance, the Administration inevitably gave highest priority to maintaining America's side of this balance. The missile programme was urgently reappraised but it was in fact in another area that the real gap proved to lie. A major Soviet onslaught on Western Europe or any other area could, in the Administration's think-ing, only portend nuclear war; but there were exposed positions, notably West Berlin, with regard to which there was a flagrant discrepancy between the Western commitment and the Western willingness to risk nuclear war. The Administration increased

America's effective conventional forces in Western Europe and in reserve, and throughout 1961-2 urged its NATO allies to do the same.

Only West Germany crept slowly ahead towards its twelve divisions. In his 1962 State of the Union Message, Kennedy declared: 'We have rejected an all-or-nothing posture which would leave no choice but inglorious retreat or unlimited retaliation'. But America's NATO partners at least, had done nothing of the sort. Their calculations of Soviet attitudes and their concern for their separate national economies, forces and atomic bombs, outweighed the possibility of a crisis within Berlin which might force the Soviet Union's hand. They did not think it worthwhile to insure against the patent fact that in such an event they would surrender.

The new Administration sought also to strengthen the political and economic base of the Atlantic Alliance, but still in a slow, defensive fashion. It was impeded in its efforts by the suspicions which accompanied military weakness. The building of the Berlin Wall on 13 August 1961, without Western retaliation, and the manifest preparedness of the United States and Britain for flexibility on the German question as a whole, awakened West German opinion to the realities of Western policy. Their confidence in the Atlantic Alliance was weakened, even if, as yet, no new road was apparent. Throughout 1961-2, Chancellor Adenauer and General de Gaulle drew closer together in resistance to negotiation on Germany, and a 'Paris-Bonn axis' emerged at clear cross-purposes with the 'Anglo-Saxon alliance'.

The Administration tried to acknowledge the growing power of Western Europe within the alliance, and, at the same time, to prevent the spread of national nuclear forces, by pursuing the idea of a NATO nuclear force. France had exploded a nuclear device in February 1960. The idea seemed, however, to carry no more conviction than had the tentative soundings of Secretary Herter. The will to co-operate in shaping the concept and in building an Atlantic defence community appeared to be lacking. As the United States moved towards a position in which, if it must, it could dispense with bases in Western Europe for its strategic nuclear defence, and as Western Europe moved slowly towards independent nuclear power, the conditions permitting separate policies towards the Soviet Union were being created.

Atlantic economic co-operation was pressed by the United States only to the extent of its own difficulties. Financial co-operation had become an urgent necessity in 1959-60 to offset the drain on American reserves of overseas aid and the $1 billion foreign exchange costs of American troops in Europe. Reflecting this, the President declared in his 1961 State of the Union Message: 'No Atlantic Power can meet on its own the mutual problems now facing us in defense, foreign aid, monetary reserves and a host of other areas'. That summer, Britain and others took the decision to seek to join the European Economic Community. Accordingly, while welcoming this as a grand consummation, the Herter-Clayton report now called urgently for a policy looking towards a 'trade partnership' with the Community. Confronting American industry with 'the stunning evolution of Western European economic unity', the President now, in December, had added to his list, asking: 'Will we work together on problems of trade, payments and monetary reserves?'[6]

The following year brought the successful outcome of the year-long GATT tariff negotiations and the passage of the Trade Expansion Act; but this defensive bargaining of tariff concessions, useful though it was, was not in itself evidence of an idea of Atlantic partnership. This idea was still weak on either side of the Atlantic. In an address of 4 July 1962, President Kennedy went only the distance which he felt American and European opinion would accept: 'It would be premature at this time to do more than indicate the high regard with which we view the formation of this partnership. The first order of business is for our European friends to go forward in forming the more perfect union which will some day make this partnership possible . . . we will be prepared to discuss with a United Europe the ways and means of forming a concrete Atlantic partnership.'

Some European leaders, for instance M. Spaak, appeared to favour the Atlantic idea; others, notably in France, rejected it. Even in Britain, many of those most strongly in favour of British membership of the Community, believed that Europe must be made and made equal to the United States before an Atlantic partnership was possible. Yet, at the end of 1962, there was talk in America of 'the two Europes', a large, outward-looking community which accepted Britain, and a small, restrictive community based on the Paris-Bonn axis. There was anxiety at the idea of this second Europe. It appeared to be not the precursor of an Atlantic partnership but a growing obstacle even to the old Atlantic co-operation.

While unwilling to seek an end to different national interests on an Atlantic basis and unwilling to abandon national military power, the Atlantic allies nonetheless felt that all should be consulted if one of their number were to bring its power into play in a crisis of its interests. The reason for this feeling was clear; an explosion caused by one could involve the fortunes of all. But it was not clear what effect consultation in a crisis was supposed to have so long as a country had in the end to defend its separate national interests. Doubts as to the meaningfulness even of the day-to-day consultation between Britain and the United States, fears that the standing Anglo-American 'special relationship' was only a comforting illusion were, with some reason, currently assailing British opinion. The most that could be said was that the powerful, frightened desire for consultation in a crisis might in time reinforce the necessity of striving to create a community of interests and of power.

These considerations were exemplified in the crisis of a vehemence unprecedented since the Korean War which burst upon the

West in the days from 22-28 October 1962. While seeking in agreement, as it thought, with the Soviet Union to hold the military balance of East and West, the United States was suddenly confronted with a Soviet attempt to 'tilt the balance' by action in the Western Hemisphere. In an address of 22 October President Kennedy announced the discovery that the Soviet Union was installing intermediate range missiles in Cuba. America would impose a 'quarantine' on the island. Ships carrying these weapons would be stopped.

Indignation at the Soviet Union's intrusion into the Western Hemisphere no doubt strengthened the President's decision, but it was not the basis. While the United States deeply resented and sought to resist this intrusion, it was not apparently prepared to take a 'collision course' on that account. Soviet troops and other types of missiles were not included in the quarantine. The decisive factor was the belief that the Soviet Union was seeking to alter the East-West military balance and or at any rate to alter the political balance by military means. No drastic change in the deployment of the nuclear weapons of the two powers had been made in recent years. In the American view these manœuvrings contravened in the most dangerous fashion the understanding which seemed to have grown between the powers.

Many in the West did not share American alarm that the Soviet Union was altering the military balance. In practice, it seemed no more likely than it was before that the Soviet Union would set out to destroy America and itself in consequence. The description of the Soviet intermediate range missiles as 'offensive' was, in a military sense, question-begging in an age of deterrent strategy. Despite the abortive attack of April 1961 on Cuba by rebels from the United States, and the patently aggressive mood of the United States itself, the suggestion that the missiles were relevant to the defence of Cuba was not very convincing. On the other hand, the parallel which Mr Krushchev drew with the missile bases in Turkey for the defence of the West appeared to have some justice. Cuba was the equivalent of Turkey or Formosa, and there was some indignation in the West at the thought that Americans might be alarmed to the point of war by a situation which they denied should alarm Russians and Chinese. Early in 1959, Lyndon Johnson had said: 'We have treated constant Soviet preoccupation with our overseas bases as a sort of unreasonable Soviet obsession. Speaking for myself, I am frank to admit that I might find myself plagued by an obsession against Soviet bases if their ballistic launching facilities were in the Caribbean or Mexico . . .'[7]

Yet, whatever the logic of the military situation, the idea which the world had of this situation necessarily gave the Soviet action a drastic significance. The logic was easier to see at a distance, the psychology, nearer at hand. Nuclear missiles might not be a means to power through aggression, but they were nonetheless in practice a means to power by possession, scale and deployment. The installation of Soviet missiles in Cuba would enormously enhance the prestige of the Soviet Union, particularly in Latin America, by the most tense and dangerous means. The defensive necessity for missiles on Cuba was weak; the political challenge in this advance was blatant. Confidence in the power of the United States would receive a serious blow if the challenge were to be successful. At very least, it was utterly undesirable that political influence should be pursued by such means and that further areas of the world should be infected with the same fears of nuclear destruction as haunted Western Europe. It was at the same time a fair calculation that the Soviet Union would not back its pursuit of influence by military means by further military means, that is, by war.

Simultaneously in the autumn of 1962, the United States was involved in a less acute but far more confusing crisis, the Chinese incursion in north-eastern Kashmir, reinforced by a thrust and withdrawal in north-eastern India. The confrontation of the fifties around Kashmir, with Pakistan relying on its American alliance, and India on its understanding with the Soviet Union, had already begun to shift. President Ayub of Pakistan had already shown restlessness with the American alliance and had strengthened his relations with the Soviet Union. The Chinese intervention held some possibility of a complete diplomatic revolution.

In the event, Pakistan now sought to use agreements with China on the Pakistan Kashmir border as a lever, and India accepted armaments from the United States and Britain. But India also maintained its relations with the Soviet Union, and America and Britain approved of this since they hoped to maintain the tension between the Soviet Union and China. This was a very significant change in American attitudes from the Dulles era. They also sought a Kashmir settlement between India and Pakistan to remove the core of the trouble and create unity against China.

At least up to end of 1962, there were too many cross-currents for any of the parties to see the quarrel as a grand clash after the manner of the East-West quarrel in Europe. Even the United States was muted in its references to the free world and Communism. China's attack on India was, from one point of view, Asia's Czechoslovakia *coup d'état*; but the methods and circumstances of Asia were too different for the results to be necessarily the same. There appeared to be some prospect of maintaining the fluidity of the situation, of continuing to operate on the level of a border dispute, of avoiding the growth of a Cold War and an arms race which could only be ruinous to the Asian countries concerned.

Certainly India appeared to have awakened to a very different picture of China; but whether China, India and Japan would now begin the struggle for influence in South East Asia which the Colombo Powers feared, remained to be seen. On the other hand, the United States, and to a lesser extent, China, had already for some years pictured a rivalry between India and

China. In the American view, it was the rivalry of economic development in freedom or in slavery.

Within the ring, the 'ground rules' of military coexistence, the Kennedy Administration, like its predecessors, saw world events as a grand struggle for freedom. 'For our nation is commissioned by history', said the President 'to be either an observer of freedom's failure or the cause of its success.'[8] With the acceptance of non-alignment and of economic rather than military battle, however, there came a marked shift of tactics.

In planning aid to the underdeveloped countries, the Republican Administration to the very end, and to some extent Congress thereafter, continued to lay heavy emphasis on whether an overseas government was aligned against the East for the protection of the country's international freedom. The Kennedy Administration now began to place heavy emphasis on whether a government was in tune with the aspirations of the country towards internal freedom, at this stage, social justice. The President's message to the Punta del Este conference of August 1961, called to begin the work of the Alliance for Progress, linked economic progress with increasing social justice. It was now believed that seizure of power by Communists 'can be stemmed only by one thing. And that is Governments which are oriented and directed towards assisting the people, and identified with causes which mean a better life for the people of those countries.'[9] Such governments must be aided. As to the others, whatever their fate might be: was it worthwhile to buttress them?

The Kennedy Administration went further than this in flexibility. It sought with far more energy than its predecessor to cross the economic and cultural frontiers with the East. The attitude to China showed little relaxation, but, in the case of Poland and Yugoslavia, the Administration battled with Congress for the continuation of aid despite political quarrels in which these countries took the Soviet Union's part. The Presi-

dent believed, as also in his efforts to foster scientific co-operation with the Soviet Union, that the breaking down of barriers,
the loosening of exclusive ties in the Eastern *bloc* must in the
long term assist the growth of freedom.

The American belief in the ultimate victory of freedom over
tyranny was beset with difficulties. There was in the first place
some tendency to equate this with the victory of democracy
over Communism, of current Western political institutions over
those of the East and of the rest of the world, an historical
absurdity which necessarily produced frustration at the course
of events. It was certain that the example of the Communist
countries was helping to fashion the institutions of the West and
of the rest of the world just as the reverse was the case. The vital
point was that the Western countries should seek the essentials
of freedom, and thereby be capable of judging and urging what
was to be done and what was not.

In this respect, the outlook in the Western world was doubtful. The European movement had generated the ideal of a community but no political philosophy for that community, and not
all the omens were good. The vigour of American belief in freedom was not matched by clarity. In American rhetoric it was
usually obscure whether the reference was to free institutions
or to independence; it was uncertain what the former might
mean in the contemporary world, particularly the southern
world; and equally, how the latter was to be reconciled, particularly by nationalists, with the idea of co-operation, interdependence and unity. These difficulties were not perhaps the fault
of American politicians; to clarify the idea of freedom was not
perhaps their job; but certainly the result was that the American
call to freedom roused only a feeble echo in many to whom it
was addressed.

While the changes of method made by the Kennedy Administration in the struggle for freedom were an increase of flexibility,
they were still far from representing maximum flexibility. The

centres of the struggle were no longer confined to the frontiers of the West and might appear anywhere in the world. Neither East nor West was the solid grouping it had once appeared to be. The kaleidoscope was shifting. But the United States still considered itself to be holding or advancing across 'a frontier' with the East. It now seemed more essential than ever before, within the field created by a military balance, to abandon such rigid imagery from the period of containment and to adopt an open strategy, to seek the advance of the Communist powers into the world outside their borders. But there were as yet few signs of this conception in American policy. Almost any extension of the activity of the Communist powers across 'the frontier' was still greeted with indiscriminate, frontal resistance.

So far as Soviet and Chinese activity in the political movements of the southern countries of the world was concerned, the problem of discriminating resistance for American and other policy-makers was appalling. Each situation was different, involved a different Western stake and was surrounded by different national and international attitudes to reaction or inaction by the Western powers. Nonetheless the experience of the fifties appeared to reinforce certain general principles.

The seizure of power by Soviet or Chinese sponsored leaders, enjoying negligible local support from the population or the ruling classes, might well be expected to lead to the binding of the country's resources to those of the Soviet Union or China and the closure of the country to the rest of the world. In such cases, the initial presumption that the Western powers should resist, just as much as in the case of armed attack, was strong.

On the other hand, no such presumption was justified where a national leader, actual or potential, Communist or non-Communist, enjoying considerable local support was befriended or supported by the Soviet Union or China. However repugnant a Communist or other dictatorship might be, it would in many a case be meaningless for the Western powers to seek in effect to impose or support a puppet of their own. Their cause for concern with the independence of a country was always clear, but it was not to be assumed that a leader, Communist or otherwise, who was the enemy of free institutions was also necessarily and irrespective of the reactions of the Western powers and other international circumstances, the enemy of his country's independence.

Hostility by the Western powers to a Communist or other hostile régime could be expected to reinforce the very result which they most feared, the closure of the country to them. Conversely, an open attitude could be expected gradually to assist access to the country. Not only in the case of the Soviet Union but of all hostile countries, it seemed essential to seize any opportunity to foster diplomatic, economic and cultural relations precisely because they were hostile.

Americans easily assumed that the activities of the Communist powers in the diplomatic, economic and cultural fields, the attempts by the Soviet Union and China in particular to increase their standing in other countries and in the world, were illegitimate and dangerous and to be resisted. Americans and to some extent the Russians and Chinese contrived to picture even these activities as assisting the growth of a world Communist system. What the danger might in fact be to free institutions and to independence was not however clarified. By the late fifties, many of America's allies were seeking to loosen the apron-strings of America and to diversify their international relations. The countries of Latin America were now at least prepared to join in the neutralist Belgrade Conference of August 1961. Countries like Japan, Thailand, Pakistan and Iran found that their hostility to local Communists need not in itself prevent strengthened relations of one sort or another with the Soviet Union and China, and believed that, if they could be achieved, such relations would be beneficial. It was not clear in what way they were wrong.

It was certain, on the other hand, that it would be to the advantage of the southern countries and of all others including the United States to encourage the growth of trade and aid and technical exchange with the Communist countries as part of a general growth. It also seemed wise to many in the West that every effort should be made to involve these countries in the problems of national development and international effort. The effect of encouraging the Soviet Union and China to make good their claims to automatic understanding in these problems with the peoples of Asia, Africa and Latin America could only be beneficial; to oppose such relations could only foster crude alleigances. The traditional isolation of the Soviet Union and China from the southern world, their ignorance of its complexities, contributed greatly to the grossness of their picture of the world and of their methods of intervention in it. To seek to draw the Communist powers into the conventional activities of the world was as difficult an idea in practice as the idea of containment, but it seemed a less dangerous and far more promising approach.

The new example under the Kennedy Administration of America's instinct to ostracize its enemies was Cuba, an example which the six largest Latin American countries resisted at the Punta del Este Conference of January 1962 as inexpedient. The most long-standing and rigid example was China. The strongest American argument in this case was that to allow a condemned aggressor to join the United Nations Organization would undermine the conception of the Organization as an effective agent for peace. Yet this argument seems to have sprung from the persistent American belief that the United Nations Organization ought to be united, a body of countries subscribing to the same law, accepting the same obligations, and adopting the same attitudes in a crisis. This notion was exemplified anew by President Kennedy's proposal in his address to the Assembly on 25 September 1961 that all members should earmark special military units to be on call by the Organization. In practice, the Organization would always be a microcosm, and so, as far as anyone could foresee, a meeting of very divergent countries, only some of which would unite for action in a crisis with the greater or less interest or acquiescence of the others.

The Organization could still in this sense be an effective agent. It would become increasingly so, if as a world forum, it could make some contribution to the conciliation of divergent national attitudes. In a world of rapid change and of deep divisions between whole peoples, the idea of solutions by settlements was in many cases obsolete. The Western powers sometimes acted in the fifties as though they believed that the division of Germany and of Europe and of East and West might one day be solved by drawing up a document. It seemed more likely that such divisions would only be healed by the growing together of the two sides, beginning with the most tentative common action or, at most, with not a treaty, but an agreed directive of action with a common administration. It could not be expected that sufficient community of spirit would exist for such an approach necessarily to solve every violent clash of interests, Germany, Kashmir, Laos, the Congo, Cuba, Goa, New Guinea, to mention only those problems which beset the Kennedy Administration in its first two years. But the Kennedy Administration at least, did not hope for rapid or complete solutions. The idea of concord by common action rather than by settlements was the best that had so far been developed. It was, in fact, the version, fashioned by experience, of the idea of co-operation and of One World with which America had set out on the postwar years.

REFERENCES

Abbreviations

BM – James F. Byrnes, Speaking Frankly, New York, 1947. DAFR – Documents on American Foreign Relations, Council on Foreign Relations, New York, Annual. FA – Foreign Affairs, New York, Quarterly. FD – The Forrestal Diaries, ed. Walter Millis, New York, 1951. HCFA – U.S. House of Representatives, Committee on Foreign Affairs. NYHT – New York Herald Tribune. NYT – New York Times. PPAR – The Public Papers and Addresses of Franklin D. Roosevelt, ed. Samuel I. Rosenman, Volume 1944-5, New York, 1950. SCFR – U.S. Senate, Committee on Foreign Relations. SDB – U.S. State Department Bulletin. TM – Harry S. Truman, Memoirs, Volume 2, Years of Trial and Hope, New York, 1956. VS – Vital Speeches of the Day (U.S.A.), City News Publishing House, New York, Annual.

Chapter 1

[1] 24 February 1945, SDB, 25 February, 282. [2] New York, 1943, 4-5. [3] ibid., 165. [4] FD, 45. [5] TM, 68. [6] BM, 229. [7] Senate, 1 March 1945. [8] William T. Fox, The Super Powers, New York, 1944, 88, 96. [9] House of Commons, 27 October 1944, 18 January 1945. [10] BM, 98. [11] BM, 108. [12] FD, 6. [13] Edward R. Stettinius, Jr., Roosevelt and the Russians, London 1950, 283.

[14] Challenge and Response in United States Policy, FA, October 1957, 42. [15] Peace and War, U.S. State Department, Washington, 1943, 367-8. [16] George F. Kennan, Realities of American Foreign Policy, Princeton, 1954, 18. [17] 26 August 1953, VS 1952-3, 708. [18] 23 August 1944, PPAR, 232. [19] 8 March 1944,

PPAR, 99. [20]BM, 37. [21]BM, 64-5. [22]Radio Interview, The Listener (BBC London), 22 January 1959, 156.
[23]Walter Lippmann, U.S. Foreign Policy, Shield of the Republic, Boston, 1943, 120. [24]SCFR, Hearings on the Charter of the United Nations, Washington, 1945, 73. [25]ibid., 608. [26]FD, 42.

Chapter 2

[1]14 July 1947, NYT, 15 July. [2]SDB, 20 January, 1946, 51. [3]23 February 1945, PPAR, 563. [4]BM, 59.
[5]26 May 1945, SDB, 27 May, 950. [6]BM, 23. [7]Harley Notter, Postwar Foreign Policy Preparation 1939-45, Washington D.C., 1945, 592. [8]FD, 153. [9]27 October 1946, SDB, 28 October, 654-5.
[10]Hans W. Weigert, U.S. Strategic Bases and Collective Security, FA, January 1947, 251. [11]New York, 1947, 46. [12]BM, 295.

Chapter 3

[1]Bernard Brodie, How Strong is Britain?, FA, April 1948, 433. [2]Chester Bowles, Ambassador's Report, New York, 1954, 155. [3]30 June 1954, NYT, 1 July. [4]Jonathan Daniels, The Man of Independence, Philadelphia, 1950, 285. [5]19 December 1947, SDB, 28 December, 1244. [6]Walter Lippmann, The Cold War, New York, 1947, 52. [7]Joseph M. Jones, The Fifteen Weeks, New York, 1955, 141. [8]12 January 1950, VS, 1949-50, 238.
[9]Major Problems of United States Foreign Policy 1947, International Studies Group of the Brookings Institution, Washington D.C., 1947, 29. [10]Historicus, Stalin on Revolution, FA, January 1949, 214. [11]John R. Beal, John Foster Dulles, New York, 1959, 232. [12]TM. 105. [13]Op. cit. (note 7), 105-2.
[14]War or Peace, New York, 1950, 17. [15]Op. cit. (Note 9), 19. [16]Op. cit. (note 1), 432. [17]Op. cit. (note 9), 21.
[18]Gabriel A. Almond, The American People and Foreign Policy, New York, 1950, 55. [19]FD, 444. [20]11 March 1959, NYT,

12 March. [21] The National Commander of the American Legion, 21 September 1950, VS, 1950-1, 19. [22] 15 January 1951, VS, 1950-1, 267.

Chapter 4

[1] TM, 101. [2] FD, 267. [3] Walter Lippmann, The Cold War, New York, 1947, 21. [4] Chester Bowles, Ambassador's Report, New York 1954, 384, 389, 107. [5] 24 April 1954, India's Foreign Policy, Government of India, New Delhi, 1961, 398. [6] FD, 156. [7] Herbert Hoover, Broadcast, 20 December 1950. [8] 5 April 1951. [9] 18 September 1951, VS, 1950-1, 742. [10] SCFR, Review of Foreign Policy 1958, Washington, 1958. [11] Walter Millis and Others, Arms and the State, New York, 1958, 361. [12] 3 December 1957, DAFR, 78-9. [13] TM, 306. [14] FA, January 1948, 262. [15] HCFA, Hearings on the Mutual Defense Assistance Act 1949, Washington D.C., 1949, 71. [16] Richard P. Stebbins, The United States in World Affairs, 1950, Council on Foreign Relations, New York, 1951, 122. [17] 4 September 1952, VS, 1951-52 708. [18] 11 December 1952, VS, 1952-53, 164. [19] 5 January 1951, VS, 1950-1, 198-205. [20] 10 February 1951. [21] 19 April, 1951, VS, 1950-1, 430. [22] 12 January 1954, DAFR, 9-11. [28] FA, April 1954, 358-9. [24] 8 December 1955, DAFR, 15.

Chapter 5

[1] 28 April 1947, SDB, 11 May, 919. [2] 18 November 1947, SDB, 30 November, 1024. [3] European Recovery and American Aid, President's Committee on Foreign Aid, Washington, 1947, 4. [4] Walter Lippmann, The Cold War, New York, 1947, 26-7. [5] Hamilton Fish Armstrong, The Calculated Risk, New York 1947, 9-11. [6] Percy W. Bidwell and William Diebold Jr., New Aid for Europe, FA, October, 1947, 186. [7] Stacey May, Measuring the Marshall Plan, FA, April 1948, 457. [8] 18 November 1947, SDB, 30 November, 1024. [9] 7 June 1948, SDB, 20 June, 810.

[10] TM, 243. [11] Abram Bergson, Russian Defense Expenditure, FA, January 1948, 373. [12] TM, 248. [13] ibid.
[14] Stability in Our Foreign Policy, FA, October 1948, 35.
[15] 27 January 1953, VS, 1952-3, 266. [16] 14 December 1953, NYT, 15 December.

Chapter 6

[1] cf. SCFR, Hearings on the Military Situation in the Far East, Washington D.C., 1951, 123-4. [2] TM, 333. [3] 29 June 1950, SDB, 10 July, 46. [4] TM, 341. [5] TM, 359. [6] TM, 362.
[7] TM, 366. [8] TM, 397-413.

Chapter 7

[1] J. C. Hurewitz, Middle East Dilemmas, New York, 1953, 33.
[2] TM, 133, 162, 149.
[3] 31 October 1953, SDB, 16 November, 659. [4] SDB 20 February, 291. [5] 2 September 1953, NYT, 3 September.
[6] 30 June 1954, NYT, 1 July. [7] 21 July 1954, NYT 22 July.
[8] 17 October 1950, SDB, 30 October, 701. [9] House of Commons, 23 June 1954. [10] 18 September 1951, VS, 1950-1, 742.
[11] 7 October 1951, SDB, 22 October, 646. [12] Richard P. Stebbins, The United States in World Affairs 1950, Council on Foreign Relations, New York, 1951, 307. [13] 10 October 1951, SDB, 22 October, 647. [14] 1 June 1953, SDB, 15 June, 831-5.
[15] Anthony Eden, Full Circle, London, 1960, 221.
[16] ibid., 336. [17] 9 June 1956, SDB, 18 June, 999-1000.

Chapter 8

[1] 8 February 1950, NYT, 9 February. [2] 16 February 1950, NYT, 9 March. [3] 19 December 1947, SDB, 28 December, 1244.
[4] TM, 245. [5] Dean Acheson, 26 March 1952, NYT, 27 March.
[6] 24 July 1951, SDB, 6 August, 203. [7] 18 April 1953, VS, 1952-3, 421. [8] Anthony Eden, Full Circle, London, 1960, 60, 70.

[9] 21 April 1956, 21. [10] SCFR, Review of Foreign Policy 1958, Washington D.C., 1958, 792. [11] Op. cit. (note 8), 499.

[12] 20 February 1957, NYT, 21 February. [13] NYHT, 10 November 1958. [14] John R. Beal, John Foster Dulles, New York, 1959, xiii. [15] Life Magazine, 16 January 1956. [16] Challenge and Response in United States Policy, FA, October 1957, 34.

[17] Interview with Joseph Alsop, NYHT, 21 February 1957.

[18] SCFR, Review of Foreign Policy 1958, Washington 1958, 804. [19] 13 November 1957, NYT 14 November. [20] 23 April 1956, DAFR, 102. [21] 16 November 1959, NYT, 17 November.

Chapter 9

[1] SCFR, Hearings on the South East Asia Collective Defense Treaty, Part 1, Washington D.C., 1954, 15. [2] The Sino-Soviet Economic Offensive in the Less Developed Countries, Department of State Publication, 6632, Washington D.C., 1958, 3. [3] 17 March 1959, Committee on the Mutual Security Programme, NYT, 18 March.

Chapter 10

[1] 16 April 1959, John F. Kennedy, The Strategy of Peace, New York, 1960, 163. [2] cf. 25 September 1961, Address to U.N. Assembly, NYT, 26 September. [3] 21 June 1962, SDB, 9 July, 47. [4] ibid. [5] 6 June 1961, NYT, 7 June. [6] 6 December 1961, NYT, 7 December. [7] U.S. News and World Report, 13 February 1959, 87. [8] State of the Union Message, 11 January 1962.

[9] President Kennedy, 16 June 1961, NYT, 17 June.

INDEX

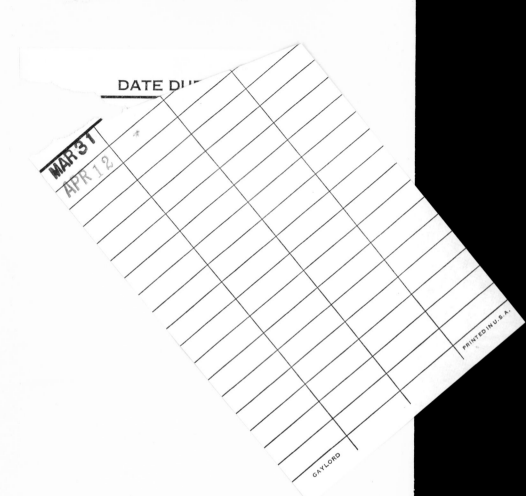

DATE DUE

MAR 31
APR 12

GAYLORD   PRINTED IN U.S.A.